The Supreme Court and Labor-Management Relations Law

The Supreme Court and Labor - Management Relations Law

Alvin L. Goldman
University of Kentucky

Lexington Books

D.C. Heath and Company
Lexington, Massachusetts
Toronto   London

Library of Congress Cataloging in Publication Data

Goldman, Alvin L
  The Supreme Court and labor-management relations law.

  Includes index.
  1. Labor laws and legislation—United States. 2. United States.
Supreme Court. I. Title.
KF3369.G6   344'.73'0189   75-42953
ISBN 0-669-00496-0

Published simultaneously in Canada.

Printed in the United States of America.

International Standard Book Number: 0-669-00496-0

Library of Congress Catalog Card Number: 75-42953

To Joseph and Emma Goldman
with love and gratitude

Contents

Acknowledgments   ix

Introduction   xi

Chapter 1   **Historic Perspective**   1

      Constituion of 1787   1
      The Worker as Property   1
      The Worker as a Contracting Party 2
      Legislative Regulation of Employment 2
      Rise of Collective Bargaining   5
      Early Court Decisions   6
      Impact of Early Federal Legislation 12
      Adoption of Current Legislation 22

Chapter 2   **Regulation of Picketing and Other Union Organizing Activities**   41

Chapter 3   **Supremacy of Federal Power**   59

Chapter 4   **Regulating Economic Warfare**   71

      The Limited Protection of Economic Strikers 73
      Unprotected Concerted Activity 75
      Union Waivers of Statutory Protection 84
      The Employer's Right to Initiate a Work Stoppage 87
      Disciminatory Treatment of Union Militants 93
      Consumer Boycotts   97

Chapter 5   **Creating a Law of Labor Arbitration**   105

Chapter 6   **Change of Ownership and Other Business Alternatives**   127

      Runaway Shops   128
      Contracting Out   129

| | Plant Closings | 133 |
| | Business Transfers and Bargaining Status | 137 |

Chapter 7   **The NLRB as Overseer of Personnel Arrangements**   **151**

	Antifeatherbedding Provision	151
	Machinery for Resolving Jurisdictional Disputes	155
	Contractual Arrangements to Promote Union Membership	164
	Divided Loyalties of Employees	168

Chapter 8   **Conclusion**   173

Index   187

About the Author   193

Acknowledgments

A considerable portion of this book was prepared while the author was on sabbatical leave in Louvain, Belgium. The author is most grateful to the Rechtsfaculteit and the staff of the Groot Begijnhof at the Katholieke Universiteit for the kind and generous courtesies extended to him and to his family during that stay. A special and most emphatic statement of thanks is also owed to our friend Dr. Eric Suy who very generously made his office available to the author and thereby made this work possible. And most of all, to our dear friends Dr. Roger Blanpain and Gabby Blanpain, and to the entire staff of the Instituut voor Arbeidsrecht, we can only begin to express our gratitude for their warm and gracious hospitality, encouragement, guidance, and aid.

The author also wishes to acknowledge the efforts of Donnie White, who assisted the author in various stages of the manuscript preparation, and to thank Bunnie Scutchfield and Pam Johnson for the many hours of tedium endured in typing the manuscript.

Introduction

This book describes and analyzes typical dimensions of the decisional process of the United States Supreme Court encountered in labor relations litigation. A book of this size cannot provide total coverage of the labor relations field even if the discussion is confined to Supreme Court decisions. Fortunately, total coverage is not necessary to examine the more interesting facets of the Court's decisional process in this area. A selective sampling can accomplish that purpose. And, by careful selection of the cases for discussion, it is possible to explore a variety of ways in which social, political, economic, and institutional factors both influence the Court's judgment and are in turn influenced by the exercise of judicial power.

The Supreme Court of the United States has the final power to interpret and apply the laws of Congress (including treaties). It also provides the ultimate interpretation and application of the Constitution of the United States. This latter authority encompasses, when necessary, the power to reject as constitutionally invalid, statutes passed by Congress and those passed by the state legislatures. It also includes the power to reject as unconstitutional the actions of the executive branch of the federal government and of the executive and judicial branches of the state governments. Therefore, whenever the role of the Supreme Court of the United States is discussed in relation to the development of a body of law, it is wise to begin by examining the specific Constitutional constraints upon, and guidelines for, such decision making.

The Supreme Court and Labor-Management Relations Law

1

Historic Perspective

Constitution of 1787

The original constitutional charter of 1787 dealt only indirectly with the relationship between the worker and his employer. Involuntary employment—that is, slavery and indentured service—was a matter of political concern, and that concern is reflected in two constitutional provisions.

Article I, section 9, of the Constitution withheld from Congress until 1808 the power to prohibit the migration or importation "of such persons as any of the states now existing shall think proper to admit" and limited to $10 per person the duty Congress could impose on such importation. This provision was designed to delay for twenty years Congressional termination of slave trade across state and national boundaries. Related to this provision was the language in section 2 of Article I that permitted states to count persons bound to servitude for a term of years together with free persons and to count three-fifths of the enslaved population, for the purpose of determining the number of members a state was entitled to elect to the House of Representatives. Both of these provisions were concessions to those states, such as Virginia, in which enslaved and indentured employment were widespread.

Although the above constitutional provisions were not designed to shape the law governing the employment relationship, they did have the impact of delaying the confrontation over the termination of involuntary employment and, of course, thereby played an important role in our nation's political, economic, and social history. In addition, the constitutional references to involuntary servitude reflected a stage in the development toward our present law of employment in that they recognized that, at the time the Constitution was framed, the law of property had a significant affect upon employment relations.

The Worker as Property

When our nation was founded, slavery as a legal institution was based on the enslaved person's status as property owned by the master. In contrast, the legal status of the indentured servant and of the free worker was based on the law of contracts.

Theoretically the property relationship is purely one of status; the law fixes the respective rights, privileges, duties, and responsibilities of the parties in accordance with their relationship to the item in question. Thus, the slave's terms and conditions of employment, insofar as they were fixed or affected by law, were set by the slave owner's property rights in the enslaved person. The law, not the parties, controlled the legal nature of the relationship. Needless to say, those terms and conditions of employment left very little in the way of rights or privileges on the part of the enslaved worker, although some basic protection was afforded to safeguard the slave from gross brutality.[1]

The Worker as a Contracting Party

In theoretical contrast to a property relationship between employer and worker is the contractual arrangement between two such parties. In a contractual relationship, the parties are supposed to be able to themselves govern their respective rights, privileges, duties, and responsibilities. Lawyers sometimes speak of this as the private law enacted by the parties to regulate their own particular relationship. As previously noted, the free worker's employment status and the indentured servant's employment status were regarded as matters of contract, not property. But here, too, the law has always intervened to some degree. For example, at the time our Constitution was framed, the common law prohibited beating a servant and guaranteed a right to wages — though generally the amount of the wage was left to the parties.[2] Thus, the worker was free to condition his employment upon receipt of satisfactory terms and conditions of work. Despite this theoretical advantage to the employee whose status was based on contract, the pressures of economic crisis or personal misfortune often forced employees to accept wages and conditions of employment that were appropriately characterized by the Marxist phrase "wage slavery." Similarly, at other times, labor shortages facilitated exhorbitant wage demands.

Legislative Regulation of Employment

For this reason, and for other reasons, legislatures sometimes intervened by statutorily restricting or specifying particular terms of the employment agreement. Thus, within a year of its settlement, the Massachusetts Bay Colony set maximum wage rates for the building and other trades. This was soon abandoned (apparently as too rigid to meet the reasonable needs of either worker or employer), and after some years it was decided that wage disputes would be resolved by a board of three men.[3]

During the Revolutionary War, a number of states and townships sought to keep prices from rising too rapidly by fixing wage ceilings. But in an economic system in which barter was not only practical but also widely practiced, enforcement of such controls was extremely difficult. Frequently the only effective means of enforcement were extra-judicial techniques; public villification, ostracism, and occasionally mob action substituted for judicial decree.[4]

Various statutory requirements continued to be imposed on employment contracts after the Revolution. For example, the early laws of Virginia guaranteed that an apprentice receive payment of $12 upon discharge from service. Also, the discharged indentured servant was by law entitled to a new complete suit of clothes plus his wages.[5] By 1859, Kansas was fixing such statutory benefits at a new Bible, two new suits of clothes (to be worth $40 for a male; $20 for a female) and $10 currency.[6] Illinois was more generous with respect to the cash benefit ($20) but did not specify the value of the two suits of clothes.[7] Both states additionally required that apprenticed servants be given a basic education in reading, writing, and arithmetic.[8]

Working conditions, too, sometimes evoked legislative and judicial inter-position into the private law of the employment contract. In Virginia, for example, in the postrevolutionary period, a master was entitled to use moderate correction of an apprentice, but could lawfully whip an apprentice only with approval of a Justice of the Peace.[9] Further, an employer was held liable for failure to provide a worker with suitable means and appliances "to work as safely as the hazards of the employment permit."[10] This included the obligation of providing a suitable and reasonable place in which to perform the work and fellow workmen sufficient in number and skill to avoid exposure to unnecessary risk.

With the adoption of the Thirteenth Amendment in 1865, which prohibited involuntary servitude, American labor relations law moved out of the area of property relations. But this did not mean that the law would henceforth leave the employer and worker totally to their own contractual devices. Instead, the law became increasingly involved in shaping both the structure and substance of that relationship.

As early as the 1830s, workingmen's parties had succeeded in getting some states to pass laws imposing a maximum 10-hour work day. In 1840, labor pressure induced President Van Buren to establish a 10-hour day in Naval shipyards. In 1868, Congress passed a law limiting laborers and mechanics employed by the federal government to an 8-hour work day. State legislatures continued to pass laws affecting working hours, though one can readily question whether the measures were always sufficiently generous to provide any meaningful benefit for employees. For example, an Act of 1891 adopted in Colorado prohibited railroads from working a person for more than 18 consecutive hours without providing a rest period of at least 8 hours. One cannot help wonder as to whether this law was intended to assure 8 hours of rest or to sanction 18 consecutive hours of work.

Moreover, until well into the twentieth century, it was often authoritatively asserted that a number of constitutional provisions barred legislatures from fixing the terms and conditions of employment. One restraint thought to prevent such legislation was the provision in Article I, section 10 of the Constitution prohibiting states from making laws "impairing the obligation of contracts." Another was the prohibition in the Fifth Amendment prohibiting the federal government from taking liberty or property without due process and from taking property for public use without just compensation. It was similarly asserted that the Fourteenth Amendment's prohibition against states taking liberty or property without due process of law prevented states from passing laws interfering with the right of the employer and worker to privately fix their own terms of employment.

The demise of these purported constitutional barriers to legislation that sets terms and conditions of employment, or regulates the process by which employers and employees fix those terms, began with *Holden v. Hardy*, 169 U.S. 366 (1898). In that case, the Supreme Court of the United States upheld a state law limiting the daily hours of work in underground mines. The holding of the case, however, was later given a very limited interpretation, and it was not until another four decades had passed that constitutional doctrine became settled as permitting broad legislative intervention in fixing employment conditions.

In addition to the constitutional obstacles to those legislative reforms that sought to benefit American workers, a further barrier was posed by the very considerable influence business interests had over the legislative process. Lobbying at the state legislative level in nineteenth-century America often took the very crude form of purchased votes, and management clearly had the superior buying power.[11] Moreover, so long as the nation was expanding westward, the disgruntled worker could envision limitless opportunity for improving his lot by seeking his fortune elsewhere — possibly by farming homestead land, possibly by panning for gold, or by trapping, trading, and the like.

In contrast, other industrial nations often developed legislative reforms concerning the terms and conditions of employment decades before similar laws were adopted in the United States. Such regulatory schemes for fixing the terms of employment evolved from early practices designed to protect employers, rather than workers. For example, the English Ordinance of Labourers, pronounced by Edward III in 1349 and confirmed by Parliament in the Statute of Labourers, required all able-bodied persons under age 60 to be employed either as a merchant, craftsman, or laborer at no more than the wage rate customary in 1346. This law was designed to assure a supply of labor at a reasonable cost after the Black Death had reduced England's population by about one half. The Statute of Apprentices of 1563 attempted to stabilize the labor market by providing for the annual fixing of wage scales by the courts and the standardization of hours of employment at 13 1/2 hours per day for laborers; 14 1/2 hours for farm workers. But, with the rise of the factory system and the enclosure of grazing lands in Britain, the terms of hiring had by the late eighteenth-century become governed, as in the United States, by the parties themselves.

Nevertheless, by the mid-nineteenth century, Britain, like other European countries, was looking for legislative solutions to the multitude of grievances being voiced by the working class. Thus, Britain established, during the first half of the nineteenth century, a series of statutory limits upon the number of hours a worker could be required to work during a day or a week. In 1883, Germany adopted a program of compulsory health insurance to aid the working class, and the next year it instituted a compulsory program to provide insurance benefits to workers injured through accidents. Germany also established a compulsory pension program in 1889 to assure income for those too old or infirm to work. Minimum wage legislation, too, became a major focus of reform outside the United States by the late nineteenth century. And in the early part of the twentieth century, compulsory systems for providing unemployment insurance were being adopted elsewhere in the industrialized world: in Great Britain in 1911; Italy in 1919; Germany in 1927. It was not until the mid-1930s that such legislative reforms became a significant factor in shaping the terms of employment in the United States.

Rather, because statutory reform beneficial to labor moved so very slowly in the United States, labor leaders sought and achieved progress in the conditions and remuneration of work largely by following the path of collective bargaining.

Rise of Collective Bargaining

As early as 1794, American workmen were banning together for the purpose of making group demands for improvements in their employment contracts. The first such effort is usually attributed to the journeyman shoemakers of Philadelphia whose organization in 1799 maintained a strike for about 10 weeks against their employers who were master shoemakers. Actually, however, about half a century earlier, a strike had been used by journeymen bakers in New York City in an effort to raise wages.[12] In 1803, an organization of shipwrights was formed in New York City, and within a few years other trade laborers, such as carpenters and tailors, joined together in trade unions for the purpose of obtaining greater benefits from their employers. These groups, though, were weak and usually died out after a few years.[13]

By the late 1820s, efforts to improve worker bargaining strength by engaging in united action to set contract demands had accelerated to the point of looking toward national associations.[14] The strategies of these groups were diverse. Some looked to political victory and legislative reform as the best means for improving wages and working conditions; others sought their victories in the form of concessions from employers that would be reflected in more generous employment contracts. As indicated above, the philosophy of the latter group eventually gained clear dominance.

The modern era of labor union activity can probably be dated from 1881 when the Federation of Organized Trades and Labor Unions of the United States and Canada was formed as a means of bringing local labor groups together. By 1886, the structure of this organization was altered, its functions broadened, and the name changed to the American Federation of Labor. Samuel Gompers, who led the predecessor organization for three years, was chosen president of the A.F. of L. and remained in the post for some forty years. Gompers strongly favored the process of bargaining directly with management as the best method for obtaining improved worker benefits. Further, he generally regarded government intervention as improper or, at least, too frequently detrimental rather than beneficial to employee interests. His was a philosophy of *laissez-faire*: the role of law was to let the parties battle over the terms of employment by using their respective economic strength and weapons, though refraining from violence.

Early Court Decisions

Early litigation respecting labor union activity in the United States did not involve the invocation of either the Constitution or federal statutory law and therefore was resolved without the aid of the Supreme Court of the United States. However, because those cases set the background and tone for both the legislation and the litigation that eventually thrust the High Court into the midst of labor-management relations controversies, they deserve brief examination.

There is a generally held, though mistaken, notion that American law has evolved steadily from a position of great hostility toward organized labor to one of sympathy and accommodation with collective labor action. However, despite how one characterizes present legal policies toward organized labor, the earliest American decisions often were not hostile.

Criminal Conspiracy Theory

It is true that the trial judge's instructions to the jury in the first known case, *Commonwealth* v. *Pullis*,[15] asserted that the law condemns combinations of workmen, whether for the purpose of improving their own conditions or for the purpose of injuring those who do not join their collective. However, in that prosecution the charged misconduct focused largely on the injury that the strikers sought to do to those who did not join the concerted action — which is a form of conduct still legally condemned in most situations. More significant, as pointed out in the classic study by Felix Frankfurter and Nathan Greene,[16] the *Pullis* doctrine, condemning all collective labor efforts seeking improved benefits, was a short-lived thesis.[17] During the thirty years after *Pullis*, of eighteen prosecutions of workmen for unlawful conspiracy, in only one did the court concur in that part of the *Pullis* decision that condemned even those combinations of workmen designed merely to improve their own situation.

Workers were convicted in most of these eighteen cases, but not for the mere act of acting in concert. Rather, conviction was because their concerted action involved elements of physical coercion.[18] For example, in 1810 a New York court expressly withheld decision on the question of whether a strike not accompanied by unlawful conduct would itself violate the law.[19] Moreover, even in some cases in which the trial judge instructed the jury that the union's conduct had been unlawful, the jury returned a verdict of acquittal.[20]

It was not until the decision of the Massachusetts Supreme Judicial Court in *Commonwealth* v. *Hunt*,[21] in 1842, that a widely accepted doctrine was formulated for restraining certain concerted labor activity on a criminal conspiracy doctrine. Although that decision provided the rationale used by courts for surpressing union activities during the next few decades, it was not wholly antagonistic to unions. The Massachusetts court's opinion by Chief Judge Lemuel Shaw held that it was lawful for workingmen to join in a society and refuse to work for an employer who employs persons who are not society members. The power resulting from such concerted action, explained Shaw, might be exerted for honorable purposes such as to give aid and comfort to their fellows in times of sickness or distress or to raise the standards of their art. By analogy, the Chief Judge suggested that it would not be an unlawful conspiracy if workers favoring temperance were to collectively insist that their employer discharge a fellow workman who persisted in "the use of ardent spirit."

Shaw's opinion contained several illustrations of the distinctions to be drawn between lawful and unlawful conspiracies. He indicated, for one, that it would be unlawful for either an individual or collective to refuse to work unless the employer discharge an employee prior to the expiration of that employee's contracted term of employment. He further stated that it would be unlawful for workers to make demands or threaten to quit during a period for which they had contractually engaged to remain in their master's employ. On the other hand, he stated that the mere fact that a refusal to work financially injures the employer is not enough to make out a case of criminal conspiracy. Suppose, he suggested, that a village's sole baker was charging too high a price and the villagers demanded that he lower the price or else they would bring in a new baker and patronize the newcomer. Such a conspiracy, explained Shaw, having a laudable object, would not be unlawful.

The *Hunt* decision not only left the criminal conspiracy doctrine intact, though with limiting refinements, it also had the dual affect of placing the prestige of one of the nation's most respected courts behind both the criminal conspiracy doctrine and behind the concept that unionization is lawful so long as it is not for the purpose of engaging in unlawful conduct. Moreover, as we can see in the preceeding paragraph, some of the Massachusetts court's discussion supported the idea that, at least in some instances, workers can lawfully withhold their labor in support of demands for improved benefits.

Whether Judge Shaw in fact intended to give support to the idea that strikes

are lawful for some purposes has been a matter for debate.[22]   In any event,
legislators in subsequent years attempted to give statutory definition to the
distinction between the lawful and unlawful purposes of concerted labor
activity. Some of these statutes treated almost every form of concerted worker
conduct as unlawful in purpose. Other of these enactments were designed to
broaden the scope of lawful collective labor activity. The courts, however, frequently gave narrow interpretations to the latter statutes with the result that
labor union conduct continued to run the gauntlet of criminal conspiracy
trials.[23]   As a result, it became a common theme of unionists to demand the
total repeal of the criminal conspiracy doctrine in labor-management disputes.

Tort Theory

Another legal impediment faced by unions, which sought to place collective pressure on employers in order to receive improved benefits, was the suit to
recover damages resulting from a tort. A tort is conduct that violates a person's
or entity's right to exist free from harm. Thus, employers argued that the
freedom of the marketplace includes the right to be free from interference in
obtaining the employment services of others. If that definition of the market is
accepted, then invasion of the described freedom will arguably give rise to a traditional right to recover damages in tort. For example, in an 1871 decision,[24]
the Massachusetts Supreme Judicial Court held that an employer was entitled
to recover money damages from a group that induced some of the employer's
workers to leave his employ and induced others to refrain from entering his
employ.

Injunctive Remedies

By the 1880s, employers no longer looked to criminal conspiracy prosecutions or to damages suits as the means of restraining collective employee
activity. Rather, they sought relief through the injunctive remedy. An injunction is a court order requiring someone to do or refrain from doing some act.
The first American injunction against strikers dates back to the railway strike
of 1877, a national dispute accompanied by the calling out of state troops and
the use of gatling guns.[25]
In 1883, courts in Maryland and Ohio issued injunctions to prohibit the
Knights of Labor, a national labor organization of some prominence in the
latter part of the nineteenth century, from inducing European contract
laborers to quit their employment.[26]   By the mid-1880s, injunctions were
being issued with frequency against a wide variety of union activities. One
authority explains that "it was not until some years later, however, that the

modern well-rounded theory in justification of the issuance of injunctions in labor disputes was developed."[27]

That explanation of the grounds for injoining union activity was provided by the New Jersey Court of Chancery in an 1894 decision.[28] The situation before the court arose when a Newark, New Jersey, newspaper petitioned for judicial relief from the actions of a group of trade unions, which the newspaper asserted had called for a work and patronage boycott in order to force the newspaper to cease using printing plates prepared in New York City. The newspaper's owners averred by affidavit that the affect of the boycott was to reduce both patronage and advertizing.

Citing to a statement by the Supreme Court of the United States in the *Slaughterhouse Cases*, 16 Wall. 36 (U.S. 1873), the New Jersey court declared that a person has a right to be protected in carrying on his business without interference respecting the manner in which he disposes of his business capital. Further, explained the New Jersey court, such freedom of investment and management benefits all of society. Accordingly, the New Jersey court concluded that although the newspaper's employees were within their legal right to collectively quit work in protest against the use of plates produced elsewhere, they went beyond their lawful prerogatives by imposing a boycott that was intended to force the newspaper to adjust its business practices in accordance with the union's dictates.

Up to this point in the New Jersey court's reasoning, it was following the traditional approach for justifying a money damages remedy based upon the commission of a tort. The court, however, upon concluding that a legal wrong had been committed against the newspaper, proceeded to determine whether the proper remedy would be money damages or whether it was more appropriate to issue an injunctive order requiring the union to cease its unlawful activity.

If the tort remedy was to be the form of relief, the newspaper owner would have to persuade a jury to grant the money verdict against the union — a very uncertain prospect if the case were to be tried in a jurisdiction in which unions received general popular support. Moreover, the employer would have to await the exhaustion of the trial, and perhaps the appellate process as well, before he could collect the money award even if he were successful. Further, there was always the possibility that the employer would not be financially able to withstand the boycott pressure during this wait. Thus he might have to capitulate to the unlawful demand or face ruin.

On the other hand, if the proper form of remedy was found to be an injunctive decree, then under proper legal procedure the relief would be determined without the participation of a jury and it could even be granted on a temporary basis pending a trial. Such temporary relief could even be given without a hearing on the disputed facts and without thorough argument of the legal issues. Moreover, the trial court's order would normally not be subject to a stay, which means that it would have to be obeyed pending the outcome of any appeal to a higher court. Failure to obey would be punishable as a contempt to court.

It should be noted, here, that the general experience is that once a strike is enjoined for but a few days, it is very difficult to renew it — even though a higher court later reverses the decision to issue the injunction. Thus, in a situation in which the union is imposing economic pressure upon an employer, the injunctive remedy provides distinct advantages for the employer and distinct disadvantages for the union.

Traditionally, however, the courts take the position that an injunction is not available if the wrong can be remedied by a damages award. Also, under the normal standard, in determining whether an injunction is appropriate, the court is required to "balance the equities" — that is, to weigh the burdens of the wrong against the burdens of the injunctive remedy.

The New Jersey court concluded that the newspaper was entitled to injunctive relief. It explained that a damages remedy would not adequately relieve the employer both because damage to a newspaper's reputation and good will cannot be accurately measured in money and because there was a threat of a continuing nature that would require a series of suits to remedy fully the wrong even if damages were measurable. In such situations, held the New Jersey court, an employer need not await collection of a damages award before receiving judicial protection.

A couple of years after the previously discussed case, Oliver Wendell Holmes, Jr., then a judge of the Massachusetts Supreme Judicial Court, offered a rebuttal to the foregoing rationale by attacking the underlying assumption that the employer has been subjected to a legal wrong. Holmes challenged the notion that the law protects a business from all coercive efforts: "[T]he policy of allowing free competition justifies the intentional inflicting of temporal damage, including the damage of interference with a man's business by some means, when the damage is done, not for its own sake, but as an instrumentality in reaching the end of victory in the battle of trade."[29]

Holmes viewed economic intercourse as an arena for conflict with the end result working to the public benefit: "One of the eternal conflicts out of which life is made up is that between the effort of every man to get the most he can for his services, and that of society, disguised under the name of capitol, to get his services for the least possible return. Combination on the one side is patent and powerful. Combination on the other side is the necessary and desirable counterpart, if the battle is to be carried on in a fair and equal way."[30] Holmes concluded from this that absent violence or breach of contract, a union was entitled to use any form of argument, persuasion, or the granting or withholding of advantages, to improve the economic position of its members: "The fact that the immediate object of the act by which the benefit to themselves is to be gained is to injure their antagonist does not necessarily make it unlawful, any more than when a great house lowers the price of goods for the purpose and with effect of driving a smaller antagonist from the business."[31]

Holmes' opinion, however, represented a minority position not only on the Massachusetts bench, but generally in the United States. No better evidence of that fact was to be found than the unanimous decision of the Supreme Court of the United States only a year earlier, which had upheld the order of a federal district court enjoining the American Railway Union's strike against the Pullman Company.

The Pullman strike was called by the union, under the leadership of Eugene V. Debs (later Socialist candidate for the presidency), in an effort to reverse the company's previously imposed 20 percent wage reduction. In support of the strike, sympathetic union members refused to operate trains containing Pullman Company cars. The strike quickly spread West and South from Chicago, then the hub of major railroad activity, with the result that the Attorney General of the United States applied in federal court for an injunction against any interference by Debs and his followers with the operations of named railroads. Debs and his supporters denounced the court order as "government by injunction" and refused to obey. Federal troops were called out by President Cleveland to enforce the court order. Debs was charged with contempt of court for having failed to obey the injunction and was sentenced to six months' imprisonment. Because his refusal to obey was a contempt of court, Debs was tried without a jury.[a] With Debs' arrest, the strikers were demoralized and the strike abandoned.[32]

The basic argument against the federal court's order was that the court lacked authority to intervene in the dispute. It is an axiom of American constitutional law that federal authority is limited to those powers expressly granted by the Constitution. Therefore, it was necessary for the Supreme Court to establish a constitutional basis for the lower court's exercise of jurisdiction over the railroad strike.

The Court found such justification for the injunction against the stoppage of railroad traffic in the national government's expressly granted power over interstate transportation and over the movement of the mail (which was largely handled by rail). The power to regulate such matters is given to Congress in Article I of the Constitution. Thus, reasoned the Court, the executive branch has a responsibility to aid Congress in protecting interstate commerce by requesting judicial assistance in removing obstructions to the flow of railroad traffic and mail carriage. Moreover, the Court reasoned, by creating an impediment to Congress's control over interstate traffic, the strike was in the nature of a public nuisance. Accordingly, since public nuisances are subject to abatement by judicial order at the request of the government,[33] the federal court had authority to enjoin the railroad strike.

The injunction issued in the *Debs* case, as noted above, broke the momentum of the Pullman strike and the Supreme Court's unanimous approval of the injunction multiplied the extent of that blow to labor unionists. Nevertheless, in the long run, it had a countervailing beneficial impact upon the labor movement in

---

[a]Contempt traditionally has been tried by the court without a jury.

that it focused national attention on the injunction weapon and generated considerable political support for labor's demand that this sort of judicial intervention into labor-management conflicts be curbed. That political response was
reflected in the 1896 Democratic National Platform that read, in part: "[W]e
especially object to government by injunction as a new and highly dangerous
form of oppression by which Federal Judges, in contempt of the laws of the
States and the rights of citizens, become at once legislators, judges and execu-
tioners; and we approve the bill passed by the last session of the United States
Senate, and now pending in the House of Representatives, relative to contempt
in Federal courts and providing for trials by jury in certain cases of contempt."[34]

As we shall see, it was decades, however, before the political challenge to
labor injunctions made a lasting inroad upon the legal system. In the meantime,
courts continued to enjoin all sorts of union activities with little consideration
to traditional standards either for justifying the use of the injunctive remedy
or for cautious constraints on the breadth of the injunctive order. As Charles O.
Gregory once observed:

> [M]any courts using the injunction against the activities of labor unions
> fell into the bad habit of overlooking the need for proof of specific and
> independently unlawful conduct, either already committed or threatened,
> on which to base their injunctive orders. They came to look at much of
> organized labor's economic coercive activity as enjoinable in itself, with-
> out bothering to find or to state in their opinions that it was also unlaw-
> ful. This was an unfortunate tendancy which fed on itself. It seemed
> to lead many courts to grant sweeping injunctions on the basis of
> personal or class dislike of organized labor's economic program instead
> of in accordance with settled standards of law.[35]

Impact of Early Federal Legislation

In 1908, the Supreme Court of the United States dealt two more blows to
labor union supporters. Both involved consideration of federal statutes enacted
under Congress's power to regulate interstate commerce. The first case to be
decided concerned the constitutionality of part of the Erdman Act of 1898.
This statute, which was a byproduct of the report by a presidential commission
appointed in 1894 to investigate the Pullman strike, reflected Congress's
attempt to adjust several aspects of employer-employee relations in the nation's
railroad industry. In large part, the Act was designed to avoid strikes by requiring the Interstate Commerce Commission to mediate controversies involving
wages, hours, or other terms of employment. It also provided for a procedure
by which the parties could submit their disputes to arbitration, and the means
by which an arbitration award could be enforced in the U.S. courts. Further, it

required that when the parties agreed to arbitrate their differences they would, for a stated period, refrain from work stoppages. Finally, the Erdman Act prohibited railroads from engaging in a variety of activities designed to discourage union membership. Included in the banned practices was discrimination against, or discharge of, an employee because of union membership. It was this last provision that was challenged for want of constitutionality in *Adair* v. *United States*, 208 U.S. 161 (1908).

Adair had been found guilty of threatening a railroad worker with discharge because of the latter's membership in a labor organization. Reviewing that conviction, the majority of the Supreme Court of the United States concluded that that part of the Erdman Act used to convict Adair was unconstitutional. The Court explained that the Fifth Amendment protection against the taking of property without due process includes the right not to have one's freedom to contract interferred with by the government, absent justification reasonably related to serving the common good. There could be no such justification for this law, stated Mr. Justice Harlan in his opinion for the court, because the rights of employers and employees to contract for employment must be equal in order not to be arbitrary and this law placed restraints on the employer that were not placed on the employee.[36] Further, Harlan asserted that the restraint on the employer imposed by the Erdman Act was unjustifiable because it did not involve conduct directly related to the carrying on of interstate commerce and, therefore, was not within the legislative power granted to Congress by the Commerce clause of Article I.[37]

In separate opinions, Justices McKenna and Holmes dissented from the Court's holding. In part, McKenna relied on prior decisions in which the Court had recognized the validity of Congress's power to regulate other aspects of a railroad's freedom of contract — that is, such aspects as rate regulation and prohibitions on price fixing. Further, McKenna rejected the majority's contention that this law did not involve conduct directly affecting interstate commerce. This law, he rebutted, "will prevent or tend to prevent the stoppage of every wheel in every car on an entire railroad system"[38] and therefore clearly did deal with conduct directly affecting such commerce. Finally, McKenna drew a distinction between the protection of private business rights and the protection of the rights of businesses such as railroads, which, he stated, are quasi-public.[39]

Holmes' dissent argued that freedom to contract is not absolute; that that freedom can be restrained when required by important public need. Congress, he concluded, can determine whether facilitating unionization of railroads serves the public need and that having so found, the Court should not interfere with the corrective legislation adopted by Congress.

In *Adair*, the Supreme Court placed the railroad unions back in the situation —shared by other unions—of having to organize under the constant threat of discharge of union supporters. A week later, adding salt to the wound, the Supreme Court, in *Loewe* v. *Lawlor*, 208 U.S. 274 (1908), introduced a new hurdle for union activity.

Loewe, which arose out of a strike at a hat plant and a boycott of those dealing with the company, became popularly known as the *Danbury Hatters* case. The purpose of the strike and boycott was to get union recognition for a group of hatmakers employed in Danbury, Connecticut. In response, a suit against the union was brought under the Sherman Antitrust Act of 1890 to recover money allegedly lost because of the strike and boycott. The union lost the suit and was eventually assessed treble damages (as called for in civil suits under the Sherman Act) in the amount of $252,000 — an enormous sum in the early part of the century.[40] The Supreme Court unanimously refuted the contention that labor activity is not business and therefore was not intended to be covered by the Sherman Act. To support its conclusion, the Court noted that Congress had rejected various proposed amendments that would have exempted workers and farmers from the Sherman Act. Moreover, the Court proclaimed, "the act made no distinction between classes;" its prohibitions were applicable to *every* contract, combination or conspiracy in restraint of trade.[41] Because the union members were jointly liable for payment of the judgment amount, the company was able to, and did, attach savings accounts and place judgment liens on the members' homes. Fourteen years after the litigation began and under the threat of foreclosure of the liens, the judgment was satisfied, largely with money raised from the voluntary contributions of A. F. of L. members.[42]

There were those who bitterly complained that the Court's decision in the *Danbury Hatters* case added labor disputes to the coverage of the Sherman Antitrust Act, although that had not been intended by Congress. Others insisted that the Court correctly discerned congressional intent from Congress's failure to expressly provide for the exclusion of workers and farmers when the Sherman Act was promulgated. But any deficiency in the Court's result probably should, as Harry Shulman once suggested,[43] be attributed not to the Court but to Congress. Congress had an opportunity to carefully weigh the implications of the Sherman Act as it related to labor union activities and to expressly announce its intended policy in that area. Yet it adopted a statute that left to the Court the task of resolving this issue.

Six years after the *Danbury Hatters* case, Congress adopted the Clayton Act, an expansion and refinement of the Sherman Antitrust Act. Sections 6 and 20 of this statute were regarded as performance on a pledge that the Democratic Party made in its Platform of 1912 when it committed itself to the withdrawal of labor and farm organizations from the shadow of the Sherman Act.[44] Section 6 of the Clayton Act states that "the labor of a human being is not a commodity or article of commerce." Further, it declares that the antitrust laws are not to be construed as forbidding the operation of labor organizations, nor as restraining them from carrying out their lawful objective. Section 20 prohibits the federal courts from issuing restraining orders or injunctions in labor disputes "unless necessary to prevent irreparable injury to

property or to a property right." Further, it forbids any such order from prohibiting the refusal to work or of efforts to peacefully persuade others to stop
work. President Wilson characterized the provision as a "veritable emancipation" of workers, and Samuel Gompers hailed it as the "industrial magna charta
upon which the working people will rear their construction of industrial freedom."[45]

But despite these superlatives, the Court eventually had to determine the
meaning of sections 6 and 20 as applied to particular facts, and once again
Congress provided little guidance respecting the specific intent of its grand
proclamations. In the words of Frankfurter and Greene: "With a legislative
history like that which surrounds the Clayton Act, talk about the legislative
intent as a means of construing legislation is simply repeating an empty formula.
The Supreme Court had to find meaning where Congress had done its best to
conceal meaning."[46] That interpretive task came before the Court in *Duplex Co.*
v. *Deering*, 254 U.S. 443 (1921), and unionists were not at all pleased with the
result.

The International Association of Machinists had demanded recognition as
the collective bargaining representative of the employees of Duplex Company,
a printing press manufacturer. Amongst other things, the union sought a closed
shop in which only union members would be employed and demanded certain
improved work benefits. The union had already succeeded in obtaining all of
the terms demanded of Duplex from the latter's three competitor manufacturers
of printing presses.

Duplex rejected the demands with the result that the union resorted to
various forms of economic pressure. For one, it called a strike of Duplex workers.
This was not too effective inasmuch as only about one out of twenty workers
responded to the strike call. The union also called upon potential buyers of
Duplex's presses not to deal with Duplex, urged a trucker not to haul the presses,
and urged union members neither to install nor repair Duplex presses until Duplex
complied with the union's demands. In response to these pressures, Duplex
sought injunctive relief from the federal district court based on the theory that
the machinists' union was violating the Sherman Act by seeking to place restraints
upon its trade. The requested injunction was denied by the lower courts, but that
denial was reversed by the Supreme Court with Brandeis, Holmes, and Clarke
dissenting.

The thrust of the majority's position was that the Clayton Act's restriction
upon federal courts issuing labor injunctions applied only to activity directly involving the disputing employer and union. The Court concluded that coercive
union pressure on third parties, such as customers of an employer with whom a
union has a conflict, was not intended to be exempt from the Sherman Act's
prohibitions against restraints of trade.

Mr. Justice Brandeis prepared the opinion in which the three dissenters took
issue with the majority's assumption that workers employed by employers other

than Duplex could not have an interest in the product produced by Duplex. "[I]t is lawful," asserted Brandeis, "for all members of a union by whomever employed to refuse to handle materials whose production weakens the union."[47] The union's boycott efforts were characterized by Brandeis as self-defensive actions in the form of refusing to deal with the product of an employer who had refused to deal with the union.[48] Moreover, the dissenters rejected the majority's interpretation of Congress's intentions in adopting the Clayton Act. Emphasizing the events leading to the effort to have sections 7 and 20 included in the Clayton Act, Brandeis insisted that Congress's design was to substitute its own policy for the policies previously determined by judges with regard to the use of injunctions in any form of industrial struggle between workers and employers. Thus, he concluded, the restrictions placed by the Clayton Act on injunctions in labor disputes were aimed at any conflict between labor and management in which labor pursues its group self-interest.

In the next decade the Supreme Court reiterated its limited reading of the Clayton Act's protection against federal court injunctions issued in labor disputes.[49] And, in the lower federal courts, at least 20 injunctions were granted against union activities within a half dozen years of *Deering.*[50]

Ironically, although the adoption of the Clayton Act was originally proclaimed as the bulwark against federal courts being able to utilize the Sherman Act so as to enjoin peaceful union action, in fact it became the function of the Clayton Act to provide the very authority for issuing such injunctions. The reason for this is that injunctive relief under the Sherman Act was available only upon the petition of the Department of Justice. Commencing in 1913, Congress regularly attached to the appropriations bill funding the enforcement of the Sherman Act, a rider prohibiting the use of such funds to prosecute suits against labor groups.[51] Accordingly, all of the injunctive actions referred to in the previous paragraph were suits brought by employers based on section 16 of the Clayton Act, which authorized private actions, as contrasted with government actions, for injunctive relief against restraints of trade. Such actions were not available to private litigants prior to adoption of the Clayton Act. Commenting upon this turn of events, Frankfurter and Greene stated: "The Clayton Act was the product of twenty years of voluminous agitation. It came as clay into the hands of the federal courts . . . . The result justifies an application of a familiar bit of French cynicism: the more things are legislatively changed, the more they remain the same judicially."[52]

Injunctions against strikes, picketing, or boycotts were not the only legal burdens placed upon union growth and influence during the first third of this century. A contractual device — earning the union epithet of "Yellow-Dog Contract" (only a miserable cur would ask a man to sign one, and only a dirty yellow dog would agree to sign it) — came into vogue in the 1890s.

To employers the notion of these contracts was simple, fair, and reasonable. When a person comes to work for you, you assume that he or she is satisfied with the terms of hire. The "yellow-dog" contract merely formalized those expectations by requiring the employee to accept the condition of working in a nonunion shop. To assure this, the agreement stated that the employee would quit any union to which he belonged when hired and that he would not join or become involved with any union during his employment. Some contracts went so far as to forbid any dealings or even communications with union members respecting union activities.[53]

It was just such a yellow-dog contract, giving rise to the charges of discrimination against union activity, that had been the focus of the dispute in the previously discussed *Adair* case. Whereas the federal law struck down in *Adair* had indirectly sought to outlaw yellow-dog contracts by prohibiting employer discrimination against union activities, *Coppage* v. *Kansas*, 236 U.S. 1 (1915), involved a state statute that sought directly to outlaw such contracts.

The Kansas legislature in 1903 had adopted an act prohibiting any person from coercing, requiring, demanding, or influencing another to enter into "any agreement, either written or verbal, not to joint or become or remain a member of any labor organization or association, as a condition of securing employment or continuing in the employment of such individual, firm or corporation." Coppage, a railroad supervisor working in Kansas, ordered a switchman to sign an agreement to withdraw from membership in the Switchman's Union of North American. As a result, Coppage was charged, tried, convicted, and fined for violating the Kansas statute. He challenged the state law's constitutionality by asserting that it amounted to taking liberty and property without due process of law. The Kansas Supreme Court upheld the act. However, Coppage persuaded a 6-3 majority of the U.S. Supreme Court to declare the Kansas law unconstitutional. In essence, the Court divided over the meaning of constitutional liberty to contract. To the majority, it meant the right to exploit one's superior bargaining power; to the dissenters, it meant the right to deal in a manner not inconsistent with the legislature's reasonable definition of the public welfare.

Relying on the *Adair* decision, the U.S. Supreme Court concluded that part of constitutionally guaranteed liberty is the right to stipulate the terms of employment. The Court conceded that the state could infringe that liberty of contract if it was necessary in order to aid the general welfare. However, because unions are not "public institutions, charged by law with public or governmental duties," the Court could find no such state interest involved in this legislation. The inequities of economic fortune, explained the Court, are a normal and inevitable result of contractual freedom and therefore the state may not intervene simply for the purpose of removing such inequities. Further, the Court suggested that the employer's protected right to refuse to keep union men in his employ is but a counterpart of the union member's right to refuse to work for employers who hire nonunion people. "[C]an there be one rule of liberty for the labor organization and its members, and a different and more restrictive rule for

employers? We think not . . . ."[54] Finally, the Court cited to decisions of five
state courts of last resort striking down similar statutes for want of constitutionality and claimed that earlier Kansas decisions followed a rationale inconsistent with the state court's decision in *Coppage.*

Justice Holmes dissented in a short separate opinion. He asserted that
liberty of contract begins with equality of position between the parties.
Accordingly, he argued, it is consistent with that liberty to adopt legislation
protecting the worker's right to join a union in order to acquire such equality
of bargaining position.

A much longer dissent, offered by Mr. Justice Day and joined by Justice
Hughes, emphasized that "the right of contract is not absolute and unyielding,
but is subject to limitations and restraint in the interest of public health, safety
and welfare . . . ."[55] The legislative judgment respecting the needs of public
health, safety and welfare, asserted Day and Hughes, should be set aside only
if it is clear that the legislation is so divorced of reasonableness as to be arbitrary
and capricious. Accordingly, they concluded that the Kansas statute, which
was designed to protect the individual's privilege of becoming a labor union
member, was valid because it in fact did bear a reasonable relation to carrying
out the state's interest in protecting the right of people to associate in such
organizations. Moreover, they rejected the argument that *Adair* required the
majority's result in this case. Being free to refuse someone employment does
not give the right to insert any stipulation you choose into a contract of
employment, argued Day and Hughes.

As one of several illustrations of this point, they suggested that it would be
appropriate for a state to prohibit employers from conditioning employment
upon the workers' agreeing to quit the state militia, or to prohibit employers
from conditioning employment upon quitting membership in a particular
political party. Finally, Day and Hughes contended that the majority had made
an erroneous comparison in suggesting that the employer's right to refuse to
employ union members is a counterpart of the worker's right to refuse to work
in a nonunion shop. The privilege being protected under the Kansas law, they
explained, was the freedom to associate with other workers in an effort to
promote their mutual interests. Therefore, the analogous employer right is to
join with other employers in an effort to promote their mutual interests. Just
as the state protects the organizational rights of workers, they argued, so too it
should protect the organizational rights of employers and thereby provide the
equity sought by the majority.

Of course, at the heart of this controversy was the issue of whether the
constitutional protection of liberty and property reflects an enshrinement of
laissez-faire economic principles. The majority position gave constitutional
status to such principles, whereas the dissenters regarded the choice of market
system as a matter for legislative discretion.

One might wonder why the yellow-dog contract generated all of this fuss
in the first place. If the governing legal rule acknowledged the employer's right

to discharge a worker for union activity, did the worker lose or the employer gain anything by using a yellow-dog contract to formalize the employer's right to discharge? In fact, such contracts antagonized unionists from the standpoint of both morale and vulnerability. For one thing, the contracts reminded workers of their employers' displeasure with, and reaction to, union activities. For another, the contracts placed a moral deterrent in front of workers to keep them from engaging in union contacts, not because of their fear of discharge, but because their sense of honor might cause them to adhere to their agreement. Still another aspect was to give the fence-sitter a new excuse for not getting involved in union activities. But perhaps more than anything, the unions feared and hated this contractual device because it opened new avenues through which employers could use the institution of law to destroy the unions themselves. The basis for this last concern was well illustrated in *Hitchman Coal & Coke Co. v. Mitchell*, 245 U.S. 229 (1917).

Hitchman operated a mine in West Virginia employing 200 to 300 men. It was unionized after about a year's operation and continued to operate as a union mine for several years. During the period of operations as a union mine, there were several strikes. In April of 1906 the mine was shut down by a strike. In early June some workers approached management and requested an end to the strike. The company agreed to resume operations so long as the mine was run nonunion. Work resumed on June 12th, with the employees agreeing not to remain members of or be represented by a union.

By the early 1900s, the United Mine Workers Union of America had been quite successful in organizing miners in Ohio, Indiana, and Illinois, where the entire industry operated on a union-members-only basis. Part of the industry was organized in Pennsylvania as well, and all of these areas made up what the union referred to as the Central Competitive Field. Most coal mines in West Virginia, in contrast, were nonunion. The union had considerable difficulty in gaining benefits in the Central Competitive Field because low-cost coal from the nonunion mines of West Virginia competed with union-produced coal and thereby made it difficult for unionized operators to be able to provide the increased benefits demanded by the United Mine Workers. Accordingly, in 1907 union officials decided that it would be necessary to unionize the mines in West Virginia and that this could best be accomplished by imposing an assessment on union members working elsewhere in order to financially support workers in West Virginia called out on strike for the purpose of gaining union recognition from the mine operators.

The union learned of the yellow-dog contracts at the Hitchman mine when it sought voluntary recognition from the company. Nevertheless, the union engaged in organizing activities and informed the company that as soon as there was enough union support, they would close down the mine through a work stoppage that would continue until the union was recognized as the miners' bargaining agent.

The Hitchman mine owners went into federal court seeking injunctive relief

against what they termed a threat to their legally protected contractual relationship with their workers. The contracts referred to were the agreements requiring
the workers to refrain from union activities. An injunction was granted and was
upheld by the Supreme Court over the dissent of Justices Brandeis, Holmes,
and Clarke. Stated the Court: "The same liberty which enables men to form
unions, and through the union to enter into agreements with employers willing
to agree, entitles other men to remain independent of the union and other
employers to agree with them to employ no man who owes any allegiance or
obligation to the union."[56] The Court relied on case law applying to labor cases
the maxim "use your own property so as not to injure the rights of another."[57]
Enticing an employee away from service in breach of that employee's contract of
employment had, by the early part of the century, become well recognized as an
actionable tort. Thus, the Court concluded that the mine owner's were entitled
to the requested relief from the union's attempted interference with the mine
workers' contractual commitment to keep clear of union activities.

One might wonder why the Clayton Act, adopted in 1914, did not bar the
injunctive relief given in *Hitchman*. After all, unlike the *Duplex* case, at issue here
was a dispute directly involving the employees of the complaining employer.
Interestingly, the union's lawyers did not assert that the Clayton Act barred the
federal court from enjoining the union's actions. Perhaps, as Frankfurter and
Greene have suggested, the union's lawyers assumed that because the injunction
had been issued prior to adoption of the Clayton Act, the *Hitchman* suit was
unaffected by that statute. However, such an assumption was not compelled by
the language of the Act. Moreover, a few years later, in *American Steel Foundaries*
v. *Tri-City Central Trades Council*, 257 U.S. 184 (1921), the Court held that the
Act was applicable to a decree that, even though issued prior to enactment of
Clayton, was still in litigation on appeal when the Clayton Act became law.

Nevertheless, had the Clayton Act question been raised and had the Court
treated it as relevant to weighing the *continuing* validity of the injunction in
Hitchman, the Court's probable response would have been to note that the Clayton Act exempts only "lawful" union activities from federal court decrees and
that because the conduct in question constituted the tort of inducement to
break a contract, the union's action was not lawful and, therefore, was not protected by the anti-injunction provisions of Clayton. Thus, the Court's willingness to protect the sanctity of the yellow-dog contract clearly spelled legal doom
for the union's efforts against Hitchman and any other employer using this
form of employment agreement.

Brandeis's dissenting opinion in *Hitchman* pointed out that the yellow-dog
contract at issue created an at will employment agreement – that is, a contract
which either party can terminate at any time – and, therefore, the employee
was free to terminate it at any time. This being so, he noted, the only contractual
breach would be if an employee became a union member without withdrawing

from employment with Hitchman. But the union's campaign was directed at getting the miners to agree to join the union and, upon getting sufficient agreement, to sign them up as members and then have them withdraw from employment—strike—in order to force union recognition. Thus, the union was not interfering with Hitchman's contractual interests. Moreover, Brandeis rejected the suggestion that the union's scheme for gaining recognition was coercive in a legal sense: "If it is coercion to threaten to strike unless plaintiff consents to a closed union shop, it is coercion also to threaten not to give one employment unless the applicant will consent to a closed nonunion shop. The employer may sign the union agreement for fear that *labor* may not be otherwise obtainable; the workman may sign the individual agreement for fear that employment may not be otherwise obtainable. But such fear does not imply coercion in a legal sense."[58]

As a result of the decision in *Hitchman,* employers were put on notice that by having yellow-dog contracts with their workers, the federal courts would be available to help them keep unions at bay. The importance of having such contracts was reinforced by the Court's decision in the *American Steel Foundaries* case[59] in which it held that an injunction against unionizing was not available if the employer did not have a yellow-dog contract with its employees.

Employers took to the offensive by encouraging each other to adopt a nonunion shop policy in an approach they called "the American Plan." It is estimated that by the end of the 1920s, well over a million workers had signed yellow-dog contracts and that over 60 injunctions had been issued pursuant to the authority of *Hitchman.*[60] Labor, however, was not the only victim. There were political repercussions that had an adverse impact upon conservative forces as well. An example was the response to the nomination of John J. Parker, a judge of the U.S. Court of Appeals, to the position on the Supreme Court vacated by the death of Mr. Justice Edward Sanford in 1930.

Judge Parker's nomination was attacked in the Senate confirmation process both by the National Association for the Advancement of Colored People, because they considered Parker to be a racist, and by the American Federation of Labor, because Parker had, on the authority of *Hitchman,* voted to affirm a lower court injunction against organizing employees covered by yellow-dog contracts. When the nomination of Parker failed, President Hoover submitted the name of Owen J. Roberts, a very prosperous corporate lawyer who had gained acclaim for his leadership in the prosecution of corruption involving the leasing of government-owned oil lands, which had become known as the Teapot Dome scandal. Labor leadership was favorably inclined toward Roberts because he had, on occasion, provided legal services for some unions at nominal fees. The Roberts nomination was confirmed by the Senate. Although Roberts' initial performance on the Court left union supporters convinced that he was, after all, no less conservative than Parker, he ultimately redeemed his reputation with labor by casting the swing vote in upholding the constitutionality of the National Labor Relations Act.

Adoption of Current Legislation

Two major pieces of federal labor legislation preceeded the enactment of the National Labor Relations Act. The first was the Railway Labor Act, which was adopted in 1926 with the joint support of railroad unions and management. The policies adopted through this Act were largely a reflection of standards of conduct imposed on the industry by the government during the First World War when the railroads were government operated. In addition, the Railway Labor Act was a byproduct of persistent efforts to find a legislative formula that would promote labor peace and pass constitutional muster. The Erdman Act of 1898, which had fallen beneath the judicial axe, was followed in 1913 by the Newlands Act. This law created a permanent board of mediation that had, over the next few years, successfully averted work stoppages on a number of occasions.

With America's entry into the First World War, President Wilson created a Board of Railroad Wages and Working Conditions to assist the Railway Administration. The latter was a government agency given temporary control of the nation's railroads. Also influential was the National War Labor Board, co-chaired by the then former President and later Chief Justice, William Howard Taft. When Congress transfered control of the railroads back to their owners in 1920, it adopted the Transportation Act, which provided for continuation of existing collective agreements. It also established a Railway Labor Board with mediatory responsibilities. But due to a lack of enforcement powers, the board was relatively ineffective. This experience led to the series of conferences between the railroad unions and owners that produced the proposals adopted as the Railway Labor Act in 1926. The Railway Labor Act was amended in 1934, and in 1936, most of its provisions were extended to cover airlines. It was again amended in 1940, and further changes were made in 1951, 1964, and 1966.

The Act as amended prohibits employers from interfering with the workers' right of self-organization. When the majority of workers are union represented, the Railway Labor Act requires the employer and union to bargain prior to making any changes in the terms and conditions of employment. The Act also establishes procedures for determining whether a majority of employees wish to be collectively represented by a union, procedures for mediating differences and for arbitrating unresolved disputes concerning the interpretation or application of collective bargaining agreements between the unions and the railroads.

A challenge to the Railway Labor Act's constitutionality reached the

Supreme Court in *Texas & New Orleans Railroad Co.* v. *Brotherhood of Railway & Steamship Clerks*, 281 U.S. 548 (1930). In that case the lower federal courts had enjoined a railroad from interfering with the unionizing rights of its workers. The railroad's interference consisted of sponsoring a union of its own despite the fact that the majority of its workers were already represented by the Brotherhood of Railway Clerks. The injunction was based on the Railway Labor Act's prohibitions against such interference with union activity.

Relying on *Adair* and *Coppage*, the railroad argued that the Act unconstitutionally infringed upon its inherent right to contract with its employees on whatever basis it chose. Moreover, and with considerable irony, the railroad argued that section 20 of the Clayton Act barred the federal courts from authority to issue an injunction concerning this labor dispute.

Without dissent, the Supreme Court upheld the Act's constitutionality. Congress's authority to adopt this law was explained as an appropriate measure to protect interstate commerce by recognizing the right of workers to collectively organize to secure agreements with the railroads. "Such collective action would be a mockery if representation were made futile by interferences with freedom of choice. Thus the prohibition by Congress of interference with the selection of representatives . . . instead of being an invasion of the constitutional rights of [the workers or railroads], was based on the recognition of the rights of both."[61]

Chief Justice Hughes, writing the Court's opinion, expended but a few lines on the *Adair* and *Coppage* cases, which were treated as inapplicable on the grounds that the Railway Labor Act did not interfere with the railroad's right to hire or fire its employees, but merely protected the workers' rights to decide for themselves whom their representatives would be. With similar dispatch, the Court disposed of the Clayton Act contention by explaining that the requisite irreparable injury had been shown by the union in this case. Moreover, the Court suggested that the intent of Congress in adopting Clayton was not to withhold injunctive relief in support of an expressed statutory right such as that created by the Railway Labor Act. The Court, by dealing with *Adair* and *Coppage* as involving principles distinguishable from the constitutional issues raised by the Railway Labor Act, avoided overruling those cases. In fact, however, as a practical matter the *Texas & New Orleans* case had the impact of overruling *Adair* and *Coppage*.

The Railway Labor Act, as did the Erdman Act, regulated employer demands respecting the terms of the employment contract. The nature of the prohibited employer conduct (i.e., placing restraints upon union activity) were the same under both statutes and in both instances were justified on the grounds that Congress can take steps to stabilize labor relations in an industry serving interstate commerce. Yet these restraints were held unconstitutional with respect to the Erdman Act in *Adair*, but valid with respect to the Railway Labor Act in the *Texas & New Orleans* case. The only real difference between the two decisions was the personnel on the Court. Of the justices on the bench when *Adair* was decided, only Holmes was still on the Court in *Texas & New Orleans*. Moreover, Holmes had been amongst the dissenters in *Adair*.

A similar observation can be made in comparing *Coppage* and *Texas & New Orleans*. Although *Coppage* involved a state, rather than a federal statute, the Court had used the *Adair* rationale in overturning the Kansas anti-yellow-dog statute. It will be recalled that the majority's reasoning in *Coppage* essentially was that the legislature cannot constitutionally interfere with an employer's exploitation of its economic advantage by prohibiting the employer from negotiating an employment contract that limits employment to those who refrain from union activities. Yet, in *Texas & New Orleans,* the Court was upholding the constitutionality of a statute that placed the very same sort of restraint on the employer's exercise of superior bargaining ability. Four of the members of the bench that had decided *Coppage* were still on the Court in 1930. McReynolds and VanDevanter had been part of the majority in *Coppage*, whereas Holmes and Hughes had dissented. When the test of the Railway Labor Act came before the Court in *Texas & New Orleans,* Hughes, now Chief Justice, gave himself the task of writing the opinion upholding the Act's constitutional validity and was joined amongst others by VanDevanter as well as by Holmes. Mr. Justice VanDevanter did not attempt to explain the seeming inconsistency of his vote; Chief Justice Hughes having removed that chore by discussing *Coppage* as though it was not inconsistent with the *Texas & New Orleans* decision. Mr. Justice McReynolds did not hear the oral argument of the *Texas* case and, therefore, as is customary, did not participate in the decision.

Perhaps encouraged by the constitutional success of the Railway Labor Act and clearly acting in response to the very urgent political climate caused by the economic crisis known as the Great Depression, Congress within a few years of the *Texas & New Orleans* decision undertook further legislative reordering of labor-management relations.

Its next legislative step was designed to undo the results of decisions such as *Debs, Loewe, Adair, Deering,* and *Hitchman.* Despite the Supreme Court's decisions in those cases, legislators identified with labor union philosophy had continued to press for limitations upon labor injunctions. In 1927, for example, a bill limiting the use of such injunctions was submitted by Senator Henrik Shipstead. Shipstead's bill was modified after hearings were conducted by the Senate Judiciary Committee, but it was never adopted.

Charges of abuse of the labor injunction had, by the summer of 1928, become sufficiently persuasive so that both political parties called for reforms concerning this area in adopting their respective national platforms. The legislative approach suggested was similar to that taken in the Erdman and Clayton Acts, but this time, the statutory language was to be more precise and more comprehensive. The political impetus for this renewed legislative effort, as noted, was greatly accelerated by the Great Depression that began late in 1929.

Whereas national income in 1929 had been in excess of $83 billion, by 1932 it had declined to a little under $40 billion. Industrial production in 1932 was barely over half of the 1929 level, and the total of wages earned in the United States was less than half the amount for 1929. The reduction in wage earnings was a result both of decreased wage levels and massive unemployment. By 1932 nearly one out of four persons in the United States wanting a job was unemployed. In Malvern, Arkansas, lumber workers were paid 10 cents per hour; in Tennessee textile mills, women received as little as $2.39 for a 50 hour work week. United Mine Workers' President John L. Lewis charged that the economic system was a competitive design whose purpose was to see how little a worker could eat and still survive. One scholar, summing up the resulting political climate observed:

> There was as a result a widespread loss of confidence in the ability of unregulated free enterprise to maintain full employment and the rising standards which had been foreseen during the twenties. . . . Measures to promote greater equality of bargaining power, therefore, began to appear proper public policy, in order to increase wages. Among workers themselves, moreover, the experience of depression and mass insecurity turned them toward unions.[62]

Thus, in 1932 it became possible for two progressively oriented Republicans, in a Republican controlled Congress faced with an up-coming presidential election, to sponsor successfully a bill designed to remove serious obstacles to union organizational efforts. The legislation was proposed by Senator George W. Norris and Representative Fiorello LaGuardia. The bill was reputedly drafted by then professor and later Supreme Court Justice, Felix Frankfurter. Justification for the legislation had already been provided in a book co-authored by Frankfurter in 1930 and in journal articles and a book published in 1932 by Edwin E. Witte[63] These works presented, in the form of scholarly criticism, the picture of the federal bench using labor injunctions in situations not meeting traditional standards for this form of extraordinary relief. Both Frankfurter and Witte, as well as several other academicians, plus Donald Richberg, a Chicago attorney, were called in as consultants by Senator Norris's committee.

The Norris-LaGuardia Act was passed by the House 363 to 13, and by the Senate 75 to 5. President Hoover signed it into law in March of 1932. Its central policy is an enshrinement of the *laissez-faire* philosophy of labor-management relations that had for so many years been espoused by Samuel Gompers.

The Act contains a declaration of policy proclaiming the equity of protecting the laborer's right of self-organization as a counterpart to governmental protection of capital collectively organized into corporations and business associations. To carry out this policy it declares yellow-dog contracts to be unenforceable and contrary to the public policy of the United States. Further, and even more importantly, the Act removes from the federal courts the power to issue injunctions in labor disputes except for narrowly defined situations and only after specific standards of proof and strictly confined procedures have been satisfied. Specifically exempt from federal court injunction under Norris-LaGuardia is such conduct as refusing to remain in any relationship of employment, publicizing the existence of or facts involving a labor dispute, and advising or urging others to engage in conduct such as picketting and work stoppages.

The procedural restraints imposed by Norris-LaGuardia include placing a five-day time limit upon the life of a restraining order issued upon one side's allegations of substantial irreparable harm where circumstances do not permit notice to the other side and proof by testimony subject to cross examination. For the most part, the remaining procedural restraints on labor injunctions constitute a statutory restatement of the traditional rules of equity limiting the availability of extraordinary relief granted in the form of an injunctive decree.

One particular departure from those traditional rules, however, is the Norris-LaGuardia provision entitling anyone charged with violation of an injunction arising out of a labor dispute to be tried by a jury rather than by the judge issuing the decree. This variation from the traditional approach to the trial for contempt of court clearly indicated congressional sympathy with union assertions that the federal bench had abused its authority in dealing with labor organizations.

Later that same year, Franklin D. Roosevelt was elected President of the United States together with Democratic majorities in the House and Senate. The Democratic campaign pledged that the government would take major new steps to combat the grave economic depression. As Governor of New York, Roosevelt had developed a close relationship with several of the nation's most influential union leaders, and in the election of 1932 he received their strong support. Within a few months, the new administration successfully pressed through Congress the National Industrial Recovery Act, section 7 of which was thought to be of particular benefit to labor organizations. United Mine Workers President John L. Lewis, with characteristic gusto, pronounced it the most significant legal document since the Emancipation Proclamation.[64]

If one takes a detached retrospective view, the National Industrial Recovery Act can more accurately be described as a step in the direction of economic fascism in the sense of creating a system of "state-capitalism" or a corporate state. The N.I.R.A., as a result, was adopted over the expressed misgivings and negative votes of some of Roosevelt's staunchest supporters such as Senator, and later Supreme Court Justice, Hugo Black and Senators LaFollette and Norris.[65]

The National Industrial Recovery Act was designed to allow business leaders to stabilize commercial and industrial activity under government supervision. Associations were to be formed on an industry basis to draw up codes of fair competition standardizing such things as promotional and marketing activities, financial practices, pricing practices, and the like. These codes were required to be submitted through an agency, called the National Recovery Administration, to the president who could approve them if they were found to comply with the basic policies of the Act. Once approved, violation of the code was made a misdemeanor. Section 7 of the Act required such codes to guarantee the right of employees to unionize free from employer interference.

With this encouragement, labor unions stepped up their organizational efforts. Those efforts produced conflicts over the meaning of the section 7 guarantees with the result that by August of 1933 the president established a National Labor Board with Senator Robert F. Wagner serving as chairman. The board's charge from the president was to mediate or arbitrate disputes between labor and management that interfered with the purposes of the NIRA. If the majority of workers wished to be collectively represented and the employer refused to deal with the union on behalf of all the workers, the board treated the employers' conduct as a violation of section 7 responsibilities, and this was reported to the National Recovery Administration and to the attorney general for appropriate action.

Employers, led by the National Association of Manufacturers, soon began resisting the National Labor Board. It became apparent that the board was not really able to effectively enforce its orders. The NIRA, by its language, did not compel employers to deal with the unions or to cooperate with government mediators. Enforcement proceedings relying on action by other agencies or departments meant administrative delay, at the very least, and possibly resistence by those other public officials who were not always in agreement with the board's conclusions and were reluctant to have the legality of the entire NIRA challenged for the sake of enforcing such determinations. For numerous reasons, there was serious question concerning the constitutionality of the National Industrial Recovery Act and thus a desire to avoid legal confrontations.

Further, employers hit upon the device of encouraging and recognizing company dominated unions as a means of satisfying the compliance demands of NIRA officials. The company union was not a new concept, but by November of 1933 the National Industrial Conference Board was able to report that nearly two-thirds of the company unions then in existence had sprung up after enactment of the NIRA.[66]

Senator Wagner set to work to get separate legislation detailing the legal responsibilities of employers with respect to unionizing and to give a new federal agency the power to enforce findings of violation by itself securing orders from the federal courts. Employer groups mounted a strong counterattack against Wagner's efforts, thereby slowing down the progress of the legislation. Nevertheless, prompted by increased strike activity, Congress did accede to a plea from Roosevelt by issuing a Joint Resolution in June of 1934 that called upon the president to establish a board to investigate controversies under section 7 of the NIRA and to conduct employee elections respecting representational demands.[67]

The agency established pursuant to the Joint Resolution was called the National Labor Relations Board. (For reasons soon to become clear, it is now referred to by labor historians as the First National Labor Relations Board.)

Designated as chairman was Lloyd K. Garrison, Dean of the University of Wisconsin Law School. He resigned after a few months and was replaced by Francis Biddle, a Harvard educated Philadelphia lawyer. There were two other public members of the board.

A major issue for the board was whether a union winning a majority of votes was entitled to represent only its supporters or to represent all of the workers involved in the election. A conflict had arisen between the NLB and the National Recovery Administration over this issue. The NLB had supported the concept of exclusive representation by the winner and was followed in this policy by its successor. For a while the new agency gained cooperation from the NRA. But, as with its predecessor, the National Labor Relations Board's chief problem was obtaining compliance with its decisions. Its principal weapon was to have the National Recovery Administration remove the offending company's Blue Eagle. (The Blue Eagle was an official symbol designating enterprises in compliance with an approved NIRA code. To induce compliance with the codes, a national campaign had been mounted to persuade the public that it was a patriotic duty to avoid doing business with those who did not possess the Blue Eagle.) But public response to the Blue Eagle campaign had begun to decline by late 1934, probably reflecting disappointment with the slow pace of economic recovery. Many who had previously endorsed the Act now joined in referring to the NRA as the "National Run Around." Moreover, by late 1934, Donald Richberg, who had played an active role in the promulgation of the Norris-LaGuardia Act and who was general counsel of the NRA, became publicly critical of the majority-rule concept and undertook, successfully, to reduce the scope of the board's jurisdiction.[68]

As for the other potential enforcement weapon, the Department of Justice was uncooperative in prosecuting those charged with noncompliance. Of the 33 cases referred to the Justice Department by the National Labor Relations Board, only one was prosecuted. Moreover, that case was still being litigated when the codes established under the National Industrial Recovery Act were unanimously held unconstitutional by the Supreme Court in *Schechter Poultry Corp. v. United States*, 295 U.S. 495 (1935), a decision issued but a few months prior to the Act's statutory expiration date in June of 1935.

Although Roosevelt had asked Congress early in 1935 to extend the NIRA for two years, support by the Executive Branch was generally considered half-hearted and public opinion was unenthusiastic. Accordingly, Senator Wagner renewed his effort to enact separate legislation to cover labor-management relations. He was assisted by his own staff counsel Leon Keyserling, later to become chairman of the Council of Economic Advisors, and by the general counsel of the National Labor Relations Board, Calvert Magruder, later to become a most respected judge of the United States Court of Appeals for the First Circuit.

Despite affable relations with union leadership, Roosevelt gave little initial support to Wagner's proposal. Business leadership labelled it as courting disaster.

Interestingly, while newspaper editors and business associations were damning Senator Wagner's bill as communistic, the American Communist Party denounced it as a weapon to destroy the economic power of worker organizations.[69] Nevertheless, aided by his own eloquence and the testimony of labor leaders and academic labor relations experts, Wagner brought the bill to Senate adoption by a roll call vote of 63-12.

Arguing his case before the Senate, Wagner cited to a long string of Supreme Court decisions, including the *Danbury Hatters'* case, *Adair, Coppage, American Steel Foundaries*, and *Deering* and stated: "These cases which I have cited are not mere records of mock trials in moot courts. They are the external evidence of sweeping political and economic developments completely out of line with our professed desires to make opportunity equally available to all."[70]

The House version of Senator Wagner's proposal was still in Committee when the Supreme Court issued its decision invalidating the National Industrial Recovery Act codes. This shed a new light on the urgency of the proposed legislation and the House Committee quickly reported favorably on the bill. By now Senator Wagner had persuaded the president to give more active support to the bill, and although it faced vigorous opposition in the House, it passed without a roll call vote. Some who voted for it no doubt expected that the Supreme Court would strike it down as unconstitutional.

The official name of the Wagner Act is the National Labor Relations Act, and with substantial amendment, it continues to be the basic statute structuring labor-management relations in the United States. In the form passed in 1935, the Act established the National Labor Relations Board as an independent, impartial, three-member administrative agency. The board was empowered to hire a staff, including persons authorized to conduct hearings, and was given the basic procedural tools for investigating and prosecuting charges of unlawful conduct. The Act declared it to be the public policy to favor the right to freely unionize and to encourage the practice of collective bargaining. Certain forms of employer conduct interferring with unionization, including employer domination of, or assistance to, company unions and the refusal to bargain collectively with a union representing an employee majority, were made unfair labor practices subject to the remedial orders of the NLRB. Those orders, in turn, were made enforceable by judicial decree upon the application of the board. In addition, the statute gave the board authority to determine which grouping or unit of employees constitutes the appropriate group for collective bargaining. In the event of an employer refusal to recognize a union claiming to represent a majority of workers in such an appropriate bargaining unit, the board is authorized to conduct an election and certify the majority choice. The majority-rule concept became a basic feature of American labor relations policy under the Act. Finally, the Act was to apply to controversies "burdening or obstructing the free flow of commerce, or having led or tending to lead to a labor dispute burdening or obstructing commerce or the free flow of commerce."

As Gregory once observed: "Congress virtually ordered employers to stop resisting the spread of unionism, telling them that the desire of their employees to organize was none of their business and to keep their hands off . . . . This was a bitter pill for rugged individualists brought up in the tradition of American economic free enterprise."[71]

Thus, whereas the Norris-LaGuardia Act had in effect declared the government a neutral in the battlefield of industrial conflict, the Wagner Act placed governmental prestige and power behind the organizational drives of the labor movement. This became a common theme emphasized by union organizers and, not surprisingly, union membership experienced its most dramatic period of growth in the first ten years under the National Labor Relations Act.

But first the Act's opponents challenged its constitutionality. In this effort they were encouraged by the fact that eleven pieces of economic legislation, including the National Industrial Recovery Act, had recently been struck down by the Supreme Court as involving regulation beyond the scope of Congress's power. Thus, two weeks after the Wagner Act became effective, a brief signed by 58 prominent lawyers who declared the NLRA unconstitutional was publicly released under the sponsorship of the American Liberty League, a conservative organization. It took a bit longer for the constitutional question to reach the Supreme Court of the United States, and when it did, the Court upheld the Act.

The constitutional issues were presented to the Court in five cases argued orally over the course of three days. The decisions were issued two months later, on April 12, 1937. One case involved the finding that a major steel producer had engaged in discriminatory and coercive action by discharging union supporters. The National Labor Relations Board determined that such conduct was an unfair labor practice in violation of the National Labor Relations Act and ordered the discharged persons reinstated with back pay. It also ordered the company to post notices assuring all employees that it would not discriminate against workers engaged in union organizing activities. Another of the cases, which also involved the NLRB's finding of unlawful discharge and the remedies of reinstatement with back pay plus posted notices pledging the employer to future obedience to the law, had been prosecuted against a major manufacturer of truck trailers. In still another case, the employer had been found guilty of unlawful surveillance of union activities as well as of having made antiunion threats and discharges. The employer was a moderate-sized clothing manufacturer employing about 800 persons. The fourth case arose when one of the leading newswire service companies discharged an employee for union activities, and the fifth case again centered on a discharge for union activities, this time involving an employer engaged in carrying passengers on buses operating between Virginia and the District of Columbia.

With respect to this last case, the Court unanimously upheld as constitutionally valid the application of the National Labor Relations Act and the decision below enforcing the NLRB's order. As to the remaining four cases, the court split 5 to 4, with Mr. Justice Roberts providing the swing vote between the so-called conservative and liberal wings of the Court. Chief Justice Hughes assigned to himself the task of writing the majority opinion in the first three cases and gave to Mr. Justice Roberts the task, or perhaps honor, of preparing the Court's opinion in the newswire and interstate busline cases.

As previously noted, a series of constitutional objections had been raised as to the validity of the NLRA. These included assertion that Congress's delegation of authority to the NLRB was excessive, thus handing legislative power over to the agency, and the charge that the right to trial by jury was abridged by the Act's system of administrative adjudication. But in the end, the division on the Court centered on two different but no less fundamental issues.

One issue was confined to the newswire service case. It concerned the extent to which the First Amendment protection of the freedom of the press was abridged by the Act. The other issue, which cut across all of the cases and on which the justices were in full accord only in the interstate busline case, was whether the nature of the labor-management relations being regulated by the NLRB was within the scope of congressional authority under the commerce clause of the Constitution.

To explain its resolution of the commerce clause issue, the steel manufacturing case, *National Labor Relations Board* v. *Jones & Laughlin Steel Corp.*, 301 U.S. 1 (1937), provided the majority with an ideal vehicle. The constitutional contention with which the majority had been confronted was that under settled doctrine the power of Congress to regulate commercial activities was limited to that directly involving interstate carriage or exchange of persons or goods. All other regulation of commercial activity is the exclusive domain of the state governments. Accordingly, the argument continued, transactions that are local in nature are beyond the power of congressional regulation. Applying that approach to the NLRA, the argument went, labor-management relations deal with matters of purely local concern — wage rates, hours of work, shop conditions, job security, and the like — and thus the NLRA deals with matters that are beyond the scope of congressional power.

In support of the position that Congress does not have the power to regulate labor-management relations involving persons manufacturing goods, the various employers challenging the National Labor Relations Act and the dissenting justices were able to cite as authority the Court's very recent decisions in the *Schechter* case, supra, and in *Carter* v. *Carter Coal Co.*, 298 U.S. 238 (1936). Inasmuch as the *Schechter* decision was unanimous and was presented in an opinion by Chief Justice Hughes, the discussion there concerning the constitutional limits on the power of Congress to regulate commercial relations posed a most serious obstacle to upholding the NLRA.

In striking down the National Industrial Recovery Act's codes, Hughes had said: "In determining how far the federal government may go in controlling intrastate transactions upon the ground that they 'affect' interstate commerce, there is a necessary and well-established distinction between direct and indirect effects. . . . [W] here the effect of intrastate transactions upon interstate commerce is merely indirect, such transactions remain within the domain of state power."[72] Applying that doctrine to the facts in the *Schechter* case, Hughes had explained that in regulating the hours of employment and wages paid to persons employed in the slaughter of chickens for distribution to local butchers, the NIRA code, there under challenge, affected matters having no direct relationship with interstate commerce and therefore was constitutionally invalid as an attempt to exercise power where the federal government had none. "The question of how many hours these employees should work and what they should be paid differs in no essential respect from similar questions in other local businesses which handle commodities brought into a State and there dealt in as a part of its internal commerce. . . . If the federal government may determine the wage and hours of employees in the internal commerce of a State, . . . it would seem that a similar control might be exerted over other elements of cost . . . . If the cost of doing an intrastate business is in itself the permitted object of federal control, the extent of the regulation of cost would be a question of discretion and not of power. . . . But the authority of the federal government may not be pushed to such extreme as to destroy the distinction, which the commerce clause itself establishes, between commerce 'among the several States' and the internal concerns of a State."[73]

Chief Justice Hughes discerned a path whereby he could uphold the constitutional validity of the NLRA without having to reject *Schechter*. Indeed, he even cited *Schechter* for support. The National Labor Relations Act, Hughes explained, was carefully drafted so as to avoid the exercise of power not available to Congress under the commerce clause. Only that which burdens or obstructs the flow of commerce or tends to lead to such burden or obstruction is covered by the Act according to its own definition of its scope. "[T] hus qualified," stated the Chief Justice, "it must be construed as contemplating the exercise of control within constitutional bounds."[74] It is that direct burdening or obstructing affect upon the flow of commerce, not the source of the injury, he stated, that determines that the conduct in question comes within Congress's regulatory power. In each individual case, therefore, the Act requires the NLRB to determine whether the requisite affect upon commerce is present so as to place the conduct within the scope of congressional power, and thereby within the scope of the Labor Act's coverage.

But although the Act may have theoretically been confined by its own language to regulating only that directly burdening or obstructing interstate commerce, and thereby is within the scope of congressional power, it still remained for the Court to determine whether in any of the cases it was reviewing, the labor relations being regulated by the NLRB came within that defined scope of federal regulatory power.

In the case of the interstate bus carrier, the Court was able to unanimously agree that the labor-management relations of the company directly affected

interstate commerce.[75]   There seemed to be similar agreement regarding that
aspect of the newswire service case as well.[76]   But with respect to the three
cases involving manufacturing operations, the four dissenting justices, Van
Devanter, McReynolds, Sutherland, and Butler, insisted that the affect of the
labor relations in question upon interstate commerce was no more direct than
it had been in previous cases, such as *Schechter*, in which the Court had rejected
the constitutional validity of federal regulation. As a result of the majority's
decision, they complained, the NLRB would have "power of control over purely
local industry behond anything heretofore deemed permissible."[77]

Whereas the majority used the steel case to illustrate its point, the dissenters
chose to emphasize the case involving the smallest operation, the clothing manufacturer's case. Examining the facts involved, the dissenting opinion of Mr.
Justice McReynolds, which he reportedly read in open court "in bitter and
incisive tones,"[78] found that "the Company is so small that to close its factory
would have no direct or material effect upon the volume of interstate commerce
in clothing."[79] As a result, he concluded, "Any effect on interstate commerce
by the discharge of employees shown here, would be indirect and remote in the
highest degree."[80] Carrying the majority's argument to the extreme, he declared
that "Almost anything — marriage, birth, death — may in some fashion affect
commerce."[81] At the close of his delivery, McReynolds added the extemporan-
eous comment: "The cause is so momentous, the possibilities for harm so great,
that we felt it our duty to expose the situation as we view it."[82]

In contrast, Chief Justice Hughes emphasized the far flung and yet highly
integrated structure of Jones & Laughlin's activities. Its iron ore was supplied
from Michigan and Minnesota, its coal from West Virginia and Pennsylvania. It
owned four ore ships operating on the Great Lakes and had a railroad line linking
it with three major interstate railway systems; it smeltered and processed its
products in Pennsylvania, shipped three quarters of them out of state, and ware-
housed much of it in Chicago, Detroit, Cincinnati, and Memphis. Accordingly,
the majority accepted the NLRB's finding that a stoppage in those operations
would have "a most serious effect upon interstate commerce."[83] In view of the
company's structure and operations, stated Hughes, "[I] t is idle to say that the
effect would be indirect or remote."[84] The Court could not, Hughes insisted,
deal with such facts in an intellectual vacuum. "When industries organize
themselves on a national scale, making their relation to interstate commerce the
dominant factor in their activities, how can it be maintained that their industrial
labor relations constitute a forbidden field into which Congress may not enter
when it is necessary to protect interstate commerce from the paralyzing consequences of industrial war?"[85] Referring back to the description of the Jones
& Laughlin operation, the Chief Justice observed: "[I] t presents in a most
striking way the close and intimate relation which a manufacturing industry
may have to interstate commerce . . . ."[86] Clearly the *Jones & Laughlin* case
provided an ideal vehicle for illustrating a substantial relationship between

labor conflict in a manufacturing enterprise and the burdening of interstate commerce.

But could these same observations be made as persuasively with respect to the other employers whose cases were before the Court. Most particularly, could the Court sustain its analysis with regard to the clothing manufacturer's business? In reaching its decision in that case, Hughes chose simply to reiterate the NLRB's findings respecting the interstate nature of commerce in the clothing industry — raw materials coming from several states, most goods sold to out-of-state retailers. He then merely cited to the decision in *Jones & Laughlin* to support his conclusion upholding the NLRB's authority to remedy the company's unfair labor practices. By implication, therefore, the majority was giving approval to the power of Congress to regulate economic activity not only where the individual being regulated has a direct impact upon interstate commerce, but also where that individual is part of a larger pattern of economic structure in which interstate activities play a dominant role.

As for the freedom of the press issue raised in the *Associated Press* case, the employer's contention was that by imposing rules for management in dealing with editorial employees, the government was unconstitutionally interfering with the publishers' protected right to determine editorial content and policy. Mr. Justice Roberts' majority opinion rejected the purported relationship between the Labor Act's restraints upon interference with union activity and the publisher's freedom to determine editorial content and policy. Summing up the Court's response, Justice Roberts stated: "The act does not compel the petitioner to employ anyone; it does not require that the petitioner retain in its employ an incompetent editor or one who fails faithfully to edit the news to reflect the facts without bias or prejudice."[87]

With the decision in *Jones & Laughlin* and its companion cases, the National Labor Relations Act was on its way to becoming a major factor shaping labor-management relations in the United States. The following year, 1938, saw an enormous spurt of unfair labor practice cases and NLRB representation elections. The unfair labor practice cases tapered off a bit as employers became more knowledgeable concerning the restrictions imposed by the Wagner Act, but the number of elections conducted grew at a rather steady pace even through the war years of 1941 to 1945.

The labor union movement received another significant legal victory in 1938 when the Court gave the language of the Norris–LaGuardia Act broad construction in limiting the power of federal courts to issue labor injunctions. In *New Negro Alliance* v. *Sanitary Grocery*, 303 U.S. 552, modified 304 U.S. 542 (1938), a 6-2 majority concluded that Norris-LaGuardia prevented a federal court from enjoining picketing in support of a boycott against stores that discriminated on the basis of race in hiring workers.

Having lost the constitutional battle and faced with a Court that was now prepared to interpret federal statutes in a manner that supported a policy favoring collective bargaining, those who were antipathetic toward labor unions turned to the legislative forum as a means of combatting the evil they perceived in union growth. Their basic political theme became the assertion that although the law may have been unfairly supportive of management prior to the Wagner Act, the new balance had swung too far in the opposite direction.

The political environment in which the campaign for changes in the Wagner Act's legislative policy was to take place had been shaped in the first instance by the termination of World War II. During the war, unions, despite their leadership's no-strike pledge, had engaged in some highly publicized walkouts, a tactic that produced considerable public antagonism. Moreover, during the economic readjustment of the postwar period, a rash of strikes broke out throughout the nation. In addition, a split in the federation of national labor organizations had occurred in the late 1930s when a group of unions left the American Federation of Labor in conflict over that federation's orientation toward organizing along trade lines. The new federation formed by those leaving the A.F. of L. was called the Congress of Industrial Organizations. Its member unions adhered to the concept of industrial unionization — that is, organizing all of the workers in an industry into the same union irrespective of job skills. As a result of this break within union ranks, so-called jurisdictional strikes became a frequent occurrence as C.I.O. affiliated unions and A.F. of L. unions vied for representation of the same employee units.

Unions also frequently resorted to so-called secondary boycott activities both in support of union organizing demands and of demands for improved benefits. Included amongst these practices were such activities as boycotting retailers handling goods made by nonunion help, refusing to work with materials produced by nonunion personnel, and refusing to work at the same work site with nonunion workers. A dimension of these secondary pressure tactics was to expand the extent and frequency of visible union resort to economic leverage. Such tactics also created considerable confusion and inconvenience for the general public.

Finally, there were many aspects of internal union governance that conflicted with popular notions of fair treatment and democratic organization. In some situations, these were the product of paternalism; in others they were a manifestation of racketeering or adherence to totalitarian political ideals. In any event, such conduct was not consistent with the notion of "industrial democracy," a concept propagated by unions for over half a century.

With all of this, the status of labor unions had declined dramatically in public esteem by mid-1946.[88] As a result, several bills restricting various forms of union activity were adopted by Congress in April, May, and July of 1946.

President Truman vetoed one of these proposals,[b] but signed the other two into law.[c]

A newly elected Republican-dominated Congress met in January 1947 and heard President Truman deliver a State of the Union message in which the lead item was a request for reform of labor legislation. Truman specifically requested curbs upon jurisdictional disputes and certain types of secondary activity. Also, he asked for expanded government services to facilitate mediation and arbitration of labor disputes. Finally, he asked that a special committee be set up to recommend ways to reduce strikes and improve the collective bargaining process. But Congress was in the mood to do much more to alter the nation's labor relations policies.

Literally dozens of reform bills were submitted to Congress. The House committee handling these proposals was chaired by Fred A. Hartley, Jr., a Republican from New Jersey; the Senate committee was chaired by Senator Robert A. Taft of Ohio, the son of the only person to serve both as President and later as Chief of Justice of the United States. Senator Taft had distinguished himself in his own right by becoming a living symbol of the ideology of his party. Interestingly, two new members of the House committee were freshmen representatives—a California Republican named Richard M. Nixon and a Massachusetts Democrat named John F. Kennedy.

Extensive testimony was received by both committees. But the Democratic members of the House committee soon charged that the hearings were a sham. They asserted that the bill proposed by the committee majority was prepared by industry representatives, not the congressional staff, and that it was prepared without consideration of the evidence submitted to the committee.[89] These charges typified the sort of highly emotional and bitter battles that soon developed over these proposals.

Only six hours of debate was assigned to the House bill, which passed 308-107. The Republican majority was joined by the bulk of Democrats from the region that had comprised the Confederacy.

Senator Taft introduced his bill on the day the House bill was adopted. The debate on the Senate floor was deliberative and lasted for three weeks. When it was over, the Senate adopted Taft's committee proposal 68-24, again a coalition of the Republican majority joined by most Southern Democrats. There were a number of important differences between the Senate and House bills, and these were worked out by the conference committee. Both houses then adopted the conference report.

---

[b]The Case Act, which, among other things, would have required a five-day work stoppage notice followed by a thirty-day no-work stoppage period during which time a board of federal mediators would attempt to adjust differences.

[c]The Lea Act, which prohibits make-work demands on the part of musicians employed by broadcasters, and the Hobbs Act, barring labor extortion in interstate transportation.

Union leaders denounced the resulting statute as "the Slave Labor Bill." They promoted a massive campaign urging presidential veto. The Taft-Hartley legislation was condemned as well by numerous elected officials and by social action organizations ranging from the National Catholic Welfare Conference to the National Council of Jewish Women.

President Truman's political counselors were split over the course he should take, though the majority of his legal and labor relations advisors favored vetoing the bill. In the end, Truman exercised his veto power and delivered a long, detailed, and strongly worded veto message.[90]

The Senate's response was prompt. Four days after the veto message, it overrode the veto 68-25. But the Senate was most dilatory in its action when compared with the House, which had voted 331-106 to override the veto within an hour after Truman's veto message had been read.

The formal title of the thus adopted Taft-Hartley law is the Labor-Management Relations Act of 1947. It consists of five basic divisions, or titles. The first of these is a revision of the Wagner Act. This portion continues to be officially designated as the National Labor Relations Act. The 1947 revision added two members to the NLRB and made the general counsel of the agency an independent official appointed by the president with the consent of the Senate. The purpose of giving the general counsel independence was to free that official to exercise discretion separate from the board in determining which situations involve facts warranting the issuance of complaints under the Act.

Most important, Taft-Hartley emphasized that the employee is not only protected in engaging in collective action but is protected as well in refraining from participation in such activities. Consistent with this shift in emphasis, the revised Act placed limits on the extent to which a union and an employer can agree that employees will be required to be union members.

Also, Taft-Hartley introduced the concept of union unfair labor practices. Thus, the Act was no longer a control only on employers. Union coercion of employees respecting their exercise of the right to engage or refrain from engaging in concerted activity now became a basis for NLRB intervention.

Similarly, the union was placed under the same sort of responsibility as the employer to bargain in good faith where the union is the majority representative of bargaining unit workers. A description of that duty of good faith bargaining was for the first time spelled out in detail in the revised Act. Included are requirements to give notice to the other side and to government officials before work stoppage action can be taken in support of demands for changes in the existing contractual terms and conditions of employment.

Further, the Act was changed to include restrictions on the use of secondary boycott pressure. An aspect of this last change was to give the agency authority to go into federal court to seek injunctive relief in certain types of labor disputes — a partial modification of the Norris-LaGuardia Act.

Additionally, machinery was created for dealing with jurisdictional disputes, and the procedure for representation elections was remodeled in several respects, including giving employers, as well as workers and unions, the opportunity to initiate a representation proceeding. Moreover, the above list does not exhaust all of the changes introduced into the NLRA by the first title of the Labor Management Relations Act.

In addition to amending the National Labor Relations Act, Taft-Hartley established a new independent agency called the Federal Mediation and Conciliation Service charged with the responsibility of facilitating the conciliation and arbitration of labor-management differences. Machinery was also established for dealing with those labor disputes that threaten to imperil national health or safety. This national emergency process includes "cooling off" periods during which the status quo must be maintained and the parties must refrain from work stoppages while efforts are made to mediate the dispute.

In order to strengthen the collective bargaining process, another title of Taft-Hartley gives federal courts jurisdiction to entertain suits respecting asserted violations of collectively bargained agreements between labor and management. And, in order to reduce the prospects of union racketeering, Title III of Taft-Hartley places limitations on the situations in which payments can be made between employer and union representatives. The violation of this last provision is a crime. Restrictions are also made on the use of union and corporate funds to influence federal elections.

Further, the Labor Management Relations Act of 1947 gave to parties injured by unlawful secondary labor activities the right to bring a civil suit for damages in addition to the remedies provided through the orders of the NLRB. Finally, the new law prohibited federal employees from participating in any strike.

For several years after its adoption, union leaders waged a campaign seeking the repeal of Taft-Hartley. But, by the 1952 Presidential election, pro-union political leaders were content to advocate modification rather than repeal of the 1947 law. Nevertheless, the name "Taft-Hartley" continued to be mouthed as an epithet by most unionists. Whether because of the restraints imposed by Taft-Hartley, or because of reduced organizational effort, or because most of the readily organized workers were already covered by collective agreements, union membership growth as a percent of the labor[91] force came to a relative standstill in the years following 1947. To union loyalists the reason was quite clear — Taft-Hartley!

But the embitterment of union leadership over the "Slave Labor Act" did not convince others that union power had been sufficiently checked by the 1947 Act. Just as unions demanded repeal of Taft-Hartley, there were others calling for further measures to combat what they often referred to as "union monopolies."

The thrust of criticism against unions, however, began to shift away from claims that their power had become excessive *vis-à-vis* managerial power to claims that too often unions were not giving fair and honest treatment to their members. This concern was reflected in the enactment of the 1958 Welfare and Pensions Disclosure Act, an effort to protect from corrupt and inept administration the employee interests in various fringe benefits programs secured by the collective bargaining process. A much more comprehensive program of regulation was adopted the next year with enactment of the Landrum-Griffin Act — officially entitled the Labor-Management Reporting and Disclosure Act.

A significant prelude to the Labor-Management Reporting and Disclosure Act was the series of Senate hearings conducted by a special committee chaired by Senator John McClellan of Arkansas. Senators John F. Kennedy and Barry Goldwater were committee members. A young lawyer, Robert Kennedy, brother of Senator Kennedy, was committee chief counsel. He displayed considerable tenacity investigating abuses of power on the part of union leaders, especially those in the Teamster's Union.

The McClellan hearings, which lasted about two years, were highly publicized and disclosed numerous shocking examples of union corruption, often involving the leadership selling out the members' interests. Although these revelations centered on only a few unions, many people received the impression that these wrong doings reflected widespread misconduct. As a result, the public image of unions declined demonstrably, thereby causing union supporters to complain that the real goal of the hearings was to give labor a black eye.[92]

Nevertheless, many scholars and organizations such as the American Civil Liberties Union, long considered friends of the collective bargaining process, led the call for reform of internal union affairs. Their goal was to assure democratic methods and honest union governance.

In 1958 Senators Kennedy and Ives introduced a bill containing a moderate schedule of reforms. This passed the Senate 88-1, but died in the House. Senators Kennedy and Ervin introduced a new proposal early in 1959 designed to combat dishonest practices in union affairs. The bill received majority committee approval but was considerably altered by amendment on the Senate floor. These amendments expanded the extent to which the proposed law would regulate internal union affairs. The resulting bill was adopted 90-1. The House Committee on Education and Labor considered not only the Senate bill but a bill sponsored by Representatives Landrum and Griffin as well. Eventually, it adopted a slightly amended form of the Landrum-Griffin proposal by a vote of 303-125. It then asked for a conference with the Senate and, after twelve days of deliberation, the conference committee reported out a bill that largely resembled the House version. The conference measure was overwhelmingly approved and became law in September of 1959 under the official title of the Labor-Management Reporting and Disclosure Act.

The resulting legislation went well beyond the scope of the abuses disclosed in the McClellan subcommittee hearings, which are credited with having propelled this legislative effort. Included in the LMRDA were provisions amending the Labor Management Relations Act, as were provisions regulating the rights of union officials and eligibility for union office, restrictions upon the extent of national union control over their member locals, the requirement that various kinds of financial information be filed as public records, a prohibition against extortionate picketing, and various requirements for the posting of fidelity bonds.

Landrum-Griffin made several changes in the Taft-Hartley Act. Some changes were made in the structure of NLRB's operations. These were made largely to facilitate handling the increasing caseload. Further, additional restrictions were imposed on the types of payments permitted to be made by employers to union representatives. New restrictions were also imposed on secondary activities and limits were placed on the use of picketing. Finally, slightly counterbalancing the increased restraints on union tactics, a few concessions were made to unions operating in the clothing manufacturing industry and in the building construction industry. These were justified as needed to meet particular problems encountered by labor organizations due to the peculiarities of the operational structure of those industries. Also, striking employees were assured the right to vote in representation elections for a one-year period.

In addition to the major enactments discussed above, there are a number of other federal statutes that significantly influence working conditions. Among these are the Fair Labor Standards Act, which sets minimum pay and certain overtime pay requirements; the Social Security laws, which create a compulsory pension system, provide certain death insurance benefits, and set basic standards for unemployment benefits; the Occupational Health and Safety Act, which establishes minimum standards of health and safety for the work environment; and the various civil rights laws prohibiting limits on work opportunities based on race, religion, national origin, sex, and to a limited extent age. Many state laws also help shape union activities and the terms and conditions of work.

The discussion of labor statutes in this book, however, essentially deals with Supreme Court decision making concerning the National Labor Relations Act as amended. That Act is the nucleus of American union-management relations and provides the most important part of the Supreme Court's caseload involving labor law.

The issues examined in the remaining chapters, therefore, in large measure concern the Court's choice of alternative possibilities for interpreting and applying the language used by Congress in adopting and modifying this law. Frequently, considerations involving limits imposed by the language of the Constitution of the United States also must be weighed. As we examine these cases, we will observe not only how the Court analyzes the meaning of words in order to discern the legislature's intent, but also the influence that social and economic conditions as well as the judges' own experiences and predilections have upon the decisions.

2 Regulation of Picketing and Other Union Organizing Activities

The initiative and effort to organize employees for the purpose of demanding collective bargaining often comes, as we would expect, from within the employee group that is seeking to be collectively represented. Frequently, too, however, organizational initiative comes from outside the employment unit—that is, members of other unionized employment units or paid union organizers will seek to persuade unorganized workers that they would benefit from union representation. The effort to persuade workers to support the collective bargaining approach may utilize various forms of communication— conversations with employees going to and coming from work, passing out leaflets to these same employees, discussions during work or during lunch breaks, picketing outside the employer's establishment with signs urging the workers to unionize, telephone conversations, newspaper advertisements, mass meetings at which the organizers extol the virtues of collective action and the like.

Union organizers also occasionally seek to accomplish their goal not by persuading the employees of the value of unionizing, but rather by pressuring the employer into encouraging or even coercing the employees to join—that is, the union gets the employer to do the job of unionizing. Putting pressure on the employer can be accomplished, for example, by securing a consumer boycott of the employer's product or services, or by a work stoppage conducted by those employees who are already sympathetic with the union. To end the boycott or work stoppage, the employer must recognize the union as bargaining agent of the employees, whether or not the majority of workers support the union. Other such means for "enlisting" the employer's help in unionizing include interference, through boycott or violent measures, with the supplies needed for the employer's operation or with shipment of the employer's product.

Some of the above techniques for union organizing are more acceptable than others in an ordered, free society. Physical coercion, for example, is rarely consistent with the preservation of freedom. The boycott technique may give undue power to certain strategically located persons (e.g., truck drivers) so as to create irrational centers of power, thereby destroying both the orderliness of the system and the ability of the majority to control basic economic and social decisions.

Accordingly, there may be a need to regulate the techniques of unionization to assure against abuse. And state courts and state legislatures, usually at

the behest of employer groups (motivated at least as much by antiunion senti-
ments as by concern for preserving free choice), have experimented with a
variety of techniques for restricting or prohibiting union organizing activities.[a]
But inasmuch as these union organizing techniques involve the exercise of
speech, assembly, and association—all of which are modes of conduct constitutionally protected by the due process clause of the Fourteenth Amendment—
any attempt to regulate these organizational activities is subject to challenge
on the grounds that the regulations usurp constitutionally protected liberty.
Accordingly, many of the Supreme Court's decisions in the labor relations
field have involved weighing state government attempts to regulate union organizing activities against the constitutional restraints upon the power of government to encroach on basic liberties. An early example of this sort of case
was *Hague* v. *CIO,* 307 U.S. 496 (1939).

Jersey City, New Jersey, was governed in the 1930s by a political machine
under the control of Mayor Frank Hague. When the newly formed Committee
for Industrial Organization (the forerunner of the Congress of Industrial Organizations) sent union organizers into highly industrialized Jersey City, they met
various official barriers, including forceable removal from the city pursuant to
local ordinances that barred public assemblies without a police permit and that
prohibited all leafletting.

The union organizers brought a suit in the federal district court seeking an
injunction against further interference with their claimed constitutional and
statutory rights to meet with and seek to persuade potential new union members. An injunctive decree was issued by the U.S. District Court and affirmed
by the U.S. Court of Appeals. Hague secured review by the Supreme Court of
the United States where he challenged the lower court's decree on the grounds
that it exceeded federal court jurisdiction, that it was erroneous in disallowing
the ban on street meetings, and that it was impractical of enforcement.

The Supreme Court affirmed the lower courts, but modified the decree so
as to give even greater protection to the union activity. Though a majority
joined in the result, a majority of justices were unable to agree on the reasons
supporting the decision against Hague. Justice Roberts, Chief Justice Hughes,
and Justice Black relied on the "privileges and immunities" clause of the
Fourteenth Amendment and reasoned that the Jersey City ordinances regulating
speeches and banning leafletting conflicted with freedom of speech and assembly as protected by that provision of the Constitution.

Mr. Justice Stone agreed that the judicial decree was appropriate to prevent

---

[a]States have also, with some frequency, adopted laws *protecting* various forms of union
organizing activity from interference by court issued injunctions. Although initially the
Supreme Court found such protection to be violative of the Fourteenth Amendment's Equal
Protection Clause (*Truax* v. *Corrigan,* 257 U.S. 312), it later retracted and permitted such
pro-union legislation to stand. *Senn* v. *Tile Layers Protective Union,* 310 U.S. 468.

further encroachments upon constitutionally protected speech and assembly, but Stone reasoned that the source of that protection was the "due process" clause of the Fourteenth Amendment, not the privileges and immunities clause (a view that later became the prevailing majority position). Mr. Justice McReynolds dissented on the jurisdictional basis that any attack on the ordinance should have proceeded through the state courts, and not through the federal courts. And, Mr. Justice Butler dissented on the ground that the ordinances did not interfere with any constitutional rights. Neither Douglas nor Frankfurter participated in the decision.

Soon after the *Hague* case, the Court issued several rulings to the effect that the Fourteenth Amendment protects the right to picket peacefully in a labor dispute. [E.g., *Thornhill* v. *Alabama,* 310 U.S. 88 (1940); *Carlson* v. *California,* 310 U.S. 106 (1940); *A.F. of L.* v. *Swing,* 312 U.S. 321 (1941).] Thus, in *Schneider* v. *Irvington,* 308 U.S. 157 (1939), for example, the Supreme Court ruled that union pickets and pamphleteers could not be totally barred from using public streets on the excuse of preventing litter. "[T]he streets are natural and proper places for the dissemination of information and opinion; and one is not to have the exercise of his liberty of expression in appropriate places abridged on the plea that it may be exercised in some other place."[1]

It was not long after the *Hague* case, however, that the Supreme Court also issued a decision reassuring the states that *Hague* was not to be read as in any way limiting their power to regulate violent conduct even though accompanied by labor picketing or other union activity. In *Milk Wagon Drivers Union* v. *Meadowmoor Dairies, Inc.,* 312 U.S. 287 (1941), the majority of the Court found that the picketing in question had become "so enmeshed with contemporaneously violent conduct" as to justify a sweeping injunction against *all* picketing of the affected employer's stores. Violence, the Court explained, "neutralizes the constitutional immunity."

While agreeing, in *Meadowmoor,* that a state can enjoin violence that accompanies picketing, Justice Black joined by Justices Douglas and Reed dissented from the proposition that all picketing, even future picketing of a wholly peaceful nature, could be enjoined in the aftermath of violence.

The impact of *Meadowmoor* was modified somewhat in the direction of Black's dissent when, two years later, a unanimous Court struck down a New York court's injunction against pickets who criticized the food served at a picketed cafeteria and accused those continuing to patronize the place of aiding "the cause of Fascism." Explaining its reversal of the state injunction, the Supreme Court said:

> In a setting like the present, continuing representations unquestionably false and acts of coercion beyond the mere influence exerted by the fact of picketing, are of course, not constitutional prerogatives. But here we have no attempt by the state . . . to restrict conduct justifiably found to be an abusive exercise of the right to picket.[2]

That is, because the state court's ban on picketing affected conduct that had not been shown to involve the propagation of falsehoods or the use of coercion, the state injunction of the picketing went further than was constitutionally permissible.

Not all free speech free assembly cases in the labor relations field have arisen in the union organizing situation. *Bakery Drivers Local* v. *Wohl* 315 U.S. 769 (1942), presented the issue in another context. Many commercial bakeries in New York City distributed the bulk of their products in the 1920s through employed route deliverymen. The remaining distribution was handled through so-called independent jobbers who owned their own vehicles and secured their livelihood from the price difference between what they were charged by the bakeries and what they in turn charged the retailers. By the 1930s, with increased payroll taxes resulting from the adoption of social security and unemployment compensation laws, many baking companies determined that they were better off distributing through independent jobbers inasmuch as the bakeries did not have to pay social security taxes or provide workmen's compensation or unemployment insurance benefits for the jobbers. The unionized bakeries, accordingly, notified the unions that at the end of the current collective bargaining contracts the deliverymen would be terminated and would be given an opportunity to purchase their trucks and would be invited to become independent jobbers.

In 1938, a union sought to organize these independent jobbers with the object of imposing some work standards, such as the six day week, as a membership requirement. When Wohl and other independent jobbers refused to cooperate, the union picketed the bakeries that sold to them. The picket signs identified each jobber and read: "A baking route driver works seven days a week. Help us spread employment and maintain a union wage hour and condition. *Bakery & Pastry Drivers and Helpers Local 802.*"[3] The New York courts upheld an injunction against this picketing.

A unanimous United States Supreme Court reversed the New York courts, with Mr. Justice Jackson stating in the Opinion of the Court: "[R]espondents' [the jobbers'] mobility and their insulation from the public as middlemen made it practically impossible for petitioners [the union members] to make known their legitimate grievances to the public whose patronage was sustaining the peddler system except by the means here employed and contemplated . . . ."[4] Mr. Justice Douglas, joined by Justices Black and Murphy, separately concurred and argued that an injunction of picketing is available only where narrowly drawn to regulate the patrolling part of the activity and that the information being disseminated by the picketers can be restrained only where it is shown that there is clear and present danger of destruction of life or property, or invasion of the right of privacy or breach of the peace.

A dispute that was somewhat similar to *Wohl* was presented several years later in *Giboney* v. *Empire Storage and Ice Company*, 336 U.S. 490 (1949).

There a union representing door-to-door ice peddlers sought to force all such peddlers to become union members. To accomplish this it secured agreements from ice wholesalers not to sell ice to nonunion peddlers. When Empire Storage refused to sign such an agreement, the union picketed Empire's premises, thereby causing union truck drivers working for Empire's customers to refuse to pick up goods at Empire on the grounds that crossing the picket line would subject them to fine or suspension by their own unions. As a result, Empire's level of business dropped 85 percent.

Empire, thereupon, secured from the state court an injunction against the picketing. The injunction was based on a state antitrust law prohibiting concerted efforts restraining trade. In this situation, the state court held, the statute was violated because the union sought to force Empire to join a combination designed to exclude certain persons from the retail ice trade. The union, relying on the *Thornhill, Wohl and Meadowmoor* decisions, among others, argued that its activity was protected free speech. But, a unanimous Supreme Court, in an opinion by Justice Hugo Black, upheld the state injunction of the picketing. The Supreme Court reasoned that a state has the power to protect commerce from combinations that restrain trade and that speech, which is a vehicle for carrying out an unlawful purpose such as this, can itself be restrained. "The interest of Missouri in enforcement of its antitrust laws cannot be classified as an effort to outlaw only a slight public inconvenience or annoyance . . . . It is clearly drawn in an attempt to afford all persons an equal opportunity to buy goods. There was clear danger, imminent and immediate, that unless restrained, [the union] would succeed in making that policy a dead letter insofar as purchases by nonunion men were concerned. . . . [The picketers] were doing more than exercising a right of free speech or press. . . . They were exercising their economic powers together with that of their allies to compel Empire to abide by union rather than by state regulation of trade."[5]

A most interesting application of *Giboney* is found in the Supreme Court's decision in *Hughes* v. *Superior Court of California,* 339 U.S. 460 (1950). Lucky Stores, Inc. operated a store in a neighborhood comprised of about equal numbers of Negroes and Caucasians. A group seeking improved work opportunities for blacks demanded that as job vacancies occurred the store hire only Negroes—until its employee compliment of blacks equalled that of whites. When the store refused to adopt this policy, the group picketed the store carrying placards stating that Lucky refused to hire Negroes in proportion to its Negro customers. Lucky secured a state court injunction against the picketing and when the picketing continued despite the court order, contempt penalties were assessed against the pickets. These contempt convictions were appealed to the Supreme Court of the United States which ruled, without dissent, that the U.S. Constitution posed no barriers to the injunction issued against this peaceful picketing activity. Emphasizing that picketing involves more than just communication—that the very presence of a picket line may induce action by those sympathetic to unions or those fearful of them—the Court stated that picketing can be disallowed by a state if it is conducted for a purpose that the state can properly prohibit. The Court concluded that the state policy against any form of discrimination in hiring justified disallowing the use of picketing as a tactic for attempting to obtain such an unlawful goal.

A more typical application of *Giboney* occurred in *United Association of Journeymen Plumbers* v. *Graham,* 345 U.S. 192 (1953). There, pickets carried signs identifying workmen at a building construction site as "nonunion." The Supreme Court found that the record supported the complaining employer's contention that the purpose of this picketing was to pressure the general contractor into eliminating nonunion men from the job. Such a purpose placed the conduct in violation of the state's so-called "Right-to-Work" laws, thereby giving rise to the state court injunction. Rejecting the union's argument that its activity was protected speech, the Supreme Court upheld the injunction noting that the "picketing was done at such a place and in such a manner that, coupled with established union policies and traditions, it caused the union men to stop work and thus slow the project to a general standstill."[6] Justices Black and Douglas dissented in an opinion somewhat reminiscent of positions previously articulated by Holmes. The mere fact that the picketing resulted in certain behavior was of no consequence in Mr. Justice Douglas' opinion. "For it is the aim of most ideas to shape conduct."[7] He continued by explaining that the line between constitutionally protected and unprotected picketing is often tenuous. "A purpose to deprive nonunion men of employment would make the picketing unlawful; a purpose to keep union men away from the job would give the picketing constitutional protection. The difficulty here is that we have no findings of fact."[8]

The question of a state's power to control organizational picketing arose yet again in *International Brotherhood of Teamsters* v. *Vogt,* 354 U.S. 284 (1957), where a state court enjoined picketing of a gravel pit by nonemployees carrying signs reading: "The men on this job are not 100% affiliated with the A.F.L." Truck drivers making pick-ups and deliveries refused to cross the picket line causing substantial reduction in business. The state court found this conduct to be designed to coerce the employer to compel his employees to join the union—an unfair labor practice under state law. While dividing 5 to 3, the Supreme Court of the United States did affirm the state court's action by explaining that prior case law had established that states can enjoin picketing when the purpose of that picketing is to cause an employer to coerce its employees. The dissent by Douglas, Warren, and Black was short but emphatic. Mr. Justice Douglas read the prior decisions as permitting state interference with picketing only where it creates a clear danger, imminent and immediate, that a lawful state policy will become a dead letter. "[H]ere there is no rioting, no mass picketing, no violence, no disorder, no fisticuffs, no coercion—indeed nothing but speech . . . . "[9] The majority decision was denounced by Douglas as "the formal surrender" of the doctrine protecting picketing as a form of free speech.

The doctrinal positions of the majority and dissent in *Vogt* were probably not as far apart as Mr. Justice Douglas portrayed. Rather the crux of their difference was in their respective approaches to the facts. (This, of course, is often the turning point in constitutional developments.) The majority was satisfied that the state court drew a sound inference when it found that the reduction in pick-ups and deliveries was an intended consequence of the picketing and part of a concerted effort to coerce the employer into intimidating its workers. The dissenters, on the other hand, expressly found no such showing of coercion. Consequently, the majority viewed the situation as involving state regulation of coercive conduct, whereas the dissent viewed it as state regulation of expression.

State attempts to regulate union organizing have looked to the organizers themselves and not just to their activities. Texas, for example, at one point adopted a law requiring all union organizers to register with the Secretary of State. Under that law, the state of Texas, in *Thomas* v. *Collins,* 323 U.S. 516 (1945), unsuccessfully sought to penalize a union spokesman for addressing a mass rally at which he urged those present to join the union; the prosecution being based on the union spokesman's failure to register and secure a union organizer's card as required by the Texas statute. Admitting that the state could regulate union activity to protect against fraud or other wrongdoing in handling dues and other union funds, the Supreme Court ruled that this particular statute went too far because it also limited who could lawfully give speeches advocating the cause of unionism. Such general advocacy, the Court held, is constitutionally protected from state restraints.

Four members of the Court dissented from the *Thomas* v. *Collins* decision. Mr. Justice Roberts, joined by Chief Justice Stone and Justices Reed and Frankfurter, expressed the opinion that since the organizer cards were issued by the state without fee or discrimination, it was not a constitutionally improper burden to require paid union solicitors to publicly record their identity as such prior to going about their business of attempting to increase union membership.

Decisions such as *Thomas, Meadowmoor, Giboney,* and *Swing* did not resolve all of the potential permutations concerning the impact of the Constitution upon state attempts to regulate peaceful picketing and other union exercises of the rights of assembly and expression. Some two decades later, on December 8, 1965, Weis Markets, Inc. triggered yet another legal challenge to union organizing practices when it opened a supermarket in the Logan Valley Mall, a newly developed shopping center serving the Altoona, Pennsylvania, area.

Weis, which was listed on the New York Stock Exchange, operated a chain of fifty-two retail food stores. In 1965 it had sales of $111 million and a net income of $4.6 million. Prior to opening its store at the Logan Valley Mall, Weis had had many confrontations with union organizers. Weis leased its premises at the Logan Valley Mall from Logan Valley Plaza, Inc. At the time Weis opened its store, there was only one other tenant at the mall—Sears Roebuck. The new mall, however, was designed to accommodate additional tenants and by mid-March of 1968, fifteen other tenants were leasing stores in the mall.

The mall was bordered by two heavily travelled roads. Separating the mall from these roads were berms of approximately twelve to twenty feet in width. The Weis store itself was surrounded by a parking area and walkways so that the closest entrance from the highway to the store was about 350 feet. In the front of the store was a covered porch area, and immediately adjacent to that was a customer parcel pick-up zone marked off with yellow lines. The pick-up zone, approximately four to five feet wide and thirty to forty feet in length, was designed for customer waiting while store employees loaded their purchases into the customers' motor vehicles.

Several competitor supermarkets, including A & P, Quaker, and Acme, were located further down one of the roads bordering the Logan Valley Mall. On December 17, employees of those competitor stores began picketing Weis. The number of pickets varied between four and thirteen and averaged around six. They walked in the marked-off parcel pickup area carrying signs reading: "Weis markets is nonunion. These employees are not receiving union wages or other union benefits. Amalgamated Food Employees Union Local 590."[10] None of the Weis employees at Logan Valley Mall were union members, whereas the employees at the competitor A & P, Acme, and Quaker stores were union represented.

The Weis store manager testified to the effect that these pickets interfered with the flow of auto traffic in and out of the parcel pickup area and that at one point they marched four abreast in this area blocking traffic altogether. He stated that he told the picketers to leave the premises and suggested that they could use the berm along the two public roads adjoining the mall. There was also testimony to the effect that, at one point during the picketing, the manager of the competitor A & P supermarket parked in the pickup zone and spoke to some of the picketers. The picketing was peaceful, accompanied neither by threats nor violence. Nor was there any evidence that it resulted in a reduction of deliveries of goods.

On December 27, both Weis and the landlord shopping center, Logan Valley Plaza, Inc., went to the local state court seeking relief from the picketing. Upon the posting of a $500 bond by Weis and Logan, the local court issued a temporary injunction against the union and its agents from picketing or trespassing on the shopping center premises. After the injunction went into effect, the union pickets moved to the berms near the shopping center entrances.

A motion asking the state court to either dissolve or modify the injunction was filed by the union on January 4, 1966. The court heard this motion that same day and on February 14 it denied the union's motion and ordered that the injunction be continued. An appeal was taken to the Supreme Court of Pennsylvania, which upheld the decision of its lower court. Review was then sought by the union before the Supreme Court of the United States.

There was little question but that had this peaceful organizational picketing of Weis taken place on a public way, it would have been constitutionally protected. As previously discussed, the Supreme Court had long recognized First Amendment protections of free expression as being applicable to labor picketing. Thus, on various occasions the Court had previously struck down state statutes barring all picketing in public places [e.g., *Thornhill* v. *Alabama*, 310 U.S. 88 (1940)] and had similarly overturned state injunctions that interfered with peaceful, noncoercive public picketing [e.g., *A.F. of L.* v. *Swing*, 312 U.S. 321 (1941)]. Moreover, the state court injunction in this case, unlike prior decisions, such as *Giboney, Graham,* and *Vogt,* did not rely on a claim that the union's action was designed to coerce the employer into intimidating its workers to join the union. Rather, the state court treated the picketing as a trespass. Thus, because the loading area in front of Weis' store was not a "public-way" in any traditional sense of the term, this situation presented a clear choice between the property rights claimed by the store and shopping center owners and the right of free expression claimed by the union.

From the point of view of the property holders (the landlord shopping center and the tenant), the issue ultimately boiled down to whether a retailer is required to suffer the conversion of its property from the owner's designated use of it as a parcel pickup area into the union's use of it as a picket area. From the union's viewpoint, however, the issue boiled down to whether an employer can insulate its retail employees from a basic union organizing technique by surrounding that business with a strip of privately owned land in the form of a parking area. The Supreme Court's resolution of this conflict came with its decision in *Amalgamated Food Employees Union Local 590* v. *Logan Valley Plaza, Inc.,* 391 U.S. 308 (1968).

The stakes involved in the Supreme Court's review were considerable. By 1968 the Retail Clerk's International Association, a rapidly growing union, represented more than 200,000 retail employees working in shopping centers. In an *amicus curie* brief, which it submitted in support of the Amalgamated Food Employees Union, it was estimated that in 1966 alone there were over 300 organizing campaigns in such retailing complexes. It was further estimated that by the end of 1966 there would be a total of 10,112 shopping centers in the United States. One authoritative source predicted that by 1975, shopping centers would dominate the retail industry. As it was, by 1966 shopping centers were doing approximately 36.84 percent of all retail business in the United States and Canada. And, as early as 1964, retailing in six states (Arizona, Colorado, Delaware, Florida, Nevada and Texas) had already become dominated by the shopping center method of marketing.

The particular property in dispute in *Logan* was the parking and driveway area. Such space provides the key feature that distinguishes the shopping center from other retail locations. The parking area attracts customers who wish to utilize their automobiles for shopping transportation. As a result, for example, parking spaces in California shopping centers by 1965 were capable of accommodating 836,000 autos.

Except for the provision of these extensive parking facilities, the union argued, shopping centers would be no different from downtown business districts. Moreover, asserted the union, shopping center operations depend, for their success, upon imitating the environment of downtown business districts. More and more, according to the union, shopping centers sponsor a wide variety of public activities in order to attract customers. For example, many provide such things as meeting rooms, amusement facilities, parks, theatres, and assembly halls. Similarly, they sponsor art exhibits, flower shows, fashion events, and concerts.

The American Retail Federation, in an *amicus* brief, attempted to offset some of this data concerning the nature and impact of shopping centers in modern American life. It argued that half of all shopping center businesses are conducted on premises of less than 200,000 square feet in gross leasable area and asserted that these are small operations. (Of course, 200,000 square feet of leasable space would be encompassed, for example, by a one-story building that is 400 feet by 500 feet. If the surrounding parking areas are added to these dimensions, it is open to dispute as to whether such a lot can accurately be characterized as "small.")

In upholding the injunction against picketing in the Logan Mall, the Pennsylvania Supreme Court had reasoned that the invitation to the public to use the shopping center premises was limited to potential customers and was not an invitation for purposes such as those engaged in by the picketers. Accordingly, explained the Pennsylvania high court, the picketing constituted a trespass and such a trespass could be restrained by injunctive relief. Three of the state court justices dissented, with two of them joining in an opinion by Justice Cohen who cited with approval opinions by other state courts reasoning that shopping center operations are so public in nature that they are subject to the Fourteenth Amendment's restraints upon state interference with freedom of speech.

When the case came before the United States Supreme Court, the union argued that one reason for disallowing the state's injunctive relief was that it encroached upon the authority of the National Labor Relations Board to regulate labor-management disputes and that, therefore, the state court was preempted by the National Labor Relations Act from passing on such matters. The Supreme Court declined to consider this issue because it had not been raised by the union when it appeared before the Pennsylvania Supreme Court.

The union also argued that the shopping center premises could not be denied to the picketers inasmuch as this private property was the most appropriate place for communicating with respect to a labor dispute and that under the authority of *Marsh* v. *Alabama,* 326 U.S. 501 (1946), the rights of private property must give way to the exercise of the constitutional right of free expression. This latter argument was better received by the Supreme Court of the United States.

The *Marsh* case had involved a Jehovah's Witness who distributed religious literature on the sidewalk of a business street in a company-owned town. The company had posted notices stating that no solicitation could be undertaken without written permission of the town manager. Such permission was refused to Marsh. Marsh was thereafter arrested for criminal trespass when she persisted in distributing her religious literature. The Supreme Court held that the mere fact that the property in question was privately owned was an insufficient basis to justify the encroachment upon Marsh's exercise of her right to free expression.

A 6 to 3 majority of the Supreme Court agreed with the union that *Marsh* was analogous to the Logan Valley situation and, in an opinion written by Mr. Justice Marshall, reversed the Pennsylvania court: "We see no reason why access to a business district in a company town for the purpose of exercising First Amendment rights should be constitutionally required while access for the same purpose to property functioning as a business district should be limited simply because the property surrounding the business district is not under the same ownership."[11] The Court explained that because the shopping center serves as a community business block, freely accessible and open to the people in the area and to those passing through, the property could not be withheld from persons wishing to exercise First Amendment rights on the premises "in a manner and for a purpose generally consonant with the use to which the property is actually put."[12] The Court expressly reserved for a future decision the question of the extent to which shopping center owners or tenants are entitled to limit the location and manner of picketing in a shopping center or, the number of pickets within a shopping center so as to prevent interference with access areas or pickup areas.

Actually, the *Logan Valley Mall* case was not the first occasion in which the Supreme Court had to make a choice between claims to a union organizer's freedom of expression and constitutional claims to an employer's right to control the use of his property. The Supreme Court had been faced with this choice, for example, in *Republic Aviation Corp.* v. *National Labor Relations Board*, 324 U.S. 793, a case it decided in 1945.

In *Republic Aviation,* the union's claim was supported by the NLRB, which had ruled that employee solicitation of union support was protected by the National Labor Relations Act even though it had taken place on the employer's premises. The issue arose when two different employers enforced rules against various types of union organizing activity on their respective company property. In the situation involving the Republic Aviation Corporation, the employer had prohibited all solicitation of any type in the company's factory or offices. An employee who persisted in distributing union application cards to fellow employees during the lunch periods was discharged for infraction of this rule. Other employees were discharged by Republic for wearing buttons identifying themselves as union stewards. These discharges were found by the National Labor Relations Board to be in violation of the National Labor Relations Act's protections of the right to engage in union organizational activity.

In the other situation involved in the *Republic* decision, the Le Tourneau Company of Georgia suspended employees for two days because they had distributed union literature on the employer's parking lots adjacent to the company's plant. The employees had done this during their own time but in violation of a company rule prohibiting distribution of circulars or other literature on company property without first securing permission from the personnel department. Here, again, the National Labor Relations Board ruled that the disciplinary action was in violation of the National Labor Relations Act's protection of unionization activities. Although the Supreme Court, in affirming the decisions of the National Labor Relations Board, did not address itself directly to the issue of whether an employer's right to control its property can, constitutionally, be encroached upon in the interests of enhancing the opportunities for unionization, the Court did conclude that the rationale of the NLRB for reaching its result was supportable by substantial evidence. By implication, therefore, the Court approved the encroachment upon the employer's control of its property, which resulted from the NLRB treating the employer's disciplining of the union organizers as an unfair labor practice. Moreover, in its opinion the Supreme Court quoted, with seeming approval, from the NLRB's discussion of this issue where the Board had stated: "[T]he employer's right to control his property does not permit him to deny access to his property to persons whose presence is necessary there to enable the employees effectively to exercise their right of self-organization and collective bargaining. . . . [W]hile it [is] 'within the province of an employer to promulgate and enforce a rule prohibiting union solicitation during working hours,' it [is] 'not within the province of an employer to promulgate and enforce a rule prohibiting union solicitation by an employee outside of working hours, although on company property,' the latter restriction being deemed an unreasonable impediment to the exercise of the right to self organization."[13]

The issue of the competing interests between speech and property rights was involved again in *National Labor Relations Board* v. *Stowe Spinning Co.,* 336 U.S. 226 (1949), a case decided over the partial objection of Mr. Justice Jackson and the total dissent of Chief Justice Vinson and Mr. Justice Reed. In this case, a union organizer who had been denied use of the local school building where he wanted to conduct a union organizing meeting was also denied use of the local theatre on the grounds that it could be used only for motion pictures. The only other building in town at which a meeting could be conducted was one housing a post office and the facilities of a patriotic society. Initially the society told the organizer that he could rent the hall on the payment of a janitor's fee. Thereafter the employers, which owned the building, directed the society to rescind permission. The National Labor

Relations Board agreed with the union that this refusal to permit the use of
the hall was a violation of the National Labor Relations Act.

When the case came before the United States Supreme Court, the employer
argued that the board's decision flew: "in the very teeth of the Fifth Amendment.
From Magna Carta on down, the individual has been guaranteed against disseisin
of his property."[14] Rejecting this argument, the Supreme Court stated that not
every interference with property rights is within the scope of protection of the
Fifth Amendment. Inconvenience, or even some dislocation of property rights,
may be necessary in order to safeguard the statutory right to collectively bargain.
However, the discussion of the property issue in *Stowe* went no further than
this statement. In fact, the Supreme Court concluded that whereas the board's
order required the employer to give the union access to the hall irrespective of
the employer's policies in making it available to others, the basis for its cease
and desist order was the finding that the employer had discriminated against this
union by granting the facilities to other organizations while denying it to the labor
union. Accordingly, the Court concluded, the board's remedy went beyond cor-
recting the unlawful antiunion discrimination and hence should not be enforced.
The Supreme Court sent the case back to the board for an appropriate narrowing
of its cease and desist order so as to only compel the employers to refrain from
such activity as would cause the union's application for use of the hall to be
treated on a different basis than those received from other applicants.

Mr. Justice Jackson, dissenting in part, would have limited the board's order
to requiring the employers to notify the tenant, the patriotic organization, to
the effect that the employers would make no objections in the future with respect
to that organization's desire to allow the hall to be temporarily used by the union.

A variation of this same problem came before the Court in 1956 when it decided *National Labor Relations Board* v. *Babcock & Wilcox Co.*, 351 U.S. 105.
That case involved an employer's refusal to permit nonemployee union organizers
on company-owned parking lots for the purpose of distributing union literature.
The particular parking lots surrounded a manufacturing establishment on a one-
hundred acre tract located about one mile from a town with a population of
21,000. About 40 percent of the company's employees lived in that town and
the remainder lived within a thirty-mile radius of the plant. The National Labor
Relations Board had found that leaflets could not be distributed to employees
driving to and from work except in the parking lot. Traffic conditions made it
practically impossible to safely distribute such literature to the cars entering
and leaving the lot. The employer's refusal of access to the union organizers was
explained in terms of protecting against littering of its property. The employer
noted that its policy was consistently applied to all kinds of pamphleteering.

Without dissent, the Supreme Court ruled in *Babcock & Wilcox* that the
alternative channels for communicating with employees were adequate in this
situation to meet the union's needs and that, therefore, the employer could not
be compelled to allow distribution of literature on its property by nonemployees.
The Supreme Court's opinion emphasized that those seeking to distribute the

literature were nonemployees. "The distinction is one of substance. No restriction may be placed on the employees' right to discuss self-organization among themselves, unless the employer can demonstrate that a restriction is necessary to maintain production or discipline. . . . But no such obligation is owed nonemployee organizers. Their access to company property is governed by a different consideration."[15] The Court then explained that only where nonemployees cannot reasonably communicate with employees through channels outside of the place of employment can their lack of access to the employers' property properly be deemed an unlawful restraint upon the statutory right of self-organization. By implication, the Supreme Court thereby gave its approval to a number of NLRB decisions in which even nonemployees were held to have a statutory right of access to an employer's property for the purpose of union activity where the employees were so isolated (in places like lumber camps) so that lack of such access would place the employees beyond the reach of reasonable union efforts to communicate with them.

A distinction between the *Logan Valley Mall* case and the *Babcock, Stowe,* and *Republic* decisions is, of course, that in the latter three cases the union's claim was based on a statutory right of protection from employer restraints upon union activity, that claimed right arising under the National Labor Relations Act. While a similar argument had been made in the *Logan Valley Mall* case, the Supreme Court ruled that that argument was not properly preserved in the state court. Therefore, the issue in *Logan Valley* was whether the nonemployee union organizers could utilize the employer's parking lot despite the absence of a claim to statutory protection in doing so. And, the Supreme Court's answer was, as we have seen, that the union indeed did have a right to use this type of employer's premises for organizational activity.

The *Logan Valley Mall* decision raised many unanswered questions. To what extent, if any, was it modifying the rule in the *Babcock* case? *Babcock* involved a parking lot restricted to the use of employees; *Logan Valley* involved a parking lot restricted to the use of customers. Was that the critical distinction explaining the difference in result? To what extent could the *Logan Valley* decision be extended to give picketers with nonunion organizing causes similar access to shopping center parking lots? Are there any steps that a shopping center owner can take to effectively restrict use of parking areas for customer parking only? Two cases decided in 1972 provided some answers.

Central Hardware Co. v. *National Labor Relations Board,* 407 U.S. 539, involved the refusal to allow an employer's nonemployee union organizers to use its parking lots, which surrounded two stores, for the purpose of soliciting union support from the company's employees. The stores in this case were retail hardware stores each containing 70,000 square feet of floor space. Each store had parking facilities on three sides. These parking lots could accommodate approximately 350 automobiles. The stores and parking lots were maintained solely for the individual establishment and had no connection with any shopping centers.

Central Hardware had adopted a rule prohibiting solicitation anywhere on its premises, and it enforced this rule against all solicitations in its stores and parking lots. When the union organizers appeared at the parking lots, Central insisted that they leave. In one instance, it had an organizer arrested under local law as a trespasser when he presisted in his refusal to leave. The National Labor Relations Board ruled that under the principle of the *Logan Valley* case, Central Hardware's refusal of access to the parking lots was distinguishable from the situation in *Babcock & Wilcox* and that, therefore, Central Hardware was guilty of interfering with protected union organizing activity in violation of section 8(a) (1) of the National Labor Relations Act. A divided Court of Appeals agreed and enforced an order barring the employer from prohibiting use of the parking lot premises by nonemployee organizers.

When Central Hardware appealed to the Supreme Court, the Court described its own role in cases such as this as having to find a proper accommodation between the statutory organizational rights of employees and the constitutional property rights of employers. Citing to its decision in *Babcock,* the Court decided in favor of Central Hardware explaining that permissible intrusions upon property rights are limited to those which are necessary to facilitate the exercise of employee organizational rights. Such a required yielding of property rights, said the Supreme Court, is permissible only when it is both temporary and minimal.

The Supreme Court, in the course of explaining its *Central Hardware* decision supporting the employer's exclusion of union organizers, distinguished the *Logan* case on the grounds that the principle of *Logan* applies only where the privately owned property has assumed a significant degree of the functional attributes of public property devoted to public use. The mere fact that the Central Hardware parking lots were open to the public, ruled the Court, was not enough to constitute the taking on of the functional attributes of public property. Accordingly, the Supreme Court held that the *Central Hardware* case was controlled by *Babcock* and not by *Logan.* Under the *Babcock* doctrine, explained the Court, union organizers would have been entitled to use Central's parking lots only if it had been shown that no other reasonable means of communicating with employees was available to nonemployee union organizers. The Supreme Court, therefore, vacated the judgment and sent the case back to the Court of Appeals for further consideration of the facts on this last point.

A dissent written by Mr. Justice Marshall, who was joined by Justices Douglas and Brennan, agreed with the majority that the *Central* case was controlled by *Babcock* and that *Central* involved a narrower issue than that raised in *Logan.* On the other hand, the dissenters asserted that the principle involved in *Babcock* is even broader than the holding in the *Logan Valley* case. "It holds that where a union has no other means at its disposal to communicate with employees other than to use the employer's property, or where the union is denied the access to employees that the employer gives anti-union forces, the union may communicate with employees on the property of the employer."[16]

This right to use private property, explained the dissenters, is not granted by the First Amendment but, rather, is granted by Congress under the National Labor Relations Act. However, since the NLRB and the Court had erroneously decided this case on the authority of *Logan,* rather than on the doctrine of *Babcock,* the dissenters argued that the Supreme Court should have remanded the case to the National Labor Relations Board, rather than to the Court of Appeals. The dissenters, accordingly, wanted the Labor Board to have an opportunity to reconsider the case in terms of the applicability of *Babcock & Wilcox* to the facts.

Lloyd Corporation, Ltd. v. *Tanner,* 407 U.S. 551 (1972), a case not involving labor relations, is also of significance to this discussion inasmuch as it, too, dealt with important dimensions of the *Logan Valley* decision. The *Lloyd* case involved a privately owned enclosed mall-type shopping center occupying about fifty acres and including some twenty acres of open and covered parking facilities able to accommodate more than one thousand automobiles. The perimeter of the shopping center owned by Lloyd was almost one and a half miles and was bounded by four public streets. About sixty commercial tenants occupied the shopping center. This shopping center differed from that involved in *Logan Valley* not only in that it was larger, but also in the fact that the stores all opened into a large, multi-level enclosed area containing sidewalks, stairways, escalators, gardens, fountains, statuaries, benches, an auditorium, and a skating rink. These areas were technically open twenty-four hours a day and window shopping was encouraged after store hours. On the other hand, some controls were exercised over public use of the area. For example, there was testimony to the effect that someone walking in the area at three o'clock in the morning might be questioned and watched. Moreover, signs were embedded in the sidewalk at several places within Lloyd's enclosed mall area stating that these were not public ways and that permission to use the areas could be revoked at any time. Although some groups had been permitted to solicit for charitable causes in the enclosed area, the shopping center had a consistent policy prohibiting handbilling on the theory that such activity was likely to annoy customers and create litter.

On November 14, 1968, five young people, who were quiet and orderly, distributed handbills in this enclosed mall area. The handbills contained invitations to a meeting for the purpose of protesting the draft and the Vietnam War. There was no littering. A single customer complained to the management. Security guards asked the handbillers to leave and suggested that they distribute their literature on the public streets and sidewalks adjacent to the outside boundaries of the shopping center. The handbillers left so as to avoid arrest and continued to handbill outside the boundaries of the shopping center property. They brought an action, however, in the United States District Court seeking declaratory and injunctive relief to allow their re-entry into the mall to continue their leafletting activity.

Holding that such relief was not available to the handbillers, the Supreme

Court distinguished *Logan Valley* on the grounds that the holding of that case is limited to protecting picketing that is directly related in its purpose to the use to which the shopping center property is being put and to situations in which the store is located in a place where no other reasonable opportunity is available for the pickets to convey their message to their intended audience. Emphasizing that the handbilling involved in the *Lloyd* case was unrelated to any purpose for which the shopping center was built or used, the majority of the Supreme Court, in an opinion by Mr. Justice Powell, explained that these handbillers could have distributed their message on any public street or public sidewalk, in any public park, or in any public building. He stated, further:

> The invitation is to come to the Center to do business with the tenants. It is true that facilities at the Center are used for certain meetings and for various promotional activities. The obvious purpose, recognized widely as legitimate and responsible business activity, is to bring po- tential shoppers to the Center, to create a favorable impression, and to generate goodwill. There is no open-ended invitation to the public to use the Center for any and all purposes, however incompatible with the interests of both the stores and the shoppers whom they serve.[17]

The majority also emphasized that alternative means of distributing the handbills were available, including giving them to the shoppers as they came to a complete halt in their automobiles outside the shopping center prior to moving onto the public highways.

Four Justices dissented in an opinion prepared by Mr. Justice Marshall, the author of the *Logan Valley* majority opinion. Mr. Justice Marshall, speaking for himself and Justices Douglas, Brennan, and Stewart, asserted that the shop- ping center involved in *Lloyd* was even more clearly the equivalent of a public business district than was that involved in *Logan Valley*. Agreeing with the majority's proposition that the Court is striking a balance between the freedom to speak and the freedom of the private property owner to control his property, Marshall argued that the majority reached the wrong result because: "When the competing interests are fairly weighed, the balance can only be struck in favor of speech."[18] Noting the comprehensive list of services and goods avail- able at the Lloyd Shopping Center, Mr. Justice Marshall stated that many citizens "will so completely satisfy their wants that they will have no reason to go elsewhere for goods or services. If speech is to reach these people, it must reach them in Lloyd Center."[19] In this regard, the long-range impact of the *Lloyd* decision was particularly disturbing to Mr. Justice Marshall. He observed that with the growing pattern of private enterprise undertaking the construction and operation of shopping districts:

> It becomes harder and harder for citizens to find means to communicate

with other citizens. . . . When there are no effective means of communication, free speech is a mere shibboleth. I believe that the First Amendment requires it to be a reality.[20]

The decision in *Lloyd* could well be interpreted as a total rejection of the doctrine of *Logan Valley*. As Mr. Justice Marshall bluntly stated:

The vote in *Logan Valley* was 6-3, and that decision is only four years old. But, I am aware that the composition of this Court has radically changed in four years. The fact remains that *Logan Valley* is binding unless and until it is overruled. There is no valid distinction between that case and this one, and, therefore, the results in both cases should be the same.[21]

Mr. Justice Marshall's observation respecting the change in the Court's composition cannot be overlooked. Two of the six-member majority that decided *Logan* were no longer on the Court—Warren and Fortas. Similarly, two of the *Logan* dissenters had left by 1972—Black and Harlan. All four of the new Justices appointed by President Nixon—Burger, Blackmun, Powell and Rehnquist—joined Mr. Justice White to make a new majority in *Lloyd*. These new justices came to the Court with reputations as men with relatively strong predilections toward the protection of property rights. Moreover, these new members were generally not considered to place as high a priority on free expression as did the men they replaced. Thus, the question remained open after *Lloyd* as to whether the new majority would be willing to continue to apply *Logan* to labor union activity directly concerned with businesses operating at the shopping center. Or, in the alternative, would the Court focus more and more on the *Lloyd* language respecting the lack of "an open-ended invitation to use" the shopping center, thereby reducing the long range impact of *Logan* and, perhaps, eventually overruling it.[7]

The emphasis of the Pennsylvania court in *Logan* in allowing the injunction of labor picketing was, it will be recalled, upon the owner's limited invitation for public use. Had the Supreme Court, in deciding *Logan*, placed the weight upon this factor which the Court gave to it in *Lloyd*, then *Logan* likely would have been decided in favor of the shopping center owners. Therefore, it was reasonable to speculate that so long as the ideological composition of the Supreme Court remained as it was in 1972, property interests would be found to outweigh the social interests in opportunities for controversial or self-serving expression with the result that the *Logan Valley* decision would become of consequence more as history than as law.[b]

---

[b]On Mar. 3, 1976, the Court overruled *Logan*. *Lloyd,* it said, established that shopping centers are private property. It held that property rights of the shopping center should be weighed against NLRA rights to concerted activity. Marshall and Brennan dissented, reasserting Marshall's thesis from *Lloyd.*

3 Supremacy of Federal Power

The issue the Supreme Court avoided reaching in the *Logan Valley* case—that is, whether the National Labor Relations Act precluded the state from enjoining the union's organizational activity—involves an interesting line of case development that poses an alternative mode for challenging state regulatory power over labor relations. In examining this alternative, it must be remembered that the central issue in the state court cases discussed in the previous chapter was whether the state regulation or prohibition of picketing or other union activity interfered with the union's constitutionally protected freedom of expression, assembly, or association. In contrast, the alternative means for attacking the state's action involves the assertion that even if the Constitution does not bar the challenged state regulation or prohibition, nevertheless the state's action is invalid because it encroaches upon an area of regulation already occupied by federal law.

To appreciate the thrust of this alternative theory of attack upon state regulation of labor relations, it must be understood that it is well settled constitutional doctrine that where otherwise valid state and federal laws conflict, the Supremacy Clause of the Constitution requires the state law to give way. A variation or expansion of this concept is the so-called preemption doctrine that requires state law to give way to federal law, even where the two are not in direct conflict, if the federal law has pervasively "occupied" the particular area of regulation. That is, unless Congress indicates that it does not object to there being coexistent state regulation of the subject matter, a comprehensive scheme of federal regulation of an area will be deemed to be the exclusive law governing that area of activity even in those cases in which the challenged state regulation is not inconsistent with the policy of the federal statute.

As will be seen, in applying the preemption doctrine to the field of labor relations, the Supreme Court has proceeded with some degree of caution and hesitancy, and, perhaps, inconsistency.

The earliest assertion of the doctrine in a labor case reaching the Supreme Court appears to have been in *Allen-Bradley Local No. 1111* v. *Wisconsin Employment Relations Board,* 315 U.S. 740 (1942). This union unsuccessfully tried to reverse a state injunction against mass picketing in which it had been found by the state court to have used threats of physical injury to persons and property and to have involved obstruction of streets and of ingress and egress to the company premises. Speaking for a unanimous Court, Mr. Justice Douglas, in relying on statements in the Committee Reports with which the Wagner

Bill had been explained to Congress, stated that the type of conduct in question was not intended to be encompassed by the federal legislation then governing labor relations. Douglas' opinion, moreover, emphasized the lack of any conflict between the policy of the NLRA and that represented by the state injunction under challenge in this case.

A few years later, however, in *Hill v. Florida,* the Court allowed a union to prevail against a state statute that required unions and union business agents to obtain state licenses as a condition of conducting union activities. To get these licenses, it was necessary to pay a nominal fee, to supply certain information, and to satisfy the officials that the applicant had not been convicted of a felony during the preceding ten years and that the applicant was of good moral character. This requirement, held the Court, encroached upon the federally enacted right to engage in collective activity. Such state interference with federally granted rights, the Court explained, was prohibited by the Supremacy Clause of the Constitution.[1]

Chief Justice Stone, in a concurring opinion, cautioned that the Court's decision in *Hill* did not preclude the states from protecting against fraud or violence on the part of union officials, and did not bar a state from requiring unions to file reports and perform other duties that do not materially interfere with federally conferred rights. Accordingly, Stone took partial exception to the Court's result. He would have struck down only that part of the state law that required the filing of certain information and the payment of a filing fee in conjunction with the filing of information.

Mr. Justice Frankfurter, dissenting in *Hill*, went much further in his criticism of the result. Frankfurter contended that the decision was an improper interference with state sovereignty and that the Supremacy Clause could be used to strike down a state regulation only upon the showing of a precise conflict with federal law. No such conflict had been shown in *Hill,* he argued.

The invocation of the Supremacy Clause in *Hill* cannot accurately be referred to as the preemption doctrine inasmuch as the Court emphasized the existence of a direct conflict between state regulation and specific federal rights. The issue surfaced again, however, in a setting involving a more pure form of the preemption doctrine, in *Garner v. Teamsters, Chauffeurs & Helpers Local Union No. 776 (AFL),* 346 U.S. 485 (1953).

Garner, like the previously discussed (but later decided) *Logan Valley* case, arose in Pennsylvania when a local court enjoined union organizational picketing. The pickets had been carrying signs in front of Garner's loading platform urging Garner's nonunion employees to join the union so as "to gain union wages, hours and working conditions."[2] This picketing resulted in a 95 percent reduction of business because most of the drivers delivering and picking up goods were union members who refused to cross the picket line. The lower Pennsylvania court issued its injunction on the grounds that picketing violated a state statute prohibiting the use of pickets to coerce employers to force their employees to join a union. The Pennsylvania Supreme Court, however, vacated the injunction on the ground that this dispute came within the jurisdiction of the NLRB and, therefore, state remedies were precluded.

The Supreme Court of the United States granted the employer's petition for certiorari but affirmed the decision of the Pennsylvania high court in a unanimous opinion by Mr. Justice Jackson.

Jackson's opinion noted, as had the decision of the Pennsylvania high court, that the National Labor Relations Act imposes a variety of regulations upon the use of picketing as a tool for union organizing. Accordingly, he explained, if the NLRB were to find no violation by the union or dismiss a complaint against the union, the picketing directed at Garner would be lawful under the federal statute. "To avoid facing a conflict between the state and federal remedies," stated Jackson, "we would have to assume either that both authorities [state courts and the NLRB] will always agree as to whether the picketing should continue, or that the State's temporary injunction will be dissolved as soon as the federal Board acts. But experience gives no assurance of either alternative, and there is no indication that the statute left it open for such conflicts to arise."[3] Because the Constitution gives supremacy to federal law over state law, this potential conflict between state and federal authority was, accordingly, resolved by holding that the state was excluded from taking any action on the question.

The decision in *Garner* can be characterized as an application of the preemption doctrine in its full technical sense. In *Garner,* the Court excluded the state from issuing an injunction not because there was an established conflict between state and federal authority, but rather because there was a mere potentiality of such conflict due to the fact that Congress had established a policy for regulating the type of activity in question.

It is noteworthy that Mr. Justice Frankfurter, who had dissented from the Court's application of the preemption doctrine in *Hill* v. *Florida,* voted with the majority in *Garner.* Even more significantly, he wrote the majority opinion a couple of years later in *Weber* v. *Anheuser-Busch,* 348 U.S. 468 (1955), where the Court held that a state cannot enjoin a strike in which a union seeks to establish the right of its members to do particular work. Said Mr. Justice Frankfurter, "Regarding the conduct here in controversy, Congress has sufficiently expressed its purpose to bring it within federal oversight and to exclude state prohibition . . . ."[4] That "expressed" purpose, however, was a matter of statutory interpretation and not specific language in the Act. But the employer, Anheuser-Busch, made Frankfurter's path to decision a relatively simple one to follow inasmuch as the employer had argued, in state court, that the union's conduct was in violation of the National Labor Relations Act. Accepting the employer's own allegation, the only basis for rejecting the application of preemption would have been to assume that Congress intended to allow the states to exercise parallel jurisdiction over this type of union activity. Despite the reservations expressed in *Hill* v. *Florida* concerning the application of the preemption doctrine, Frankfurter was apparently willing in *Weber* to assume that Congress's silence should be read as a rejection of parallel jurisdiction. In his words: "[T] he state court must decline jurisdiction in deference to the tribunal which Congress has selected for determining such issues in the first instance."[5]

Subsequent to *Garner,* the Court found it necessary to confine the preemption doctrine so as to permit state remedies in certain situations that were in fact subject to the NLRB's jurisdiction. Thus, the Court held that where the state remedy is directed at picket-line violence, or where it is designed to give relief from a union's breach of the duty of fair representation owed to all bargaining unit employees or to remedy torts such as defamation arising in conjunction with a labor-management dispute, the preemption doctrine will not bar that state remedy.[6]

Each of the above forms of conduct involve interference with protected labor activity or the exercise of speech in connection with conduct regulated by the NLRA. Accordingly, in each instance the state suit involves matters coming under protective or restrictive sections of the National Labor Relations Act. However, the reason for carving out such exceptions from the preemption doctrine was explained by Justice Frankfurter, speaking for the Court, in *San Diego Building Trades Council* v. *Garmon,* 359 U.S. 236 (1959): "[D] ue regard for the pre-suppositions of our embracing federal system . . . has required us not to find withdrawal from the States of power to regulate where the activity regulated was a merely peripheral concern of the Labor Management Relations Act. . . . Or where the regulated conduct touched interests so deeply rooted in local feeling and responsibility that, in the absence of compelling congressional direction, we could not infer that Congress had deprived the States of the power to act."[7] Thus, the Court has relied on its own notions of probable congressional intent respecting preemption in applying the doctrine to some aspects of state regulation of labor relations but not to others.

Even without these exceptions to the general preemption approach in the labor relations area, it is necessary to resolve whether any particular form of labor relations conduct is within the scope of the federal legislation in order to know whether the preemption doctrine is applicable. The earlier cases had reserved this sort of question for the Supreme Court.[8] In time, however, the Court surrendered responsibility over this question to the National Labor Relations Board. Thus, in *Garmon* the Court said: "[C] ourts are not primary tribunals to adjudicate such issues. It is essential to the administration of the Act that these determinations be left in the first instance to the National Labor Relations Board."[9]

Pursuant to this instruction, the Court advised that the test for determining whether the courts, both state and federal, should decline to exercise jurisdiction is: If the activity is *arguably* subject to sections 7 and 8 of the National Labor Relations Act, then the federal and state courts "must defer to the exclusive competence of the National Labor Relations Board."[10] That test, it should be observed, is far removed from the suspicious regard for preemption that Mr. Justice Frankfurter, the author of the Court's opinion in *Garmon,* had expressed some fourteen years earlier in *Hill* v. *Florida.*

Elaborating on the test to be used for determining whether the judiciary must decline jurisdiction over labor relations disputes, Justice Frankfurter also stated in *Garmon* that in the absence of a clear determination as to whether the conduct in question is protected or prohibited under sections 7 or 8 of the NLRA, or in the absence "of compelling precedent applied to essentially undisputed facts," a state court cannot exercise its power over such conduct but must instead "await the necessary clarification by the NLRB."[11] This last aspect of Frankfurter's elaboration of the preemption doctrine was rebuked by Mr. Justice Harlan, joined by Justices Clark, Whittaker and Stewart. Asserted Harlan: "The threshold question in every labor preemption case is whether the conduct with respect to which a State has sought to act is, or may fairly be regarded as, federally protected activity. Because conflict is the touchstone of preemption, such activity is obviously beyond the reach of all state power."[12] In other words, this minority of the Court would invoke the preemption doctrine in labor cases only when it is apparent that there is in fact a conflict between federal law and the state regulatory effort.

The factual setting of *Garmon* helped to place in focus the difference between the Frankfurter and Harlan approaches to this issue. The finding of the California court in *Garmon* was that the union had peacefully picketed an employer to force that employer to recognize a union as his employees' bargaining agent even though the union represented only a minority of the workers. This conduct clearly violated section 8(b) (2) of the NLRA. However, because of the relatively small size of the employer's operation, the NLRB regional office had declined to issue a complaint based on the employer's unfair labor practice charge. Accordingly, the California court gave Garmon the relief he failed to get from the NLRB by awarding him damages and an injunction against the union's continued picketing. Because the conduct in this case was clearly governed by the NLRA, Harlan was able to join in the Court's decision vacating the California court's remedy. The mere fact that the regional office of the NLRB declined to proceed with the case did not mean that it was not governed by the federal law—a proposition previously settled by the Court. Nevertheless, had this dispute not come so clearly within the scope of the National Labor Relations Act, Harlan apparently would have voted against preemption whereas the majority still could have invoked preemption so long as the dispute was *arguably* subject to the federal statute.

Inasmuch as minority positions supported by fewer justices have ultimately prevailed in the history of Supreme Court decision making, it is not surprising that the *Garmon* case did not lay to rest the dispute as to the appropriate test for ascertaining when state courts must decline to exercise their power over labor relations conflicts. The preemption issue again occupied the Court's attention in *Motor Coach Employees* v. *Lockridge,* 403 U.S. 274 (1971), where the majority opinion this time was presented by Mr. Justice Harlan. Frankfurter was no longer on the Court, and Mr. Justice Stewart was the only other member besides Harlan left on the Court from the foursome who had expressed reservations about Frankfurter's Opinion of the Court in the *Garmon* case. And in *Lockridge,* as in *Garmon,* Mr. Justice Stewart joined forces with Harlan. This time, however, it was Harlan and Stewart who were coming down in favor of a broad construction of the preemption doctrine!

Lockridge was a union security case, not a union organizing dispute. Lockridge had been employed for about seventeen years as a driver for a bus company. The company's employees were represented by a union that had negotiated a collective bargaining agreement containing a so-called union shop clause, a provision requiring those employed for more than thirty days to join the union and remain union members in order to keep their jobs. Such a provision is lawful under the National Labor Relations Act.

Lockridge had been a union member for many years but became over 30 days tardy in paying his monthly union dues. The union suspended him for failure to pay his dues, informed the employer of what had happened and the company, in turn, pursuant to the union shop clause of the collective bargaining agreement, dismissed Lockridge for failure to maintain his union membership.

Lockridge argued that under the union Constitution and by-laws, failure to pay dues within thirty days of the due date removed the member's status as a "member in good standing" with the resulting loss of certain membership privileges, but that it was not proper grounds for expulsion from the union. Suspension or expulsion, he asserted, was permissable under the union's Constitution and by-laws only when the member was over sixty days late in paying his monthly dues. Lockridge made these arguments in a suit he brought against the union in state court. In that suit he sought to recover money damages against the union for the dismissal from work, which, he contended, was wrongfully caused by the union's improper assertion that he had been suspended from membership. The state court agreed with Lockridge that the union did not have proper grounds for suspending him and awarded him a judgment of $32,678.56.[13]

This state court judgment against the union was reversed by the Supreme Court of the United States; the Court holding that Lockridge's recovery was barred by the preemption doctrine. Mr. Justice Harlan used the occasion to review the history of the preemption doctrine in labor cases and to elaborate on the majority's current application of it. He stated that a primary factor in

Congress's adoption and modification of our national labor legislation has been its perception that state legislatures and state courts cannot provide an informed and coherent policy for resolving and presiding over labor relations disputes. "Conflict in technique can be fully as disruptive to the system Congress erected as conflict in overt policy. . . . The technique of administration and the range and nature of those remedies that are and are not available is a fundamental part and parcel of the operative legal system established by the National Labor Relations Act."[14] Congress, he stated, sought "to restructure fundamentally the processes for effectuating that policy" by placing the enforcement responsibility into the hands of the NLRB. This, Mr. Justice Harlan explained, has made it necessary for the Supreme Court to find ways to avoid conflicts from arising between that Congressionally established administrative authority and the state and federal judiciary. And the Court has had to accomplish this task despite the fact that the "precise extent to which state law must be displaced to achieve those unifying ends sought by the national legislation has never been determined by the Congress."[15]

Harlan argued that in the Court's resulting effort at arbitrating between state judicial and federal administrative claims to jurisdiction, neither extreme—total exclusion of state authority nor total acceptance of concurrent jurisdiction—is a satisfactory solution. Nor, he said, is it practical for the Supreme Court to resolve each particular potential conflict on a case-by-case basis. Rather, Harlan explained, the rule of the *Garmon* case was the product of experience and was designed to provide ample guidance to the lower courts concerning the appropriate situations in which to invoke the preemption doctrine. In this case, Harlan stated, the *Garmon* principle required that the state court refrain from exercising jurisdiction. Lockridge's entire claim turned on whether the union properly procured his discharge. Since union security agreements are regulated by the NLRA, the conduct involved in the Lockridge situation, concluded Harlan, was arguably protected by section 7 or prohibited by section 8 of the Act. Thus, the state was preempted from providing a remedy for the alleged wrong.

In reviewing the list of exceptions that the Court has carved out of the *Garmon* rule, Mr. Justice Harlan asserted that these represent those situations in which the Court cannot, "in spite of the force of the policies *Garmon* seeks to promote, conscientiously presume that Congress meant to intrude so deeply into areas traditionally left to local law;" or where Congress has expressly indicated that the states are to have parallel jurisdiction; or where the rule of law to be enforced by the state "is so structured and administered that . . . it is safe to presume that judicial supervision will not disserve the interests promoted by the federal labor statutes."[16]

As to why he was now embracing the *Garmon* rule, Mr. Justice Harlan noted that Congress had not seen fit to change it and that this plus additional experience with its application, added to a high regard for the concept of *stare decisis,* persuaded him that it would not be wise to disturb its established stature.

But the swing of Harlan and Stewart in the direction of *Garmon* has not materially added to the stability of the doctrine inasmuch as there were four dissenting votes in *Lockridge.* One dissent was offered by Mr. Justice Douglas, joined in his arguments by Mr. Justice Blackmun; another dissenting opinion was presented by Mr. Justice White, joined by Chief Justice Burger and Mr. Justice Blackmun.

For Mr. Justice Douglas, Lockridge's predicament posed another situation in which the application of the *Garmon* rule is inappropriate. Experience under *Garmon* has taught him, Justice Douglas stated, that the rule should not be applied to disputes between individuals and their union. This exception to *Garmon*, he explained, is proper inasmuch as section 8(b) (1) of the NLRA states that its provisions are not intended to impair the right of a labor union to prescribe its own rules respecting the acquisition and retention of membership. Such disputes are, therefore, appropriately controlled by state law. In condemning the majority position, Mr. Justice Douglas asserted that it imposed a "great hardship" on the complaining individual who is "not financed out of a lush treasury" and who must "resort to an elusive remedy in distant and remote Washington, D.C."[17] "From the viewpoint of an aggrieved employee, there is not a trace of equity in this long-drawn, expensive remedy. If he musters the resources to exhaust the administrative remedy, the chances are that he too will be exhausted."[18]

Although there are, indeed, certain relative advantages that a complaining employee would have in prosecuting his case himself in state court, as contrasted with the issue being resolved through the process of NLRB unfair labor practice litigation, Mr. Justice Douglas was at least partially inaccurate in his recitation of the relative merits of the two procedures. An aggrieved party in an NLRB proceeding does not need a lush treasury to gain redress. The government provides his lawyer free of charge in the form of the prosecuting attorney from the staff of the Regional NLRB office. Thus, attorney's fees will normally be non-existant for the employee in a case of this sort tried before the NLRB, whereas they will probably be very substantial if he sues in state court. Further, dispite Justice Douglas' assertion, the aggrieved party need not be concerned about the distance and expense of traveling to Washington, D.C., because the NLRB sends its staff and administrative law judge to the place of employment, and any decisions made by the general counsel or NLRB in Washington are normally based on the hearing transcript and written memoranda mailed to the agency—that is, neither the employee nor his attorney, if he employs one to supplement the efforts of the NLRB lawyer who prosecutes the case, has need to travel to Washington. Finally, although the process of the NLRB can probably be made to operate more quickly, the delay between the filing of charges and trial and between appeal and decision is probably less than it is for most state tribunals with their appellate processes.

Justice White's dissent from the *Lockridge* decision made a more sweeping

attack upon the presumptions underlying both *Lockridge* and *Garmon.* Mr.
Justice White stated that although Congress intended to establish a uniform
national labor policy administered by a centralized agency, this intent should
not be construed to extend to the federalization of all aspects of labor relations
law; nor, he noted, has the Court insisted on such federalization when other
issues have been presented. To illustrate his point, Mr. Justice White reviewed
the various exceptions carved out of the preemption doctrine. For example,
he observed that a labor arbitrator is not only permitted to resolve a dispute
that is arguably either protected or prohibited under sections 7 or 8 of the NLRA,
but the Court has even indicated its approval of the NLRB's policy of liberally
deferring to the arbitrator's jurisdiction and decision in such matters. He listed,
too, the Court's approval of state jurisdiction over employee suits against their
unions where the employee alleges that the union acted in breach of its duty of
fair representation, with the Court permitting these suits to be brought before
state tribunals even though the NLRB has held that such a breach constitutes
an unfair labor practice.

In some situations, but not all, in which the Court has permitted concurrent jurisdiction for remedying labor relations conflicts, the Court has been
able to rely on an express statutory grant of judicial responsibility for dealing
with the controversy. Accordingly, the NLRB can provide a remedy based on
its finding that a union has engaged in unlawful secondary activity, and the
federal courts can additionally provide relief in the form of damages when it
makes a similar finding in a suit brought under section 303 of the Labor Management Relations Act. Moreover, the Supreme Court acknowledges the existence of such parallel jurisdiction even when the federal court reaches a result
inconsistent with the findings of the NLRB in such section 303 suits. Thus,
Justice White argued, Congress as well as the Court, has demonstrated its
willingness to have the benefits of operating with a single national labor law
subordinated to overriding state interests. "To summarize, the 'rule' of uniformity that the Court invokes today is at best a tattered one, and at worst
little more than a myth."[19]

Mr. Justice White's dissent also asserted that the history and text of the
Labor Management Relations Act and the Labor-Management Reporting and
Disclosure Act, demonstrate that Congress had no intention of depriving state
or federal courts of jurisdiction over disputes between unions and employees.
As did Justice Douglas, White noted that section 8(b) of the National Labor
Relations Act as modified by the Labor Management Relations Act, expressly
disclaims NLRB authority for the policing of internal union affairs. Further,
he pointed out that the Labor-Management Reporting and Disclosure Act
introduced a whole set of substantive and procedural rights of union members
as against their unions, with these rights to be enforced not by the NLRB but
by the federal courts. Moreover, language in section 603 of the LMRDA
reads: "Except as explicitly provided to the contrary, nothing in this Act

shall take away any right or bar any remedy to which members of a labor organization are entitled under such other Federal law or law of any State." Justice
White concluded from this that, "as to union-member relations, any parallel
rights created by the States, either directly or indirectly through enforcement
of union constitutions or bylaws, were to stand at full strength."[20]

But Mr. Justice White did not stop with his assertion that *Garmon* is inappropriate for suits by employees against unions. His ultimate target was the
Garmon test itself. The thrust of his objection to the test is that it often may
leave an aggrieved party without a remedy despite the merits of that grievance.
He explained: "The essential difference ... between activity that is arguably
prohibited and that which is arguably protected is that a hearing on the latter
activity is virtually impossible unless one deliberately commits an unfair labor
practice. ...[F] or activity that is arguably protected, there is no provision
for an authoritative decision by the Board in the first instance; yet the *Garmon*
rule blindly pre-empts other tribunals."[21] That is, the only way to establish
that your conduct is in fact protected under the Act is to go ahead and engage
in it and then establish its lawfulness when you are brought before the NLRB
in an unfair labor practice proceeding. Thus, if nobody charges you with an
unfair labor practice or if for reasons not based on a finding of lawfulness, the
general counsel of the NLRB declines to issue a complaint based on such a
charge, you cannot establish the protected status of your activity under the
NLRA. In such a situation, under the *Garmon* rule even though your conduct
"arguably" is protected by the NLRA, you may nevertheless not be able to
secure a remedy for interference with your protected activity inasmuch as the
status of your right may not be clearly defined by existing precedent. "Surely"
argued White, "the policy of seeking uniformity in the regulation of labor
practices must be given closer scrutiny when it leads to the alternative 'solutions'
of denying the aggrieved party a hearing or encouraging the commission of a
putative unfair labor practice as the price of that hearing."[22]

In reflecting upon the development of the two approaches for challenging
state regulation of union activity—the assertion of infringement of constitutional
liberty and the assertion of preclusion due to federal preemption—it is clear that
both, when successful, involve the Court's invocation of the Constitution of the
United States as a barrier to state action. The first approach does this by finding
that the state has infringed rights protected by the Fourteenth Amendment's
due process and equal protections clauses; the second approach does this by
finding that the state has violated the Supremacy Clause of Article VI by en-
croaching on the federal government's domain. The Court's interpretive problem
takes on different dimensions, however, depending upon which theory of challenge is pursued.

For the Court to decide a case based upon asserted Fourteenth Amendment
liberties, it must construe the meaning of that amendment's very vague, elusive
terminology; knowing that whatever its result, the implications of its decision

will extend beyond labor relations activities and into all aspects of political, social, and economic utilization of the liberties of expression, assembly, and association. On the other hand, for the Court to frame its decision within the preemption concept, it must construe the intent of Congress based upon the relatively more precise language of the several labor relations statutes. This latter task is complicated, however, by the involved structure of those laws and the entities created by them, and by the often ambiguous or vacuous legislative history of the federal labor acts respecting the intent to provide for either exclusive or concurrent state-federal regulation. Accordingly, whichever path the Court takes, its decision is bounded by a very wide area for judgment.

Further, the Court has not always had a choice respecting the constitutional framework in which to decide these cases. In *Logan Valley,* for example, the preemption theory was not available because the union's lawyers had not properly raised and preserved that line of argument in the state courts. Similarly, had the *Vogt* case arisen in 1960, it would have been a perfect candidate for disposition under the preemption doctrine, and the result would almost certainly have gone in the opposite direction. It will be recalled that in *Vogt* the employer successfully enjoined organizational picketing that allegedly was directed at coercing the employer into recognizing a minority union. With the adoption of the Landrum-Griffin Act amendments in 1959, which added the section 8(b) (7) regulations respecting organizational and recognitional picketing, the state remedies provided in *Vogt* likely would have been held barred by preemption.

When both paths are open for striking down a state's regulation of union activity, the Court can be expected to show some preference for the preemption approach. Although it is no less complicated than the Fourteenth Amendment theory as a framework for analysis, decision, and explanation, the preemption approach leaves open the possibility for congressional review of the Court's determination through the process of further legislation designed to clarify congressional intent. Such action by Congress might eventually renew the Court's need to consider the Fourteenth Amendment challenge, but by that time, the justices can hope that their problem will have been eased by the intervening constitutional experience with civil liberties litigation in other contexts and perhaps, too, by the intervening commentary of scholarly observers.

4 Regulating Economic Warfare

The bargaining process is built upon the negotiating parties' respective power to do good or ill to the other side. In labor relations, this power includes the ability of management to grant or withhold employment and the comparable ability of labor to perform or withhold work. The ability to improve or reduce pay and other benefits, and the ability to improve or reduce work performance, too, are aspects of the respective power that the parties possess in labor negotiations to do or threaten to do good or evil to each other.

Each side, moreover, usually can increase its power to the extent that it can secure allies — that is, collectivization of bargaining efforts normally improves the prospects for success. Thus, when an employer discharges a worker for inefficiency and persuades other managers not to hire that person because of the alleged ineptitude, the employer is strengthened in his efforts to induce the remaining work force to perform in a manner superior to that of the discharged employee. Similarly, employees who withhold their work effort (strike) in support of a negotiating demand are strengthened in their purpose to the extent that others refuse to hire-on with the employer as striker replacements or refuse to purchase goods produced by the struck company.

The power techniques employed in labor-management relations are numerous. Sometimes, they are imaginative; at times they are crude. Physical attack on persons and property have on occasion been resorted to both by employers and by workers in an effort to accomplish their bargaining goals. Blacklisting of employees, discharge of union leadership, defamation of character, sit-ins, consumer boycotts, work slow downs, political leverage, appeals to patriotism or to moral or religious responsibility, and appeals to racial, regional, or religious prejudice have all been included in the arsenal of bargaining weapons deployed from time to time on the battlefield of labor-management negotiations.

In the bargaining process, in order to move the other side toward an acceptable settlement, the parties frequently substitute the threat to use such negotiating weapons in place of their actual use. The threats may be hollow bluffs, or they may be the real thing. In the course of bargaining, at times facts are distorted for tactical reasons and even wholly baseless lies told. The terminology of the battlefield — "economic warfare," "bargaining weapons," "tactics," "strategy" — is frequently utilized in describing the collective bargaining process, and the ethics of the battlefield probably characterize much of what takes place when labor and management, using their collective strength in resolving the terms and conditions for employment, engage in the negotiating process.

In adopting both the original Wagner Act in 1935 and the Taft-Hartley amendments to it in 1947, Congress expressed faith in the concept that promoting the collective bargaining process serves to reduce and minimize interferences with interstate commerce resulting from industrial strife. Moreover, only in limited situations and only with regard to certain types of tactics has Congress established direct prohibitions on the use of economic weapons as part of the negotiating apparatus. The statutes specifically acknowledge that resort to economic warfare is an acceptable and lawful norm for bargaining behavior. For example, section 13 of the Labor Management Relations Act reads:

> Nothing in this Act, except as specifically provided for herein, shall be construed so as either to interfere with or impede or diminish in any way the right to strike, or to affect the limitations or qualifications on that right.

Not only is the right to strike normally protected, but it and other forms of economic warfare have been described by the Supreme Court as fulfilling a necessary and even a constructive role in the system of labor-management relations established by Congress.

> It must be realized that collective bargaining, under a system where the Government does not attempt to control the results of negotiations, cannot be equated with an academic collective search for truth, . . . The parties . . . still proceed from contrary and to an extent antagonistic viewpoints and concepts of self-interest . . . . The presence of economic weapons in reserve, and their actual exercise on occasion by the parties, is part and parcel of the system that the Wagner and Taft-Hartley Acts have recognized. . . . . [A] t the present statutory stage of our national labor relations policy, the two factors — necessity for good-faith bargaining between the parties, and the availability of economic pressure devices . . . — exist side by side. . . . Doubtless one factor influences the other; there may be less need to apply economic pressure if the areas of controversy have been defined through discussion; and at the same time, negotiation positions are apt to be weak or strong in accordance with the degree of economic power the parties possess.[1]

Thus, rather than impose a Treaty of Peace between labor and management, Congress has designed a Code of Conduct for the waging of economic warfare in the process of collective negotiation. The desired stability is supposed to be achieved under this system, the Supreme Court has explained, through the resulting adoption of collective bargaining agreements. These collective agreements establish, at least theoretically, a mutually acceptable framework for peaceful labor-management relations, thereby reducing the prospects for further industrial strife.[2]

The Code of Conduct that Congress has imposed on labor-management relations is, for the most part, broadly and vaguely phrased and leaves to the National Labor Relations Board — subject to the Supreme Court's ultimate reviewing authority — the task of discerning the legislative purpose and discovering the most appropriate rules for applying that purpose in the regulation of specific situations. Thus, for example, the statute states that employers shall not interfere with the workers' resort to "concerted activities for the purpose of collective bargaining or other mutual aid or protection." Arguably this protection extends to any form of concerted action so long as its aim is for the benefit of employees. Accordingly, if a company replaces striking workers, the company has interfered with concerted activity — the strike — that was designed for mutual aid and protection. Does that mean that an employer violates the federal labor statutes when, in an effort to combat a strike, the employer puts people to work at the jobs of the strikers? The Supreme Court's first encounter with this sort of question under the National Labor Relations Act occured in *National Labor Relations Board v. MacKay Radio & Telegraph Co.*, 304 U.S. 333 (1938).

The Limited Protection of Economic Strikers

The *MacKay* case arose out of an attempt by the American Radio Telegraphists Association, a union, to secure simultaneous agreements respecting both marine telegraph operators and point-to-point telegraph operators. The union assumed that its bargaining strength was enhanced by putting the company under pressure from both groups of key employees at once. A national strike was called by the union in order to force the employer to acceed to this demand. In San Francisco there was a total walkout. However, the strike call was relatively ineffective elsewhere, and after three days the San Francisco workers, too, were offering to return to work. During the brief strike, the company kept its San Francisco office operating by bringing employees in from its New York, Los Angeles, and Chicago offices. The company promised eleven of these replacements that they could remain in the San Francisco office if they desired. Only five of the eleven elected to stay after the strike was over. The company took back all but five of the strikers. It declined to take back the five on the grounds that their jobs were occupied by their strike replacements.

Each of the five strikers whom the employer declined to take back had been active in the union and prominent in organizing the strike. The union filed charges against the company asserting that the failure to take back a striker interferes with the employee's protected right to engage in concerted activities and that the manner in which MacKay selected those who would not be reinstated constituted unlawful discrimination due to union activities. It should be observed that if the company is not permitted to replace strikers on the grounds that this interferes with the employees' concerted activity, then a strike would normally close down the business, with the result that the test of strength would concern which side could hold out longer without income derived from the business.

Another possibility would be to hold that strikers can be replaced temporarily only — that is, they must be reinstated when they end the walkout. This would make it possible for an employer to keep the business going to the extent that temporary replacements can be found. In such a situation, the economic test would be which side could hold out longer without income derived from the employment of the strikers.

In the *MacKay* case, the NLRB found the employer guilty of violating the Act by selecting those strikers who would not be reinstated on the basis of their union activities. Such conduct by the employer was held to be unlawful discrimination under the Act. The Supreme Court agreed with the NLRB's decision.

Although it could have limited its discussion of the case to the facts evidencing discrimination because of union activity and thereby have avoided the question of the right of an employer to permanently replace strikers, the Court's opinion encompasses the broader issue as well. The employer's conduct did not constitute an unfair labor practice, said the Court, insofar as it involved efforts to continue business operations in the midst of a strike. The employer is entitled to try to keep its business going, the Court explained; and the employer is not required, when the strike is over, to terminate the employment of those hired during the strike in order to create places for the strikers. Accordingly, explained the Court, it was proper for the employer to reinstate only those strikers for whom vacant positions existed. However, in selecting those who will be reinstated, the employer must not make its choices based on union activities. "It might have refused reinstatement on the grounds of skill or ability . . . , it might have resorted to any one of a number of other methods of determining which of its striking employees would have to wait . . . ."[3] But the employer could not make its choice guided by the purpose of discriminating against those most active in the union.

In going out of its way to clarify the nature of the employer's right to hire striker replacements, the Supreme Court selected an alternative that swung the bargaining options even further in the employer's direction than either of the possibilities previously stated. Because the employer can permanently replace a striker, under the *MacKay* dictum, the test of strength during a strike takes on the potential added burden for the union of whether it can hold out while the striking employees' jobs disappear into the arms of striker replacements. Though only dicta in the *MacKay* decision — that is, not a rule of law the Court was compelled to reach in order to decide the case — it has since become well-settled law that a struck employer can hire permanent replacements for employees who walk out over a bargaining dispute.

Prior to the Wagner Act's adoption, an employer was free to not only replace strikers in order to keep the business going, but also could discriminate against union activists in determining which strikers, if any, to take back when the walk-out ended. Thus, although the Court's interpretation of the new federal protections respecting union activity did little to aid the bargaining position of labor, it did materially insulate union leaders from the employer's opportunity for retribution.

Unprotected Concerted Activity

February 27, 1939, was an especially busy Decision Monday[a] for the Supreme Court. It handed down thirteen decisions with full opinion, including three cases involving review of NLRB orders. The first of those cases, *NLRB v. Fansteel Metallurgical Corporation*, 306 U.S. 240 (1939), involved the rights of sit-down strikers.

The workers at Fansteel had been rebuffed by the company when a majority sent a committee to demand that the company recognize a local of the Amalgamated Association of Iron, Steel and Tin Workers of North America as their collective bargaining representative. The employer's position was that it would not deal with a union that included "outsiders." This refusal was clearly a violation of the newly enacted National Labor Relations Act.

The employee committee decided to resort to a sit-down strike. At its call, about 95 employees seized two of the company's key buildings. This brought a halt to work throughout the plant. The plant superintendent went to each of the buildings and ordered the men to leave. He was accompanied by police officials and the company's counsel. When the men did not leave the building, the corporation's lawyer announced to them that all were discharged because of their conduct.

The workers occupying the two buildings received supplies from other striking workers who were outside the buildings and the sitdown strikers remained for ten days despite an order issued by a state court and despite an attempt at forceful ejection mounted by the local sheriff. The sheriff made a second attempt, using a larger force of deputies, and this time was successful. The ousted sit-down strikers were placed under arrest and most were eventually fined and given jail sentences for having disobeyed the state court injunction.

Some days after the sitdown strikers had been oustered, the company resumed operations. It offered to take back a large number of the strikers, including many who had participated in the sit-down. The company even offered to give the men backpay, but it continued in its refusal to recognize the union.

---

[a]In those days the Court normally issued its decisions each Monday morning. In recent years it has changed to a practice of normally issuing decisions on any morning on which it hears oral argument.

Some accepted the company's offer, others rejected it and insisted that the employer recognize the union and reinstate all of the employees. The employer hired new personnel to replace those who remained on strike and about a month later, with the employer's help, an "independent" union was formed by plant employees. Charges were filed, and the NLRB found Fansteel guilty on a number of counts.

The Supreme Court had little difficulty upholding those parts of the board's order that involved finding Fansteel guilty of interfering with the employees' union activities and of unlawfully aiding and dominating the so-called independent union. Thus, the NLRB's order was affirmed to the extent that it required the company to cease its interference with union activities and to withdraw recognition from the "independent" union. However, the Supreme Court required modification of the other aspects of the board's order.

The NLRB had found that the sitdown strikers were entitled to reinstatement because their conduct was provoked by the employer's unlawful refusal to recognize the Iron Workers' union. Rejecting this reasoning, the opinion by Chief Justice Hughes stated: "But reprehensible as was that conduct of the [company], there is no ground for saying that it made [the company] an outlaw or deprived it of its legal rights to the possession and protection of its property. The employees had the right to strike but they had no license to commit acts of violence or to seize their employer's plant. . . . To justify such conduct because of the existence of a labor dispute or of an unfair labor practice would be to put a premium on resort to force instead of legal remedies . . . ."[4] Congress, the Court continued, had no intention of granting to strikers a shield of immunity irrespective of their conduct. Here the strikers made unlawful use of the employer's property and therefore the employer had good cause to discharge them. Although an employer cannot terminate strikers merely because they resort to that means of pursuing their collective goals, the Court reasoned, the statutory protection of collective activity does not prevent an employer from discharging strikers based on other causes. By resorting to unlawful conduct, the strikers took themselves out from under the Act's protection and assumed the risk of discharge. By ordering these sitdown strikers to be reinstated, the Court held, the NLRB was undermining the very purpose of the Act, which is to provide workers with avenues to redress their collective rights other than through use of force and defiance of law.

The fact that the company was willing to reinstate some of the sitdown strikers was of no benefit to the rest of them, said Hughes. He asserted that once the strikers resorted to such unlawful activity they lost their right to receive protection under the Act. Accordingly, the employer was free to grant or withhold its grace in selecting some of the strikers for offers of reinstatement. In addition, the Court held that the loss of protected status extended to those who aided the sit-down strikers as well as to those who actually engaged in the occupation of the buildings.

Mr. Justice Stone, although concurring in most of the Court's decision, would have permitted the NLRB to require reinstatement of those strikers who aided the sit-down but who did not themselves occupy the buildings. His reasoning was that until a person ceases to be an employee under the Act, that person is entitled to resume work at the end of a strike if work is available. Because of their unlawful occupation of the company's premises, the sitdown strikers were subject to discharge and once discharged, as they were by the company's lawyer, could no longer be ordered reinstated inasmuch as they were no longer "employees" under the Act. Those who aided the sitdown, however, had never been discharged. Therefore, Stone argued, they continued to be "employees" under the Act and thus the NLRB was entitled to order them reinstated if it thought this to be an appropriate remedy.[5]

Finally, a brief partial dissent was submitted by Mr. Justice Reed who was joined by Justice Black. Under the specific definition of the National Labor Relations Act (which was adopted while Justice Black was still a member of the U.S. Senate), one's status as an employee does not cease as a consequence of any current labor dispute: "Without this assurance," asserted Justice Reed, "the striking employee would be quickly put beyond the pale of its protection by discharge." As a result of the majority's holding, Reed complained, the security of the striking worker, specifically provided for by Congress, was being undermined. "Friction easily engendered by labor strife may readily give rise to conduct, from nosethumbing to sabotage, which will give fair occasion for discharge on grounds other than those prohibited by the Labor Act."[6] Requiring reinstatement of the sitdown strikers, he urged, does not constitute protection of unlawful activity. "Every punishment which compelled obedience to law still remains in the hands of the peace officers."[7] Thus, Reed urged, the law should punish these wrong doers in the normal manner. However, that was no reason to make them outlaws without rights insofar as the Labor Act was concerned. Reed did allow that the board could decline to extend the protection of the Act, if in the board's judgment it would serve industrial peace not to require reinstatement of workers who were guilty of acts of sabotage.

It may not be without significance that Reed and Black were the only two Roosevelt appointees who participated in the *Fansteel* decision. The majority opinion in *Fansteel* conveys a sense of the sort of moral indignation that one would expect from individuals who identify with the employer's situation under the circumstances of the case. The partial dissent by the two Roosevelt appointees, on the other hand, conveys a contrasting concern for the frustration and insecurity of a labor force, which sees its crude attempt to obtain their employer's obedience to the law rebuffed not only by the company's own economic might, but as well by the authority of the local court and the physical threat of the local police. If the two opinions were boiled down to emotional caracatures, the Hughes opinion representing the majority could probably be summed up in the phrase: "Shame on you!" And, the Reed dissent might similarly be described as: "Haven't they suffered enough?" Yet, as we see elsewhere in examining the Court's voting pattern in the labor field, it is an oversimplification to analyze such decisions based upon the axiom that "while justice may be blind, judges are either Democrats or Republicans."[8]

In the years immediately prior to *Fansteel*, sit-down strikes were occurring with considerable frequency. The peak year was 1937. Early in that year a highly publicized sit-down strike had resulted in the United Automobile Workers Union securing recognition from General Motors Corporation. Whether the sitdown was but a short-lived fad of the American labor movement, or whether *Fansteel* struck the critical blow will never be known. It is clear, however, that after *Fansteel* the technique quickly declined into almost total disuse.

The *Fansteel* sitdown decision was just the beginning of doctrinal development respecting the risks borne by striking employees. For example, in *Southern Steamship Co. v. National Labor Relations Board*, 316 U.S. 31 (1942), an employer asked the Supreme Court, on the authority of *Fansteel*, to reverse a finding by the board that the company had unlawfully dismissed five striking seamen. These seamen refused to work while the vessel was docked in Houston, Texas. The work stoppage was designed to protest the employer's refusal to bargain with the National Maritime Union even though that union had been certified by the NLRB as the crew's bargaining representative. In defense of its discharge, the company asserted that because the vessel was away from its home port of Philadelphia at the time of the work stoppage, the stoppage was an unlawful act of mutiny in violation of the laws of the United States governing the conduct of crews aboard American vessels.

A majority of the Supreme court agreed that the discharges in question were permissable under the doctrine of the *Fansteel* decision. Despite the fact that the refusal to obey the captain's order to perform their jobs occured while the ship was docked and that there was no violence, the Court explained that under American maritime law the seamen's conduct constituted mutiny.

Reviewing the statutory history of the Mutiny Act, the Court assured itself that Congress clearly intended that the seamen's duty to obey his officers' orders applies whether or not the ship is at sea. The Court stressed that the seamen had other means for securing redress of their grievance against the employer (e.g., they could have filed charges with the NLRB, or they could have picketed the vessel). But to engage in a work stoppage under the circumstances was illegal as a matter of law and, therefore, they could not be reinstated by the NLRB after the shipping company fired them for their unlawful conduct.

Four members of the Court dissented. Unlike *Fansteel*, however, the dissenters could not be identified as the Roosevelt appointees because by this time all of the justices had been nominated by FDR. On the other hand, as in *Fansteel*, Mr. Justice Reed authored the dissenting opinion. Reed's dissent accepted the *Fansteel* holding as controlling and did not dispute the Court's conclusion regarding the Mutiny Act's applicability. Nevertheless, Reed urged that under the *Fansteel* doctrine, the NLRB is still entitled to exercise its discretion regarding the propriety of remedying an unfair labor practice by reinstating discharged union supporters. "*Fansteel* teaches that there are extremes of conduct which leave no discretion to the Board."[9] In contrast to that case, Reed argued, the seamen's conduct in *Southern* did not affect safety and did not involve a trespass or a disorderly situation. Thus, the dissenters reasoned, the mere fact that the seamen's conduct was unlawful was not enough to place the case under the *Fansteel* rule.

In carving exceptions to the employee's statutory right to engage in concerted activity, the Supreme Court has not stopped at strikes involving unlawful conduct. In *National Labor Relations Board v. Local 1229, International Brotherhood of Electrical Workers*, 346 U.S. 464 (1953), a majority of the Court voted to allow an employer to discharge picketing employees whose conduct demonstrated disloyalty to the enterprise. In that case, collective bargaining negotiations between a broadcasting company and the union representing its employees were deadlocked. The employees did not go on strike but instead engaged in off duty handbilling and picketing. At first the handbills and picket signs simply described the dispute. After a while, however, the messages contained attacks upon the alleged low quality of the company's programming. As a result, the company discharged ten of the technicians who had distributed such handbills. The NLRB dismissed the union's charges, which asserted that these dismissals violated the National Labor Relations Act, and, as noted above, the union was equally unsuccessful in its appeal to the Supreme Court.

In the years since *Fansteel* and *Southern Steamship*, Congress, in the course of adopting the Labor Management Relations Act of 1947, reviewed the status of the law as developed during the first twelve years of the National Labor Relations Act. In the Conference Report on the Taft-Hartley bill, it was stated with approval that the courts in enforcing the right to engage in concerted activity had refused to apply that right to unlawful "or other improper conduct." Further, the Taft-Hartley amendments to the National Labor Relations Act added a sentence expressly stating that the Board's power to reinstate does not extend to those workers who are suspended or discharged "for cause." Both this legislative history and the "for cause" language were emphasized by the Court in upholding the board's refusal to reinstate the discharged technicians in the *Electrical Workers* case. "The legal principle that insubordination, disobedience or disloyalty is adequate cause for discharge is plain enough."[10] By publicly disparaging their employer's performance, the majority held, the attacking employees removed themselves from the protection of the Act and gave their employer good cause for their dismissal.

Three members of the Court, Frankfurter, Black, and Douglas, filed a dissent disputing the majority's reading of Congressional intent. Congress did not make "disloyalty" a cause for discharge, the dissenters asserted. "Many of the legally recognized tactics and weapons of labor would readily be condemned for 'disloyalty' were they employed between man and man in friendly personal relations."[11]   Further, argued the dissenters, the majority was ignoring the rough and tumble atmosphere surrounding strikers with their often loose and even reckless use of language.   Finally, the dissenters protested that the purpose of the Act was not to confine protected placards and handbills to trite conventional language such as the typical sign reading "unfair."

A different form of harassment was resorted to by a union representing insurance salesmen who, in 1956, were seeking a new collective bargaining agreement with the Prudential Insurance Company of America. In addition to the insurance agents' duties of soliciting new business, these employers were responsible for the collection of premiums. Compensation for the agents was almost entirely on a commission basis, with the salesmen receiving a percentage of the premium for newly sold policies and a percentage of premiums collected on outstanding policies. The agents' fixed work hours per week were very few. During this time the agent would report on the previous week's activities, deposit premium collections, file reports, and receive sales and other instructions. The remainder of the week, the agents fixed their own working schedule.

After several weeks of unsuccessful negotiation for a new contract, the union announced that if an agreement was not soon reached, it would engage in certain on the job harrassment tactics. This threat did not produce a new agreement and the union proceeded with its plan. The harassment consisted of refusal to perform certain of the agents' normal tasks. Initially, for a period, the agents refused to solicit new business. After a time they resumed soliciting new policies but refused to comply with the company's reporting procedure. In addition, the salesmen refused to participate in a special sales campaign, reported late for the weekly office routine, declined to submit some of the usual reports, failed to attend sales conferences, and solicited customer signatures on petitions to the company supporting the agents' bargaining position. Finally, the salesmen engaged in more traditional techniques such as picketing the district offices of the company and distributing handbills to customers.

The company did not use its disciplinary power to combat these harassing tactics. Rather, it filed charges with the NLRB asserting that the union's conduct constituted a refusal to bargain in good faith. The company's position relied wholly on the harassment tactics to prove its charge. Supporting the company's position, the board held that the union's actions violated the Act, saying that such conduct "is the antithesis of reasoned discussion."[12]

The Supreme Court ruled against the board and explained in language quoted at the beginning of this chapter that "reasoned discussion" is not statutorily mandated by the National Labor Relations Act and that the board's view of the nature of the collective bargaining process was erroneous.[13] The fact that particular tactics are used to exert bargaining-table pressure cannot, the Court held, be condemned as itself evidence of a failure to bargain in good faith. Good faith bargaining must be judged by performance at the bargaining table. It is not for the board to decide what economic weapons are available. This, Mr. Justice Brennan explained for the Court, is because Congress clearly did not want the Board to have any influence on the substantive results of collective bargaining—for the NLRB to be able to regulate the parties' economic weaponry would be to give it considerable influence over the substantive results of bargaining.

Brennan's opinion conceded that under prior decisions the agents' harassing tactics would not be protected activity. For example, the Court had previously ruled in a 5 to 4 decision that a state court could enjoin "hit-and-run" strikes—that is, intermittent strikes called without warning and lasting for only a few hours at a time.[14] But there is a distinction, Brennan asserted, between finding that activity is not protected by the National Labor Relations Act and finding that it is prohibited by the statute. If the union's tactics were not protected activities, then it would have been lawful for a state law to prohibit the conduct and for the company to secure an injunction of it under such a state statute. Similarly, the employer would not have been committing the unfair labor practice of interfering with union activities if disciplinary action were taken against the agents for employing these tactics. That does not mean, however, Brennan announced, that resort to such tactics evidences bad faith bargaining and constitutes an unfair labor practice. Accordingly, the Court's decision in the *Insurance Agents'* case leaves unions free to select unprotected economic weapons in the course of bargaining. However, such resort to unprotected economic weapons carries the additional risks of state court intervention or lawful employer disciplinary actions, which are risks a union does not bear when its arsenal is confined to protected union activities such as the traditional strike.

Three members of the Court, Frankfurter, Harlan, and Whittaker, would have sent the *Insurance Agents'* case back to the NLRB for further consideration. These justices were of the opinion that although lack of good-faith bargaining cannot be presumed from the mere resort to harassing and untraditional bargaining tactics, such tactics might have some bearing in evaluating the full record of evidence respecting the union's guilt or innocence concerning the charge that it did not act in good faith at the bargaining table. As to the conclusion to be drawn concerning good faith, Frankfurter argued, that is a task for the Board "draw[ing] on its experience in interpreting the industrial significance of the facts of a record."[15] Thus, he concluded, the Court should have remanded the case to the NLRB for reconsideration of the record in light of the Court's rejection of the board's erroneous presumption of guilt based solely on the fact of resort to an unprotected economic weapon.

The entire Court, in the *Insurance Agents'* case, appeared to accept the proposition that Congress does not want the substance of collective agreements to be influenced through governmental regulation of the weapons used to exert pressure at the bargaining table. Nevertheless, the Court, through the distinction it has developed between "protected" and "unprotected" categories of economic activity, has itself imposed regulatory qualifications upon the economic weapons available to the negotiating parties.

Under the Court's decisions, certain economic tactics are susceptible to being barred by state court injunction or discouraged by allowing employer interference through permanent discharge of participating employees. As a result, the risks of using such "unprotected" tactics are greater than are those of using protected tactics. Accordingly, it can be expected that resort to "unprotected" tactics will be less frequent than it would be had these economic weapons been treated by the Court as no different, under the National Labor Relations Act, than traditional strikes or other "protected" activities. The Court, therefore, has to this extent regulated the choice of economic weapons. In all probability this has influenced the respective bargaining power of the parties and has, thereby, influenced the final results of bargaining.

One of the other two labor cases decided by the Supreme Court on February 27, 1939, the day of the *Fansteel* decision, similarly dealt with the scope of the employer's power to replace striking workers. *National Labor Relations Board* v. *Sands Manufacturing Company,* 306 U.S. 332 (1939), involved an employer's replacement of employees who refused to work unless the company was going to apply a system of plantwide seniority by filling new job openings with previously laid-off workers. This seniority issue had been raised earlier when the collective agreement was being negotiated. The union wanted layoffs and recalls of employees to be on the basis of seniority irrespective of whether the more senior employee had prior work experience in the department of the plant in which a job had become available. The employer's position was that recognition of seniority rights beyond the department level resulted in inefficiency due to the need to place senior workers at jobs at which they were inexperienced. The resulting collective agreement provisions concerning seniority contained language such as: "That when employees are laid off, seniority rights shall rule, and by departments." When in fact such a recall situation arose, the employer insisted that this language gave it the right to recall laid off workers with regard only to departmental seniority. The union insisted that the language was ambiguous and gave the employer no such right. As a result of this stand-off, the company closed the plant and reopened it only after hiring new employees.

The Supreme Court rejected the board's ruling, which was that the replacement of the old men violated the Labor Relations Act. The Court found that there was no ambiguity in the collective agreement and that the parties fully understood that it permitted the company to lay off and recall employees without regard to plantwide seniority. When the union refused to work unless recalls were invoked on a plantwide seniority basis, the Court reasoned, "the employer rightly understood that the men were irrevocably committed not to work in accordance with their contract. It was at liberty to treat them as having severed their relations with the company because of their breach and to consummate their separation from the company's employ by hiring others to take their places. The Act does not prohibit an effective discharge for repudiation by the employe of his agreement, any more than it prohibits such discharge for a tort committed against the employer."[16] Black and Reed again dissented, this time without opinion.

Although the Supreme Court has declared that Congress intended to leave the bargaining process free from governmental influence, the regulatory impact of the "protected" activity—"unprotected" activity distinction, which the Court enunciated in the *Insurance Agents'* case, is not necessarily contrary to congressional intent. As we have seen, the origin of that distinction can be traced to the *Fansteel* and *Sands Manufacturing* decisions. Twice, since those decisions were issued, Congress has thoroughly reviewed and modified the National Labor Relations Act. Yet, Congress has not added any lanugage to the statute suggesting that the protected activity-unprotected activity distinction has had an undesired regulatory affect. Accordingly, the weakness of the Court's analysis in *Insurance Agents* probably lies not in the incompleteness of its examination regarding the regulatory nature of the choices that it made in characterizing the legal status of various forms of union economic conduct. Rather, the deficiency of the Court's explanation may instead be found in the excessive sweep of its assertion that the federal law makes no changes in the respective collective bargaining power of labor and management.

The National Labor Relations Act and related legislation do alter labor-management bargaining power. And although Congress probably did not intend that the NLRB should be able to actively supervise the deployment of bargaining weaponry in the fashion of a referee continuously umpiring bargaining tactics, Congress has structured the National Labor Relations Act so as to give the board authority, through its case-by-case application of the statute's broad phraseology, to regulate, as a practical matter, the arsenal of economic power from which the parties can find their bargaining strength.

It would be wrong to leave the impression, possibly created by the foregoing review of decisions, that the Supreme Court's exercise of its supervisory power over the regulation of labor relations weaponry always results in an employer victory if the employer resorts to disciplinary action. The Court has, at times, championed the workers as well. Thus, both the NLRB and the Supreme Court supported the employees' claim to statutory protection when an employer discharged seven employees for an unannounced walkout in *National Labor Relations Board* v. *Washington Aluminium Company*, 370 U.S. 9 (1962). The walkout in question was in protest over the lack of adequate heat in the plant. This complaint had been made previously by several machinists in the shop. One particularly cold morning the main source of heat for the plant was not operating, and at the start of the work day a group of men decided that it was too cold and went home. Upon learning of this action, the company president ordered that all of these workers be discharged. A charge was filed with the NLRB on behalf of the discharged workers, and the board, finding in their favor, reasoned that they were protected in their concerted activity by the National Labor Relations Act.

When enforcement of the board's order requiring reinstatement of the machinists was sought from the Court of Appeals for the Fourth Circuit, it was denied on the grounds that the walkout was summary and, therefore, was not part of a collective effort to secure bargaining concessions involving a labor dispute. Accordingly, the Fourth Circuit ruled, the employer was justified in dismissing the machinists for having walked out without securing permission to leave the plant.

As previously noted, the Supreme Court held in favor of the discharged employees. Emphasizing that these workers were unorganized, the Court stated that the Act protected their right to make their mutual complaint known in the very direct and dramatic manner that they chose.

Union Waivers of Statutory Protection

The doctrinal position adopted by the majority in *Sands Manufacturing* had far-reaching consequences in addition to those reflected in the *Insurance Agents'* decision. In *Sands,* it will be recalled, the Court, in holding that the discharge of strikers was lawful, despite the fact that they were collectively engaged in a peaceful labor dispute, based its conclusion on the premise that the employees had, through the provisions of the collective agreement, undertaken a contrary obligation respecting the issue in question. Thus, the collective agreement was the source of the company's authority to discharge these strikers. This rationale raised the question as to what other situations an employer can punish employees engaged in a labor dispute because of union undertakings contained in the collective agreement.

A facet of this question reached the Court some years later in the *Rockaway News* case. The Newspaper and Mail Drivers union had a collective bargaining agreement with Rockaway News Supply Co. That agreement, among other things, contained a provision prohibiting strikes, lockouts, or other forms of ceasation of or interference with work. The provision contained one exception and that was for stoppages in protest of the other side's failure to comply with an award of the Adjustment Board, which was established by the agreement for resolving disputes between the parties. Waugh, a driver for Rockaway News, was sent to pick up materials at another company's plant. When he arrived he found a picket line that had been established by the Typographers' union. Waugh contacted his employer and explained the situation by telling his employer that he would not cross another union's picket line. The management of Rockaway News warned Waugh that if he did not make the pick-up it could cost him his job. Waugh insisted that he would not cross a picket line and asked if it might be possible to have the materials he was supposed to pick up delivered to him on the other side of the picket line. This was arranged, but after two days the company insisted that Waugh would either cross the picket line or be fired. Waugh refused to cross.

Waugh's union appealed his subsequent discharge to the Adjustment Board set up under the collective agreement. The Adjustment Board upheld the discharge as being within the company's power under the contract. A charge was then filed with the NLRB to seek Waugh's reinstatement. The board decided that because the collective bargaining agreement between Rockaway and the Newspaper Drivers union contained an illegal union security clause, the entire agreement was void and hence Waugh's discharge was to be judged wholly apart from that agreement. Without the collective agreement, Waugh was not subject to a no work stoppage undertaking and, therefore, the discharge could not be explained as being based on Waugh's breach of a collective agreement. Accordingly, the National Labor Relations Board ordered Waugh reinstated with backpay on the grounds that he had been discharged in violation of his right to engage in concerted self-help respecting a labor dispute.

When the case reached the Supreme Court, *National Labor Relations Board* v. *Rockaway News Supply Co.*, 345 U.S. 71 (1953), a 6 to 3 majority ruled that although parts of the collective agreement may have been unlawful due to the illegal union security clause, the entire contract was not a nullity. Therefore, Waugh's discharge, which in no way involved the union security provision, was to be examined in light of the collective agreement. The Court then considered the impact of the no work stoppage clause upon Waugh's discharge. Citing to the *Sands Manufacturing* decision, the majority announced: "An employee's breach of such an agreement may be made grounds for his discharge without violating . . . the Act."[17] Waugh's discharge, it held, was not an unfair labor practice.

Mr. Justice Black wrote a short dissent in which he was joined by Justices Douglas and Minton. Black's dissent was uncharacteristically lacking in clarity, but it seemed to dispute that part of the Court's reasoning that was based on the principle established in *Sands*. Black asserted that the right to respect picket lines was intended by Congress to be preserved, and he appeared to argue that, therefore, this particular sort of statutory right cannot be contractually waived. Additionally, Black's dissent suggested that the particular contractual language in question was not, in any case, sufficiently clear in regard to crossing picket lines and hence was not a sound basis for finding that Waugh was unprotected in his refusal to cross the picket line.

The Supreme Court has not yet determined how far the *Sands-Rockaway News* doctrine carries. For example, can a union and employer agree in the collective agreement that no union activities of any kind shall be conducted anywhere on the company premises? An incumbent union, which is fearful of a rival, might be willing to agree to such a provision as a means of reducing its rival's organizing opportunities. Normally, the Act protects employees who engage in union organizing activity in nonwork areas during nonwork time. In such a situation, however, arguably under the *Sands* and *Rockaway News* decisions, an employee who used his lunch break to solicit support for a rival of the incumbent union could lawfully be discharged for having breached the collective agreement.

Dealing with a peculiar fact setting and without discussing *Sands* or *Rockaway News,* the Supreme Court has held that there are definite limits to the types of employee rights that can be waived by the collective agreement.[18] In the *Magnavox* case, the employer had a rule prohibiting all distribution of literature on the company premises. Although this rule was an unlawful restraint upon the right to distribute union literature in nonwork areas during nonwork times, the Court of Appeals refused to enforce the NLRB's order in favor of the incumbent union on the grounds that that union had waived its right to object by agreeing in the collective agreement to the company's right to issue rules for the "maintenance of orderly conditions on plant property." The Supreme Court reversed, holding that the NLRB could properly assure that all employees have access to reasonable in-plant means for communicating concerning collective activity. Justices Stewart, Powell, and Rehnquist, in a partial dissent, agreed that the union could not waive the right of employees to distribute in the plant literature expressing dissatisfaction with the incumbent union. However, they contended that the incumbent union did have the power to waive the distribution rights of its own supporters in the bargaining unit.

In terms of regulating the use of economic warfare in labor-management relations, however, the Court in *Magnavox* reaffirmed the doctrine underlying *Sands* and *Rockaway News.* The significance of that *Sands-Rockaway News* doctrine is that it enables the parties to contractually impose restraints upon the use of economic sanctions that are more rigorous than are those established by the National Labor Relations Act itself. To illustrate, if a group of employees covered by the National Labor Relations Act decide that a fellow employee has been unfairly disciplined, they can walk out in protest. They can do this whether or not their interests are represented by a union. If they are not covered by a collective bargaining agreement, or are covered by one that does not prohibit work stoppages, the employer can hire replacements in order to keep the business operating. And, the employees who walked out bear the risk that these replacements will remain at work when the walkout has ended, thereby depriving the strikers of reinstatement. However, the strikers cannot be discharged outright for having walked out and the strike cannot be terminated by injunction.

On the other hand, if the employment of the protesting employees is covered by a collective bargaining agreement that prohibits strikes, then the employer can discharge the strikers, irrespective of whether the employer hires replacements. Moreover, as we see elsewhere in this book, if the collective agreement also provides for arbitration of the sort of dispute that gave rise to the walkout, the employer is in a position to secure a court order requiring the strikers to end their walkout. Finally, the employer can sue or go before an arbitrator to secure additional relief in the form of damages.

Thus, the *Sands-Rockaway News* doctrine enables an employer to obtain contractual concessions that increase the union's and employees' risks in resorting to economic warfare during the term of the contract. Similarly, a union can obtain contractual protections from the employer's resort to economic weapons, which would otherwise be available to the employer during the term of the collective agreement. As a result, in American labor-management relations, the parties have an opportunity to set some of their own ground rules for the economic battlefield and receive administrative and judicial aid in enforcing their private Code of Conduct.

The Employer's Right to Initiate a Work Stoppage

Dismissal or displacement with replacements are not the only weapons available to management in the struggle over establishing terms and conditions of employment. The very power to maintain the status quo—that is, the power to say "no" to demands for improved employee benefits—is of considerable advantage to the employer. It forces the union to always mount the energy and resources of an offensive thrust. The employer's arsenal further includes the option to itself initiate a work stoppage. This tactic is called a "lockout."

Unions have long argued that lockouts are unfair inasmuch as they give the employer excessive power. The ability to maintain the status quo, it is said, is management's appropriate counterpart to the strike. The lockout, unions have argued, is one weapon too many in the employer's armory.

For many years there was, in fact, considerable disagreement as to whether the National Labor Relations Act permits employers to lock out. Although the Supreme Court has not settled all facets of this issue, the Bench has now removed much of the uncertainty and has established the basic lawfulness of the lockout under the NLRA.

The first situation used by the Court to clarify the status of the lockout arose in *National Labor Relations Board* v. *Truck Drivers Local Union No. 449*, 353 U.S. 87 (1957), better known as the *Buffalo Linen* case. Involved was a group of linen suppliers operating in the Buffalo, New York area. For about thirteen years, the union and these employers had engaged in collective bargaining on what is called a multi-employer basis. Multi-employer bargaining occurs when a union deals with a group of employers who negotiate on a joint basis. The resulting agreement controls the terms and conditions of the

workers of all of the participating employers. Employers will choose to negotiate on such a joint basis for a variety of reasons, including the desire to establish
uniform terms of employment in the industry and to secure the assumed increased bargaining strength derived from joint action.

In 1953 the union and the Buffalo linen companies started bargaining for
a new contract. Negotiations continued after the previous collective agreement
terminated. However, after three more weeks of bargaining, the union launched
its first economic offensive against the linen suppliers by striking and picketing
one of the members of the multi-employer group. This tactic is known as a
whipsaw strike.

The strategy of the whipsaw strike is to concentrate economic pressure on
one employer at a time, with the expectation that that employer will submit
to the demands ahead of the rest of the group inasmuch as during the whipsaw
strike the struck employer's business is going to its competitors—the other
members of the multi-employer group. Once the first employer breaks the
group's unity, the union shifts its strike to another member of the multi-
employer group. In the Buffalo case, to counter the whipsaw tactic, the remaining members of the Buffalo linen suppliers bargaining group locked out their
employees and notified the union that the lockout would terminate, and all of
the workers would be recalled, upon the union ending its strike and picketing
of the one employer. The union refused, but bargaining continued and in a
week an agreement on a new contract was reached and the strike and lockout
ended.

The agreement with the Buffalo linen suppliers, however, did not end the
dispute over the lockout countertactic. Maintaining that this had been unfair,
the union filed a charge with the NLRB that asserted that the lockout interfered with protected concerted activity and discriminated against union activity. The latter assertion by the union was based on the contention that its
members were locked out solely because they were members of the same union
as those engaged in the strike against a linen supplier. The board dismissed the
complaint on the grounds that absent any demonstrated anti-union motive, the
lockout constituted a legitimate bargaining tactic in defense against what appeared to be a whipsaw strike. The board was reversed by the Court of Appeals
for the Second Circuit, but that decision was in turn reversed by the Supreme
Court.

Upholding the right of the multi-employer bargaining group to use the
lockout as a defense against the union's strike tactic, the Court pointed out that
the Labor Management Relations Act seemingly assumes the lawfulness of the
lockout weapon inasmuch as the statute several times uses the term "lockout"
in describing economic weapons employed in labor disputes. For example,
section 8(d) of the Act prohibits resort to "strikes or lockouts" prior to the
expiration of a period of sixty days after notice has been given to the other

side of a demand to amend or terminate the existing collective agreement. Accordingly, the Court concluded, Congress assumed the legitimacy of lockout tactics once the sixty-day period expires. Further, the Court noted that when the Taft-Hartley amendments to the NLRA were being considered, Congress rejected a number of proposals that would have prohibited lockouts. Although the right to strike, protected by the Act, may be frustrated by the employer's taking the initiative and ordering a lockout, explained the Court, the NLRB could reasonably conclude, as it did here, that the interests of preserving the employers' opportunity to bargain through a multi-employer group outweighed the union's frustration over losing the sole ability to initiate the work stoppage.

Because the Supreme Court's opinion in the *Buffalo Linen* case spoke in terms of the reasonableness of the balance drawn by the board between the respective collective interests of the employers and the union, there was cause to speculate that the Court would similarly bow to the board's expertise in drawing the balance in other types of lockout situations. In 1965 the Court ended such speculation by rejecting, in two different cases, the NLRB's condemnation of the use of lockouts.

The first of these cases, which were decided on the same day, was *National Labor Relations Board* v. *Brown,* 380 U.S. 278 (1965), a case involving multi-employer bargaining but in a somewhat more complicated setting than that considered in *Buffalo Linen*. The multi-employer bargaining group in *Brown* operated retail food stores in Carlsbad, New Mexico. For many years they bargained with the Retail Clerks International Association on a multi-employer basis. When, during the course of bargaining over a new agreement, the union notified the employers that a strike had been authorized, the employers warned the union that a strike called against any one of them would be treated as a strike against the entire group. Several days later, when the union struck a single store, the employers responded by locking out all of the employees represented by the union at all of the stores, telling the union and the employees that the lockout would end when the strike was terminated. So far, the case resembled *Buffalo Linen.* However, an additional twist was added because all of the stores in the multi-employer group continued to do business during the strike-lockout, with the work being performed by supervisory personnel, relatives of managers, and a few temporary employees. The temporary employees were informed that their jobs would terminate with the end of the strike-lockout. This situation continued for about five weeks—until an agreement was reached and the economic activity ended. All of the strikers and locked out workers were then returned to their jobs.

A 3 to 2 majority of the NLRB held that the decision to continue operations after the lockout presented a critical distinction between the situation in Carlsbad and the *Buffalo Linen* case. The very conduct of depriving the employees of their jobs and then replacing them was sufficient indicia of punishment for union activity to constitute this conduct a violation of the Act, reasoned that board majority. This conclusion was rejected by both the U.S. Court of Appeals and the Supreme Court.

The Supreme Court, in an opinion by Mr. Justice Brennan, conceeded that the board can find an employer guilty of an unfair labor practice without first demonstrating that the employer's motive is improper. Conduct that destroys employee rights can be condemned even though motivated solely by legitimate business goals. Nevertheless, the Court stated, this was not such a situation. Because the board is not the arbiter of the sort of economic weapons available in collective bargaining, argued Brennan, it cannot guage the lawfulness or unlawfulness of particular economic tactics on the basis of the impact upon the union's bargaining position. Here the tactic chosen was not inherently destructive of employee rights but rather was a defensive measure to preserve the group against the union's selection of the whipsaw strike technique. Since the struck employer can lawfully continue to operate by using replacements, Brennan explained, the other group members who have had to use the lockout to maintain group solidarity are entitled to continue their business operations as well. While the result of the employers' countermeasures might be to severely weaken the union's strike activity, this is not evidence of a hostile motive nor unlawful discouragement of union activities. The position of the employees is not prejudiced because of union membership or support. Rather, the employees were locked out because of the union's choice of a particular negotiating tactic.

The Court's opinion emphasized both the legitimacy of the employers' goal and what it found to be a comparatively slight adverse impact on unionization activity, stating that under such a balance the employers' conduct is prima facie lawful. Finally, the Court acknowledged that here it was disturbing the "expert" judgment made by the administrative agency despite its statement in *Buffalo Linen* that it is for the board to serve as arbiter between the legitimate rights of the employees in concerted action and the legitimate interests of the employers. However, Justice Brennan explained, reversal was proper because the board's decision rested on an erroneous interpretation of its authority in drawing inferences from conduct respecting unlawful intent.

In a brief concurring opinion, Mr. Justice Goldberg, joined by Chief Justice Warren, emphasized the potential distinction of a case in which the employers in locking out the union, to counter a whipsaw strike, hire permanent rather than temporary replacements for the locked out workers. The legitimacy of the lockout technique, stated Goldberg, is based on the requirement of counteracting the whipsaw effects of the strike. Thus, the lockout with hired replacements is justified only to the extent that it does not exceed what is necessary to counteract the effects of that whipsaw strike.

A dissent was filed by Mr. Justice White who protested that the Court was departing from its policy of acceding to the board's exercise of delegated discretion in adjusting the conflicting interests to be weighed under the Labor Management Relations Act. Amongst White's stated objections to the Court's analysis is the argument that the need to resume operations at the locked out employers' premises was generated not by the union's decision to engage in a whipsaw strike but by the struck employer's decision to continue to operate by using striker replacements. Moreover, White was not satisfied that the impact of such a lockout and replacement of nonstriking workers upon freedom to choose or reject union membership is but slight.

In the companion case to *Brown,* the Court dealt with the lockout tactic in a setting divorced from the complicating factors created by multi-employer bargaining. *American Ship Building Company* v. *National Labor Relations Board,* 380 U.S. 300 (1965), involved a single employer engaged in repairing ships that sail in the Great Lakes. Because shipping on the Lakes comes to a halt during the winter months, most repair work is put off until that time. During the remainder of the year, repair work is available only in emergency situations, and there is a high premium on speed of execution so as to minimize the period of immobilization of the vessels. The board found that for this reason, customers tend to avoid sending their ships for repair at facilities at which there are unresolved labor disputes, because they fear an unnecessary delay in completion of the work due to the dispute. As a result, the union's bargaining power would be heightened if the collective agreement were to expire during or right before the winter months.

In the past negotiations with the union, American Ship Building had succeeded in securing contracts with August 1st expiration dates, a provision that advantaged the employer by minimizing the prospective amount of business lost due to a strike. In 1955, the employees had succeeded, by means of a slowdown prior to the contract expiration, in catching an $8 million ship in the yard for special repairs when the collective agreement expired. As a result, the customer lost four weeks' use of the vessel due to the strike at the busiest season of the year.

In 1961 the parties began negotiations for a new contract well before the expiration date. However, agreement had not been reached by August 1st. The union notified the employer that the members had authorized a strike but that they would agree to a six-month extension of the current contract. The employer rejected this on the grounds that it would be too vulnerable to a strike on the revised expiration date. Work continued on a day-to-day basis, with the employer twice proposing improvements in its offer. The first of these was overwhelmingly rejected by the union membership and the second was rejected by the union negotiators without taking it to the membership and without making a counteroffer. Negotiations were broken off without any specific plans made for their resumption. At this point, the employer announced a complete layoff at one of its repair yards and a layoff of all but two workers at another yard. The company explained that the layoff was due to the labor dispute and would last until further notice. The employer justified its action on the ground that it could not risk waiting until its yards were filled with ships or until the busy season in winter to bring the dispute to a resolution. Negotiations resumed after the lockout, and a new contract was reached by late October.

In defense against the union's charges that the lockout violated the employer's statutory duty to bargain in good faith and discriminated against union activities, American Ship Building relied largely on established board doctrine to the effect that an employer is permitted to lockout in defense against unusual operational problems, hazards, or losses that would occur if a threatened or imminent strike is called at a time that is particularly inopportune for the employer. The board rejected this defense by finding that the facts did not support the company's claim. Particular emphasis was given by the board to the union's statements to American Ship that it would not strike. The board also concluded that because the union offered to extend the contract for six months, the employer had no reasonable fear of an especially hazardously timed strike. Under such circumstances, held the NLRB, the employer did not satisfy the conditions justifying a lawful defensive lockout. The Court of Appeals affirmed the board's holding that the company by using a lockout had committed the unfair labor practices of interfering with lawful concerted activity and discriminating against its employees for union activity.

When the case reached the Supreme Court, it would have been possible for the High Court to find for the company on the basis of the facts concerning the employer's claim that the lockout was a defensive action and, therefore, lawful under existing doctrine. And three members of the Court—White, Goldberg, and Warren—would have disposed of the case in the employer's favor on that basis. The majority, however, chose to accept the board's findings concerning the inapplicability of that doctrine to the facts of this situation and went on to use the case as a platform for examining, in more general terms, the status of the lockout.

In its analysis of *American Ship Building,* the majority emphasized that the only issue before it was the use of a temporary layoff designed solely to put economic pressure on a union after an impasse has been reached in bargaining. It explained that such use no more interferes with unionization and collective activity than does any other form of employer resistance of union demands. Moreover, the Court said, the legislative history of the Taft-Hartley amendments provides convincing evidence that Congress intended to place the lockout on a legitimate footing. Thus, several sections of the Labor Management Relations Act make correlative use of the terms "strike" and "lockout."

Further, the Court held, the NLRB erred in trying to restrict the resort to lockouts to those situations in which its use can be economically justified in light of the union's counterbalancing weapons. Citing to its discussions in *Insurance Agents'* and *Brown,* the Court reiterated that the board has no authority to regulate collective bargaining by seeking to establish a balance in the economic weapons available to each side. Thus, the Court held in *American Ship Building* that once bargaining has reached an impasse, an employer can resort to a lockout in order to force a bargaining concession from a union.

White's concurrence asserted that the Court's reasoning would equally justify a lockout prior to a bargaining impasse. Further, he asserted that the *American Ship Building* decision would also allow an employer to use temporary and possibly even permanent replacements to keep the enterprise operating even after the lockout.

Both areas of Mr. Justice White's surmise remain open questions insofar as the Court's own ultimate determination is concerned. However, the NLRB initially seemed headed in the direction of accepting the legitimacy of the lockout tactic, irrespective of the existance of a bargaining impasse, and rejecting the lawfulness of hiring replacements after a lockout except in the special sort of defensive lockout situation such as that encountered in *Brown*.[19] However, the board shifted its position and a majority has since held that it is permissable for an employer to lockout and hire temporary replacements so long as the employer's motive is not to destroy the union. The federal appellate courts so far have approved the NLRB's decisions in this area but have indicated that the permissability of hiring temporary replacements for locked out employees must be determined based on all of the facts of each individual case.[20]

Discriminatory Treatment of Union Militants

The impact of a strike goes beyond the direct financial stakes of the work stoppage. A work stoppage is an extraordinary event in American labor relations, it is not an everyday occurrence. The work stoppage is an event marked by drama and suspense. Tales of picket line adventures and the ingenuity used to meet the exigencies of the financial crisis created by the stoppage will, for example, occupy shop talk long after the labor dispute has been resolved. Similarly, caustic remarks made to or by supervisory personnel and nonstrikers, as well as boasts of future action if certain changes are not met and the like, will often leave a lasting impression upon the participants. Hence, the post-stoppage period is one of adjustment conducted in an atmosphere marked by at least some tension.

Inevitably, at least some employees will be fearful of the long-range impact that participation in a strike will have upon their future status in the company. Mindful of this fear, an employer can dissipate the militancy of the strike effort by magnifying the uncertainties. The crudest device for accomplishing this effect is for the employer to make it known that strikers will not be returned to work. This approach is, of course, an unfair labor practice. More subtle techniques for playing upon the employee's sense of insecurity have raised close questions for the Court inasmuch as it is often difficult to determine whether the employer's conduct is directed at discouraging concerted activity per se or is directed at business survival.

For example, in the early Spring of 1963, some 350 out of 400 employees at Great Dane Trailers, Inc., walked off the job in support of collective bargaining demands. The company continued to operate by using replacements and those workers who did not join the strike, plus some strikers who later abandoned the strike effort. After the strike was in progress for about two months, a number of strikers demanded that the company give them their accrued vacation pay. The company rejected the demand on the grounds that they were not entitled to it. However, the company announced that it would give vacation pay based on its expired collective agreement to all employees who had reported to work on July 1st, some two weeks prior to its announcement regarding vacation benefits. The union charged that this constituted unlawful discrimination against those who engaged in concerted activity. The NLRB agreed, but was overruled by the Court of Appeals for the Fifth Circuit, which stated that the board had failed to establish that the company's conduct was motivated by a purpose of discouraging union membership or interfering with protected concerted activities. In a split decision, the Supreme Court reinstated the NLRB's determination in favor of the union.

The Court's decision in *National Labor Relations Board* v. *Great Dane Trailers, Inc.,* 388 U.S. 26 (1967), turned on the determination of what presumptions the board could make respecting two factors: (a) the impact of the employer's vacation policy upon employee freedom to engage in concerted activity, and (b) which side had the burden of proof respecting the counterbalancing of business justification for that policy against the impact of that policy upon employee freedom of choice. The Court of Appeals had interpreted the Supreme Court's earlier decisions as requiring proof of an unlawful motive to discourage union membership or to interfere with protected concerted activities in order to hold an employer guilty of unlawful discrimination against union activities. The appeals court stated that the board had failed to find evidence of such a motive and that the employer's conduct may have been motivated by such business considerations as reduction of expenses, encouraging present employees to stay with the company, or discouraging employees from quiting prior to the vacation period. Because such a motive would not involve an anti-union purpose, the Court of Appeals concluded that the case against Great Dane had not been proven.[21]

The majority of the Supreme Court, on the other hand, found that under the circumstances it was for the company to prove its *good* motive, not for the board to prove *bad* motive. Although it is normally for the board to bear the burden of proving improper motive in cases involving charges of discrimination against union activities, the Court explained: "[S]ome conduct . . . is so 'inherently destructive of employee interests' that it may be deemed proscribed

without need for proof of an underlying improper motive."[22]   In support of this
statement the Court cited to its discussion in *American Ship Building* and *Brown*
as well as to its holding in an earlier case, *National Labor Relations Board* v. *Erie
Resistor Corp., 373 U.S. 221 (1963)*.

In *Erie* the Court had upheld the finding of an unfair labor practice when an
employer gave to nonstriking employees seniority benefits superior to those of
the workers who went on strike despite the fact that some of the strikers were
with the company for a longer period of time. The Court explained that such
super-seniority was inherently discriminatory. However, in *American Ship Building* and *Brown,* the NLRB's finding that the employer's conduct was inherently
destructive of employee interests had been rejected and there was some thought
that those decisions marked the abandonment of the *Erie* decision.

In an attempt to clarify its position, the Court in *Great Dane* set forth what
it discerned to be the governing principles emerging from its previous rulings.
First, it said, if an employer's discriminatory conduct is inherently destructive of
important employee rights, then an unfair labor practice can be found even without proof of antiunion motivation. Further, even if the employer shows a
proper business motivation for its conduct, the board can find that that motive
is outweighed by the destructive nature of the conduct in question. Where, however, the destructive effect of the employer's conduct is not very great and the
employer has shown proper business justification, then the finding of an unfair
labor practice can be made only if the board goes forward and proves that the
employer's conduct was also motivated by anti-union considerations. In the
Brown and *American Ship* cases, according to the majority, the legitimate business consideration of maintaining operations outweighed any tendency that the
lockout tactic may have had in damaging collective employee interests. In
Great Dane, the Court stated, such a balancing was unnecessary because the
company failed to come forward with evidence of a legitimate business motive.

In considering the impact of the Court's decision in *Great Dane,* thought
should be given to the manner in which one proves good motive or bad motive.
Where the party charged must prove a legitimate motive, its proof, especially if
in the form of undocumented testimony, is likely to be treated by the fact
finder with great suspicion on the grounds that it is self-serving. Similarly,
proving bad motive can be very difficult inasmuch as the well informed wrong-
doer is not likely to openly confess his improper purpose or carelessly scatter
about incriminating evidence. Consequently, the choice made by the Court
in placing the burden upon the defendant to show good motive in cases of
discriminatory conduct, which is inherently destructive of employee rights,
was a choice that materially improved the prospects of finding employers
guilty of the charged unfair labor practice.

Dissenting from the *Great Dane* decision, Mr. Justice Harlan, joined by Mr.
Justice Stewart, charged that the decision resolved an issue that was not even
before the Court. Harlan pointed out that it would not have been discriminatory

to give vacation pay to the employees working during the strike and not to those who were on strike if the strikers had no contractual basis for receiving vacation pay. The strikers had argued that they were due vacation pay for the time worked prior to the strike, whereas the employer asserted that under the expired contract governing the work that had been performed by the strikers, no vacation pay was owing to them. Harlan pointed out that the NLRB had declined to interpret the contract in question and had instead made its ruling based on the principle that the strikers and nonstrikers had to be treated alike. Mr. Justice Harlan, noting that the expired collective agreement had an arbitration clause covering a dispute concerning the interpretation of the contract, argued that it was for an arbitrator, not the board or the courts, to decide whether the strikers were entitled to vacation pay under that expired agreement. Hence, there could be no finding that vacation pay was discriminatorily granted to nonstrikers absent a finding that the strikers were entitled to receive vacation pay. The only other possibility for finding the employer guilty, asserted Harlan, was if it is inherently discriminatory for an employer to give vacation benefits to those working during a strike, when that grant is considered independently of any vacation pay rights the strikers may have had.

The dissenters objected, too, to the Court's conclusion that the vacation benefit grant was in some way inherently destructive of employee collective rights. But even more, the dissenters rejected the evidenciary presumptions and burdens announced in the Court's opinion and protested that the stated doctrine was an alteration of the burdens established in previous decisions. Moreover, Harlan and Stewart complained that the discretion seemingly given to the board to balance the employer's business considerations against the destructive nature of the charged misconduct opens the door for the NLRB to attempt to create a balance in the respective economic positions of the negotiating parties.

The principles announced in *Great Dane* formed the framework for the Court's review of the Ninth Circuit's refusal to enforce the board's finding of an unfair labor practice in *National Labor Relations Board* v. *Fleetwood Trailer Co.,* 389 U.S. 375 (1967). As with *Great Dane,* the *Fleetwood* case arose out of a strike conducted in support of collective bargaining demands. The strike lasted about twelve days and was supported by about half of the employees. As a result of the strike, the employer cut back on production and on its orders for raw materials. When the strike ended, the employer explained that it was not in a position, due to the cutback, to immediately reinstate the strikers. About two months later, while some of the strikers were still out of work, the company hired six new employees for jobs that the unemployed former strikers were qualified to fill. The NLRB ruled that by hiring new employees without first reinstating all of the strikers, the employer was guilty of discriminating against employees because of their union activities.

In rejecting the board's decision, the Court of Appeals reasoned that the right of the strikers to reinstatement ended when their jobs were unavailable on the date they first sought to return to work. From then on, according to the Court of Appeals, the employer could treat them in the same manner as any other new job applicants. The Supreme Court reversed on the authority of *Great Dane.*

Refusal to reinstate strikers, said the Supreme Court, interferes with the protected right to strike and can be permitted only if justified by substantial business considerations. Under the specific language of the National Labor Relations Act, the Court pointed out, a striker continues to hold his status as an employee until he has obtained "other regular and substantially equivalent employment." The mere fact that the job is not available on the day the striker asks for reinstatement does not destroy his status. Thus, "if and when a job for which the striker is qualified becomes available, he is entitled to an offer of reinstatement" absent the employer's showing of legitimate and substantial business considerations for withholding that offer.[23]

Harlan and Stewart, the dissenters in *Great Dane,* supported the result in *Fleetwood Trailer,* but not the majority's rationale. The Act gives strikers a special status as continuing employees, they noted. The employer, said Mr. Justice Harlan, refused to treat these strikers on that basis and therefore was wrong. Accordingly, there was no need to apply the *Great Dane* test. Motivation and business justification were not involved in *Fleetwood Trailers,* said Harlan. The strikers were entitled to reinstatement and the company refused to recognize this protected right. This was basis enough to hold the employer guilty of violating the Act.

Consumer Boycotts

The Taft-Hartley and Landrum-Griffin amendments to the National Labor Relations Act imposed a number of restraints upon a union's use of appeals for outside help in doing battle against a resisting employer. The cases involving union attempts to secure the support of consumers or of employees who handle the supplies or product of the employer with whom there is a labor dispute, or to gain the aid of employers with whom the disputing employer does business, are amongst the most complicated decisions in the labor law field. It is outside the scope of this book to discuss all of the areas in which the Supreme Court has sought to unravel or refine the complex threads that form the legal bounds of American labor relations law. For this reason, it is best not to overtax the reader's patience or fortitude by examining the varying doctrines concerning union resort to outside pressure in support of its economic struggle with management. Nevertheless, too great a gap would be left in this survey of the Supreme Court's role in shaping the labor relations field were those cases to be totally neglected. Accordingly, let us sample the area by looking at the Court's

handling of one such significant problem—the legality of picketing directed
at consumers.

There is no question but that a union with a dispute against an employer
can picket that employer's premises in an effort to enlist the support of that
employer's customers so as to put greater pressure on the company to submit
to the union's demands. However, the National Labor Relations Act in broad
language prohibits a union from taking coercive action to get a business to refuse to handle goods made by someone else with whom the union has a dispute.
It also prohibits a union from getting employees to refuse to handle goods made
by someone other than that employee's own employer—that is, the Act forbids
a labor organization from pursuing its goals by getting one business, or the workers of one business, to join with the union to put economic pressure on another
business. Thus, if the union at company "A" has a dispute with that company,
it cannot get company "B's" workers to refuse to install company A's products
in order to put pressure on "A" to submit to the union's demands. This sort of
economic pressure, which seeks to align a business entity with the union's
cause and against the employer with whom there is a labor dispute, is referred
to as "secondary activity."

A key reason for banning "secondary" pressure in labor disputes is that this
technique places pressure on the secondary party to become entangled in a labor
dispute that grew out of management policies over which that second party had
no control. The Act contains an important exception to the broad prohibition
against secondary activity. This exception expressly states that the prohibition
against secondary pressure does not extend to a union's use of publicity, other
than picketing, to truthfully advise the public that a product is produced by an
employer with whom there is a labor dispute. In other words, the union involved
in a labor dispute can inform the general public of the existence of the dispute.
with the assumption being that some members of the public, including businesses,
might voluntarily support the union by refusing to buy the product of the employer involved in the dispute and thereby put pressure on that employer to give
in to the union's demands. The NLRB's interpretation of this provision was reviewed by the Supreme Court in two cases handed down early in 1964.

The first of these cases was *National Labor Relations Board* v. *Servette, Inc.*,
377 U.S. 46 (1964). It arose out of a strike by employees of Servette, a distributor of specialty food items. The employees sought to increase the pressure
on the company by giving handbills to stores serviced by Servette that asked
them not to do business with the company during the strike and informed them
that handbills asking people not to buy Servette's items would be passed out in
front of those stores that continued to handle goods distributed by Servette.
In a few instances, such handbills were in fact distributed in front of stores
serviced by Servette. Charges of unfair labor practices were filed against the

union but the complaint was dismissed by the NLRB. The appellate court, however, reversed the board and the case then went to the High Court.

The Supreme Court unanimously supported the dismissal of the unfair labor practice complaint. The thrust of the provision regulating such union activity, explained the Court, is "to forbid 'a union to induce employees to strike against or refuse to handle goods for their employer when an object is to force him or another person to cease doing business with some third party'."[24] Here the union was not seeking to get the handbilled store managers to cease working for their employer but rather was urging them to make a managerial decision to cease handling the struck company's goods. This sort of an appeal, held the Court, is not in violation of the Act because it neither involves a request to cease performing services for the secondary employer nor constitutes a threat to coerce the secondary employer into discontinuing business with the primary party to the labor dispute.

In support of its determination, the Court examined the legislative history of the Landrum-Griffin amendments respecting the legality of such secondary activity. It found that Congress's goal was to curb unions from using coercion rather than persuasion in order to obtain support from employers who deal with a struck company. The only "threat" involved in *Servette* was the warning to the store managers that there would be handbilling asking consumers not to buy the struck product. But this warning could not be treated as a "threat" or "coercion," the Court explained, because such handbilling is a lawful practice. To treat as a threat the forewarning that such a practice will take place, the Court concluded, would undermine the protected status of the handbilling. Thus, since in a legal sense no coercion was involved in the appeal to the store managers, the union's tactic did not violate the Act.

The Court had a bit more difficulty explaining the result it reached in the companion case to *Servette — NLRB v. Fruit and Vegetable Packers*, 377 U.S. 58 (1964), better known as the *Tree Fruits* case. That dispute arose out of a strike against 24 fruit packing companies in Yakima, Washington, which bargained on a multi-employer basis through an organization called the Tree Fruits Labor Relations Committee, Inc. Amongst the customers of the struck companies was the Safeway supermarket chain in the Seattle, Washington, area. To add muscle to its strike effort, the union called for a customer boycott against apples packed by the members of the Tree Fruits bargaining committee. As part of this effort to generate a consumer boycott, union pickets walked in front of the various Safeway stores and wore placards reading: "To the Consumer: Non-Union Washington State apples are being sold at this store. Please do not purchase such apples. Thank you." Prior to posting the pickets, the union sent each store manager a letter stating that the pickets would appear for the sole purpose of informing customers about the boycott. The letter further explained that the pickets had been expressly instructed not to interfere with store operations. In addition, the pickets were given written instructions including the statement: "You are also forbidden to request that the customers not patronize the store." The evidence showed that in fact the pickets did not interfere either with the stores' employees or customers.

Charges filed against the union asserted that its picketing violated the prohibitions against the use of secondary activities in labor disputes. The NLRB ruled against the union but was reversed by the Court of Appeals for the District of Columbia, which ordered the board to reconsider the case to determine whether the picketing had or was likely to have such a substantial impact on Safeway's business as to constitute a threat to Safeway itself. Without waiting for the board to reconsider the case, the Supreme Court granted certiorari and, by a 6 to 2 vote (Justice Douglas not participating), vacated the appellate decision and directed that the board's order be set aside.

The NLRB had ruled that the intent of the provision in question was to outlaw all picketing conducted at locations other than the struck employer's premises. In support of this position, the board was able to point to the fact that picketing is specifically excluded from the statutory language that carves an exception from the secondary activity ban and thereby expressly permits unions to engage in publicity, other than picketing, concerning the existence of a labor dispute. Examining the commentary on this provision as it made its way through Congress, the board had asserted that Congress found that picketing always has a coercive affect upon the business conducted at the picket site and that, therefore, Congress decided to curtail all labor picketing not directly involving the employer with whom there is a dispute. The examination of the provision's legislative history by the majority of the Supreme Court, however, led to a different conclusion.

The majority's findings respecting the intended purpose of the Act's regulation of publicity picketing is prefaced with an assertion that "Congress has consistently refused to prohibit picketing except where it is used as a means to achieve specific ends which experience has shown are undesirable."[25] This observation, by itself, is not very damaging to the board's interpretation of congressional intent. The board had, after all, based its reading of the statute at least in part on the proposition that experience had taught Congress that all picketing is coercive to the business operated at the picket site. But the Court relied on more than its reading of Congress's reluctance to ban picketing. It relied, as well, on a rule of legislative interpretation, which the Court stated it long followed as a result of its recognition of Congress's reticence in this area. That rule of interpretation, the majority explained, is that it will not ascribe to Congress a purpose of curbing picketing unless that result is supported by "the clearest indication in the legislative history."[26] Moreover, and perhaps more importantly, the Court noted, this caution on the part of both Congress and the Court reflects a concern that a broad ban on picketing might contravene the First Amendment's guarantees of the liberty of expression and assembly.

This last point should not be underestimated. By finding that the law did not bar the sort of picketing engaged in by the union in its dispute with the Tree Fruits Committee, the Court was able to avoid resolving the constitutional issue of whether Congress has the power to outlaw such picketing. It is a basic doctrine that the Supreme Court will avoid a constitutional issue if it can do so. In the process of such avoidance it will, if necessary, bend statutory language so as to remove the constitutional question. By the Court's own admission, the *Tree Fruits* decision was an exercise in this special form of judicial maneuver.

The goal of Congress, argued the majority, was to safeguard secondary parties to labor disputes, such as was Safeway, from being directly attacked by the union's activities simply because there is some sort of business relationship with the employer who is the primary party in the dispute. Accordingly, the Court ruled, a distinction must be drawn between a union's picketing for the purpose of urging the public to cease buying the goods of the struck company and picketing that asks the public not to do any business with the second party simply because that party is doing business with the struck company. The majority opinion cited to earlier cases in which it had noted such a distinction in different forms of picketing activity. The Court's conclusion was that only the second sort of picketing appeal to the general public, an appeal not to deal with the secondary party, is outlawed by the Act. The picketing at Safeway, the Court ruled, fell into the first category and, therefore, was not the sort prohibited by the Act.

In the Court's own words, "This is not to say that this distinction was expressly alluded to in the debates."[27] And in reviewing the legislative history of the statutory amendments that added the provisions in question, Mr. Justice Brennan, delivering the majority opinion, admitted that some senators voiced objection to the legislation on the grounds that its sweep was so great as to prohibit all consumer picketing away from the premises of the employer with whom the union has its dispute. However, such evidence against the distinction was dismissed by Brennan as the typically overstated views of an opponent seeking to defeat a particular piece of legislation. More significant, he said, was the silence of the bill's sponsors in failing to claim that their proposal would ban consumer picketing.

Justices Harlan and Stewart regarded the Court's reading of the statute as a distortion of congressional purpose. Pointing to the changes made in the bill as it went to the Senate-House Conference Committee, Harlan quoted Senator Kennedy's statements to the Senate explaining that the Senate representatives to that committee were unable to persuade the House conferees to permit picketing in front of secondary employers' shops but that the Senate conferees did succeed in getting their House counterparts to accept changes so as to allow informational activity short of picketing – such as handbilling, newspaper ads and the like. Additional statements by congressmen and senators were cited by Mr. Justice Harlan to show that Congress understood that it was prohibiting *all* picketing of employers other than those with whom there is a dispute. This led Harlan and Stewart to conclude that the board correctly found the union guilty of an unfair labor practice in picketing Safeway's stores in a dispute that was not with Safeway but with Tree Fruits.

Mr. Justice Black concurred in the Harlan-Stewart interpretation of the purpose of the provisions concerning union publicity regarding labor disputes. But, whereas this led Harlan and Stewart to support the NLRB's unfair labor practice finding, Black cast his vote with the majority in favor of dismissing the complaint against the union. Having interpreted the statute as outlawing the sort of picketing engaged in at the Safeway stores, Black, Harlan, and Stewart were compelled to weigh whether Congress can, consistent with the Constitution's guarantees of freedom of expression and assembly, prohibit such picketing. It was on this point that Black parted company with the Harlan dissent.

The first proposition underlying Black's position was that the patrolling aspect of picketing is activity apart from speech and, therefore, it is not encompassed by the First Amendment's prohibition against the regulation of expression. This proposition is modified, however, by a second one to the effect that the First Amendment restraints on infringement of free speech require that before the courts uphold regulations of conduct which is intertwined with expression, they must weigh the circumstances so as to determine whether the needs justifying the regulation outweigh the potential restraint the regulation may have upon the interrelated expression. In support of these two propositions, Black was able to cite a number of earlier decisions of the Court involving both labor and civil rights disputes.

Based on the above two premises, Black argued that the legislation in question was unconstitutional because, in his opinion, it was designed solely to curb information respecting the facts of a particular category of labor disputes. "The statute in no way manifests any government interest against patrolling as such, since the only patrolling it seeks to make unlawful is that which is carried on to advise the public, including consumers, that certain products have been produced by an employer with whom the picketers have a dispute. All who do not patrol to publicize this kind of dispute are . . . left wholly free to patrol."[28] Accordingly, Black favored striking the entire provision as unconstitutional.

Explaining their willingness to uphold the constitutionality of the provision, Mr. Justice Harlan urged that under the balancing test, described in Black's concurring opinion, it is proper for the Court to weigh the existence of other means of communication available as an alternative to the technique that Congress finds to be socially undesirable. Giving weight to that consideration and accepting the proposition that Congress's own conclusions must be given great deference in reviewing these cases, Harlan and Stewart judged that the provision was constitutionally acceptable.

Justice Black responded to the dissenters' position concerning the constitutionality of the anti-picketing provision. He stated that this reasoning was on a par with asserting that government suppression of a newspaper can be tolerated because radio and television continue to be available. "First Amendment freedoms can no more validly be taken away by degrees than by one fell swoop."[29]

Although the Court permitted the picketing weapon to be used by the union under the circumstances of *Tree Fruits*, on the assumption that Congress did not intend to prohibit such picketing, it is clear from the opinion that Congress would want the Court to enforce an unfair labor practice order where the picketing urges the public to aid its cause by not only boycotting the product or services of the employer with whom the union has its dispute, but also to boycott all retailers who handle or utilize the disputed product or service. The question remains open as to whether the Court will uphold the constitutionality of the statutory prohibition on such picketing when that case comes before it.

In their decisions subsequent to *Tree Fruits*, both the NLRB and the federal courts have found unions guilty of unfair labor practices where the struck product is "merged" into the secondary employer's business. For example, in one case a bakery's striking workers picketed against their employer's product at sandwich shops using their employer's bread. The board and at least one court have held that such picketing of secondary sites is directed at urging the public to refrain from doing business with that distributor or user of the struck goods and have concluded that such picketing is unlawful secondary activity.[30] Accordingly, these post-*Tree Fruits* cases adopt the assumption that the Harlan-Stewart dissent will ultimately prevail with respect to the issue of constitutionality.

In the course of their dissent, Harlan and Stewart questioned whether the majority was being realistic in drawing a distinction between picketing directed against the struck product and picketing directed against users or distributors of such products. Their assertion was that a picket line is a picket line insofar as the public is concerned and that it is little more than semantic game playing to draw the distinction in question. The public, so the argument goes, does not read picket signs with such a critical and exacting eye so as to draw the distinction seen by the Court majority.

The fact that unions have, subsequent to *Tree Fruits*, been found guilty of engaging in picketing using signs that do not contain the qualifying language directing the public's support only at the disputed product suggests that unions may look upon such distributor-user boycott picketing as more effective than mere product boycott picketing. This would explain the failure of such unions to insulate themselves from unfair labor practice charges—which they could do by simply incorporating the sort of picket sign language that would bring the activity within the protection of the *Tree Fruits* decision. Of course, it is possible that despite their experience in such matters, unions have erroneously assumed that the outlawed sort of picketing is more effective than the product boycott picketing protected under *Tree Fruits*. Or, it could also be that the unions involved in these later post-*Tree Fruits* cases were uninformed concerning the *Tree Fruits* technique for immunizing the secondary picket line.

Of course, it would be possible to design some empirical research to determine if the public acts differently depending on whether the picket sign makes it clear that the requested boycott is directed only at the product or service of the employer who is primarily involved in the labor dispute—that is, a carefully drawn study likely could demonstrate whether in fact the distinction drawn by the *Tree Fruits'* majority, in its interpretation of the anti-picketing exception, was based on realistic assumptions concerning actual response to the particular differences in picket sign statements. However, no such carefully collected data and analysis was available to, or underlined, either Congress's consideration of the provision or the Court's interpretation and application of the statute.

In the ideal, the Court's decisions (let alone congressional action) should not be grounded on such informational vacuums. But neither the legislature nor the Court can await ideal conditions for making their decisions. Thus, the shape of labor relations law, as well as all other areas of law, will continue to be molded, as in the *Tree Fruits* case, in part by factual premises that have their origin and support solely in the speculations of those to whom these decisional responsibilities have been entrusted.

5 Creating a Law of Labor Arbitration

Lay persons frequently confuse the term "arbitration" with "negotiation," "mediation," and "conciliation." "Negotiation" is the process whereby the interested parties themselves attempt to settle their differences or reach agreement. "Mediation" or "conciliation" is the procedure whereby a neutral party acts as a go-between trying to aid the negotiating parties in their effort to reach a settlement. In contrast, in "arbitration," the interested parties call upon a third person, a disinterested party, to resolve their differences or compose the agreement for them.

Two basic forms of problems are submitted to arbiters for resolution. One sort of problem is where the concerned parties want the neutral outsider to determine the terms of agreement regulating the future relationship between them. For example, if a union and employer are deadlocked over the number of overtime hours workers can be required to work under a new collective bargaining agreement, they might decide to resolve their deadlock by requesting a neutral third party, an arbitrator, to set that term of the contract for them. This form of arbitration is generally called "interest arbitration."

The other type of problem submitted to arbitration is called "grievance arbitration," or alternatively called "rights arbitration" or "disputes arbitration." When an arbitrator is called upon to decide a grievance arbitration problem, the parties are seeking to have the arbitrator determine their respective rights under a particular contract or custom—that is, the arbitrator is asked to issue a decision applying a contractual rule or some other sort of norm to a particular set of facts. Grievance arbitration, therefore, deals with the sort of issue that might be brought before a court through litigation. However, whereas a judge is a publicly selected and imposed neutral who resolves differences, an arbitrator is privately appointed by the parties themselves.

Arbitration proceedings generally are relatively informal and are normally conducted in private. With rare exception the arbitrator's decision, or "award" as it is usually referred to, is expected to be the sole and final decision—that is, in arbitration there is no appeal to a higher tribunal.

Although interest arbitration is only occasionally resorted to in American labor relations practice, grievance arbitration plays a very active role in union-management relations in the United States. It has been said that modern labor arbitration in the United States can be traced back to 1865, a time when the American labor movement itself had barely begun to feel its life breath. As we have previously seen, arbitration of labor disputes can even be traced back to the laws of the Massachusetts Bay Colony respecting the determination of wage rates.

By World War I, the arbitration process had become an important instrument for resolving labor relations grievances in the anthracite coal industry, in the men's clothing industry in Chicago, and in some other relatively isolated segments of the American economy. After World War I, as the Railway Labor Act evolved and was strengthened, grievance arbitration became the required method for resolving differences concerning the interpretation or application of collective bargaining agreements in the railroad and later in the airline industries. Due to the encouragement of the War Labor Board, by the end of World War II grievance arbitration had become a prominant feature throughout American labor relations practices. Indeed, the extent to which grievance arbitration is used in the United States is one of the more unique aspects of American labor relations when compared to labor relations practices in other nations.

Some of the early supporters of wider use of the labor arbitration process emphasized the voluntariness of the system by explaining that this characteristic tended to encourage a more peaceful, more cooperative, and more empathetic relationship for both sides. Through submission of disputes to an arbiter, each party, it was said, in effect implicitly acknowledged that its own position might not be the only one having merit and implicitly conceded that it might be possible to coexist even if the other side's position prevailed. This very admission by both sides, it was urged, served to promote stable labor relations. The advocates of this viewpoint considered it inappropriate for either party to resort to the courts either to compel the other side to fulfill an obligation to submit an issue to arbitration or to compel the other side to comply with an arbitrator's award. Such commentators, therefore, found comfort in the common-law rule that held that a court cannot enforce an agreement to submit a dispute to arbitration.

One theory respecting the origin of that common law rule against enforcing arbitration agreements is that it arose at a time when common-law judges received their income from court fees. It is said that they were, therefore, antagonistic to the arbitration agreement because it threatened their livelihood. In any event, though, common-law courts did enforce arbitration awards if both sides in fact participated in the arbitration hearing.

During the twentieth century the common-law antagonism toward arbitration has been eroding. Most modern American commentators in the labor relations field accept the notion that judicial enforcement of agreements to submit grievances to arbitration has a beneficial, not a detrimental, affect upon labor-management relations. In many jurisdictions the common-law antipathy toward arbitration has been replaced by a statute requiring the courts to enforce both agreements to arbitrate and the awards of arbitrators.

In 1925 Congress adopted the United States Arbitration Act, which, among other things, requires the federal courts to enforce agreements to submit controversies to arbitration where those agreements involve a maritime transaction or

involve interstate or international commerce. A specific exception is contained
in the statute, however, excluding "contracts of employment." It has been
argued that this exclusion does not apply to a collective bargaining agreement
because even though a collective agreement sets the terms and conditions for
employment, it is not of itself a "contract of employment"–that is, the determination to hire someone and the determination to work for someone (the
employment contract) is made by the employer and worker apart from the collective agreement. The function of the collective agreement is to set the terms
of employment once the worker and employer have entered into a contract of
employment. If this argument were to be accepted, then the United States
Arbitration Act would govern federal court enforcement of provisions contained
in collective bargaining agreements whereby the parties have agreed to arbitrate
any differences that might arise in the application of the collective agreement.
Indeed, the Courts of Appeals for the Second, Third, and Seventh Circuits have
held the Arbitration Act applicable to actions involving arbitration arising under
collective agreements.[1] But the Supreme Court, in constructing a federal law
favoring the enforcement of grievance arbitration agreements, has looked elsewhere than to the United States Arbitration Act.

The opening case in the development of the Supreme Court's decision
making in this area, and perhaps still the most controversial of its decisions
dealing with labor arbitration, was *Textile Workers v. Lincoln Mills*, 252 U.S.
448 (1957). The issue arose in a fairly typical setting. The Textile Workers
Union of America had a collective bargaining agreement with Lincoln Mills that
prohibited work stoppages and provided that grievances between the parties be
handled in accordance with a contractually specified procedure. Under this
grievance procedure, any party dissatisfied with the situation after the last
grievance settlement step had been exhausted could take the matter to arbitration.

The union raised several grievances complaining about certain work loads and
job assignments imposed by Lincoln Mills. The employer rejected the union's
position through each step of the grievance procedure and the union requested
that the matter be set for arbitration. This request was refused by the employer,
whereupon the union brought a suit in federal district court, thereby seeking to
compel the employer to arbitrate the grievance. The district court ordered the
employer to arbitrate but this decision was reversed by a divided vote in the U.S.
Court of Appeals, which held that the lower federal court did not have the power
to grant the requested relief. Upon appeal to the Supreme Court of the United
States, the union was represented by Arthur J. Goldberg, then a prominent union
attorney and later, of course, a Justice of the Supreme Court.

The union's position concerning the federal court's authority to grant the
requested relief relied not on the United States Arbitration Act but upon section
301 of the Labor-Management Relations Act of 1947. A key hurdle for the
union's position was the employer's argument that the Norris-La Guardia Act, by

its restrictions upon the use of injunctions to resolve labor disputes, prohibited the federal courts from ordering an employer to arbitrate a labor grievance.

Since the Norris-La Guardia Act was adopted after the United States Arbitration Act, any inconsistencies between the two statutes would appropriately be decided by giving greater weight to the most recent enactment, an approach that held little promise for the union had it placed sole reliance on the arbitration statute. Moreover, there was legislative history and a line of well-established lower court decisions supporting the argument that the exclusion in the federal arbitration statute regarding labor contracts was intended to cover collective bargaining agreements as well. Thus, by relying on the Labor-Management Relations Act of 1947, the union was able to avoid the burden of overcoming the precedent against federal court enforcement of labor arbitration clauses under the United States Arbitration Act. Also, the union could argue that any inconsistencies between the Norris-La Guardia Act and the authority claimed to be found in the more recent Labor-Management Act should appropriately be resolved by giving greater weight to the newer congressional enactment.

The union succeeded in its strategy, with a majority of the Supreme Court holding that section 301 of the Labor-Management Relations Act of 1947 gives the federal courts authority to order the parties to perform their obligation to submit disputes to arbitration if provided for in a collective bargaining agreement.

On its face, section 301 simply states that "suits for violation of contracts between employers and a" union may be brought in the federal district courts. The majority position, expressed in an opinion by Mr. Justice Douglas, was that this provision gives the federal courts not only the right to hear such suits but also the power to "fashion a body of federal law for the enforcement of these collective bargaining agreements."[2] Acknowledging that the legislative history of section 301 is cloudy, Mr. Justice Douglas found significant light shed upon the intent of Congress by its deletion of a proposed provision that would have made it an unfair labor practice under the National Labor Relations Act (the first part of the Labor-Management Relations Act) to breach an argeement to arbitrate. Further, Mr. Justice Douglas found it particularly instructive that, in rejecting that proposed unfair labor practice, the joint House-Senate Conference Committee stated: "Once parties have made a collective bargaining contract the enforcement of that contract should be left to the usual processes of the law and not to the National Labor Relations Board."[3] According to the majority of the Court, therefore, section 301 was added to the federal statutes in order to provide a means for establishing those "usual processes of the law" by which collective agreements could be enforced.[4]

In addition, the majority opinion relied for support on that part of the legislative history of the Labor-Management Relations Act in which the Senate Committee expressed concern that if industrial peace is to be promoted by the encouragement of collective bargaining agreements, then the parties should not be able to break such agreements "with relative impunity". Douglas additionally asserted that the agreement to arbitrate grievances "is the *quid pro quo* for an agreement not to strike."[5] Accordingly, the congressional goal of promoting industrial peace can only be achieved if the agreement to arbitrate grievances is enforced by the federal courts, thereby encouraging unions to surrender their right to strike in exchange for the settlement of disputes through the arbitration process.

This last statement regarding arbitration as the *quid pro quo* for the no-strike agreement has been repeated axiomatically ever since the decision in *Textile Workers*. Nevertheless, the phrase has also been strongly criticized as a naive, oversimplification of the exchanges and adjustments made at the bargaining table. Amongst other arguments, it has been noted that frequently the employer is as desirous of having an arbitration clause as is the union, thereby precluding the union's need to surrender anything for it. But this criticism has not deterred the Court from continued reliance on its notion that a no-strike clause is a trade-off for the agreement to arbitrate. In fact, in one later case, *Teamsters Union v. Lucas Flour Co.*, 369 U.S. 95 (1962), where the collective agreement contained a provision requiring that any differences arising under the agreement be decided by arbitration, the Court held that even though the contract did not contain a no-strike clause, such a clause was implicit in the collective agreement due to the presence of the arbitration provision.

Having satisfied itself that Congress's purpose in adopting section 301 included the intent to assure that the federal courts would hold the parties to their collective agreements, the Court explained that the particular substantive rules to govern such suits would have to be fashioned by the federal courts themselves by taking their guidance from the policy of our national labor legislation.

Finally, the majority opinion rejected the notion that the Norris-La Guardia Act posed any barrier to federal court orders that compel a party to perform its contractual duty to arbitrate. "The kinds of acts which had given rise to abuse of the power to enjoin are listed in section 4 [of Norris-La Guardia]. The failure to arbitrate was not a part and parcel of the abuses against which the Act was aimed."[6] Thus, for the majority, there was no conflict between the Norris-La Guardia Act's restraints upon federal court orders involving industrial disputes and the policy of the Labor-Management Relations Act to use the federal courts as vehicles for assuring that the parties live up to their collective agreements.

A lengthy dissent was filed in the *Lincoln Mills* case by Mr. Justice Frankfurter. Charging that the majority had given an "occult content" to section 301 by distorting its legislative history, Justice Frankfurter attached an appendix to his dissent in which he compiled that legislative history (this appendix covered some 61 pages in the original report of the case). Frankfurter's reading of the legislative history was that section 301 was intended to give the federal courts nothing more than authority to hear cases involving collective bargaining agreements. The substantive rules of law to be applied in such cases would have to be found in the law of the state in which the contract was executed, not through the fashioning of new rules by the federal courts. Moreover, Justice Frankfurter expressed considerable doubt respecting the wisdom of allowing courts to become involved in the enforcement of labor arbitration clauses. "Arbitration agreements are for specific terms, generally much shorter than the time required for adjudication of a contested lawsuit through the available stages of trial and appeal. Renegotiation of agreements cannot await the outcome of such litigation; nor can the parties' continuing relation await it."[7] Further, Frankfurter contended that in passing the United States Arbitration Act in 1925, Congress, by excluding employment contracts, embraced the common-law rule rejecting the enforceability of arbitration clauses in the labor field. Whatever the clouded history of section 301 might allow, he argued: "I see no justification for translating the vague expectation concerning the remedies to be applied into an overruling of previous federal common law and, more particularly, into the repeal of the previous congressional exemption of collective-bargaining agreements . . . ."[8]

Justice Frankfurter additionally objected to the *Lincoln Mills* decision on a technical basis involving the constitutional scope of the power of federal courts to entertain suits which are based on contractual rights arising under state law.

Having announced in *Lincoln Mills* that the federal courts would assume the responsibility of fashioning the substantive law governing the enforcement of labor arbitration agreements, the Court soon found itself weighing a number of such issues. Three cases, all involving the United Steelworkers of America, came before the Court in 1960. The decisions issued in these cases have come to be known amongst lawyers as the "Steelworkers Trilogy." As with *Lincoln Mills*, in each of these cases the majority opinion was prepared by Mr. Justice Douglas and, as in *Lincoln Mills*, Justice Black did not participate. In each of the cases, Mr. Justice Frankfurter simply noted that he concurred in the result, though he declined to endorse the Court's opinion. It would appear that Mr. Justice Frankfurter resigned himself to accept the rule of *Lincoln Mills* as controlling and was satisfied that the result in each case was consistent with the doctrine of *Lincoln Mills* — a doctrine with which he apparently still disagreed.

In the sequence of the decisions as issued by the Court, the first of the trilogy cases is *United Steelworkers of America v. American Manufacturing Co.*, 363 U.S. 564 (1960). In this case, an employee, Sparks, took a leave of absence from work due to an injury and while away from work sued the company for workmen's compensation benefits. The compensation case was settled on the basis that Sparks was found to be 25 percent disabled from the injury. Sparks then sought to return to his job but the employer declined on the grounds that he was too disabled for the work. Sparks' union, the Steelworkers, grieved under the collective bargaining agreement claiming that Sparks had a contractual right to return to his job. When the company rejected the grievance, the union demanded arbitration pursuant to the collective bargaining agreement. Again the company rebuffed the union. When the union petitioned for an order from the federal district court requiring the company to arbitrate, the court held for the employer on the theory that having accepted the workmen's compensation settlement, Sparks was not entitled to make any further claims under the collective bargaining agreement.

The federal Court of Appeals affirmed, but on the basis that Sparks' claim was "frivolous" and, therefore, not subject to arbitration. Sparks found a more sympathetic forum at the Supreme Court of the United States where all of the participating justices voted to reverse the lower courts.

In explaining the majority position, Justice Douglas cited to statutory authority evidencing that Congress had adopted a policy favoring the resolution of labor disputes through arbitration where the parties have voluntarily entered into such agreements. Section 203 (d) of the Labor-Management Relations Act of 1947 states: "Final adjustment by a method agreed upon by the parties is hereby declared to be the desirable method for settlement of grievance disputes arising over the application or interpretation of an existing collective bargaining agreement." That policy, explained Mr. Justice Douglas, can only be effectuated if the means chosen by the parties, such as arbitration, is given full play. Under that policy, the Court held, the judiciary cannot weigh the merits of a grievance being sent to arbitration so long as the parties have agreed to submit "all" disputes to arbitration. The meritoriousness of a claim under such a clause is irrelevant to the right to have the matter arbitrated. "[E]ven frivolous claims may have therapeutic values of which those who are not part of the plant environment may be quite unaware."[9] The merit of the claim to be arbitrated is for the arbitration tribunal, announced the Court, and that function must not be usurped by a lower court that is asked to enforce the agreement to submit the dispute to the tribunal of an arbitrator.

Justice Douglas' opinion was marked by high praise for the utility of arbitration in maintaining industrial stability and for the specialized wisdom that arbitrators bring to bear upon such disputes. Douglas' evaluation of the arbitration profession has been termed excessive by some commentators. It is not surprising, however, that Justice Douglas would hold labor arbitration in such high esteem when one considers that Harry Shulman and Wesley Sturgis, two of the superstars of labor arbitration during the 1930s, 40s, and 50s, had been colleagues of Justice Douglas during his tenure as a member of the Yale Law School faculty.

Mr. Justice Brennan, himself a specialist in the labor relations field prior to becoming a judge, though joining in the Court's opinion, added a few concurring observations. Mr. Justice Harlan joined with Justice Brennan as did Mr. Justice Frankfurter, though Frankfurter did not join in the part of Brennan's remarks that embraced the Opinion of the Court. Brennan noted that the Court's reference to the no-strike clause as a *quid pro quo* for the arbitration agreement should not be read to mean that the absence of a no-strike clause in any way affects the enforcement of the arbitration provision. Further, he emphasized that in determining whether the parties intended to give the arbitrator jurisdiction over a particular issue, the lower courts should find guidance from the nature of both the arbitration clause and any provisions involving exclusions from that part of the agreement.

The focus of the lower court's attention must be on whether the parties showed greater concern with having an arbitrator render decisions as to the meaning of their contract or greater concern in confining the arbitrator's power. If the latter, Brennan's concurring opinion asserts, then "the presumption of arbitrability would . . . not have the same force and the Court would be somewhat freer to examine into the merits."[10]

The second case in the Trilogy is *United Steelworkers of America v. Warrior & Gulf Navigation Co.*, 363 U.S. 574 (1960). This case involved a grievance protesting that the company violated its collective bargaining agreement by contracting out certain work instead of giving the work to laid-off employees. Both in rejecting the grievance and in refusing to arbitrate the issue, the employer contended that the determination of whether to contract out work is a management prerogative and that the collective bargaining agreement had specifically stated that "matters which are strictly a function of management shall not be subject to arbitration."[11] The lower courts accepted the employer's argument and refused to require the company to arbitrate.

Expanding on its discussion in *American Manufacturing*, the Supreme Court reversed and held that it was for the arbitrator, not the courts, to determine whether contracting out of work is "strictly a function of management" excluded from the arbitration process under the collective agreement. Said the Court: "In the absence of any express provision excluding a particular grievance from arbitration, we think only the most forceful evidence of a purpose to exclude the claim from arbitration can prevail, particularly where, as here, the exclusion clause is vague and the arbitration clause quite broad."[12]

The Court justified this policy of showing such a strong preference in favor of resolving labor disputes through the arbitration process by citing to the previously mentioned interpretation of the Labor-Management Relations Act. It also asserted that inasmuch as labor arbitration is a conflict resolution system adopted by the parties as the *quid pro quo* for a no-strike agreement, it substitutes not just for litigation but also for industrial strife. Stated the Court: "The choice . . . is between having that relationship governed by an agreed-upon rule of law or leaving each and every matter subject to a temporary resolution dependent solely upon the relative strength, at any given moment, of the contending forces."[13]

Justice Whittaker, alone, dissented from the Supreme Court's decision in the *Warrior & Gulf* case. For Mr. Justice Whittaker, the extent to which the Court was deferring to the arbiter's authority seemed excessive. According to Justice Whittaker, the burden is properly upon the party seeking arbitration to establish that the other side has agreed to submit to the arbitrator's jurisdiction. He found his authority for this approach in earlier Supreme Court decisions dealing with arbitration clauses in commercial agreements. Under these cases, Mr. Justice Whittaker explained, the test is whether the parties in their agreement expressed in plain language their willingness to submit the issue to an arbiter. In the instant case, Mr. Justice Whittaker could find no such manifestation of the parties' willingness to arbitrate.

The last case in the Steelworkers Trilogy was *United Steelworkers of America v. Enterprise Wheel and Car Corp.*, 363 U.S. 593 (1960). Unlike the other cases, which involved the question of whether the federal district court should order a party to submit to arbitration, *Enterprise Wheel and Car* concerned the federal district court's authority to enforce an arbitrator's award. The award in question required the employer to reinstate workers who had been suspended indefinitely after they had walked-off the job as a protest against another employee's discharge. Complicating the situation, the collective bargaining agreement under which the dispute was submitted to arbitration had expired prior to the arbitrator issuing his award.

The Supreme Court ruled that the award was to be enforced. The Court's function in enforcing arbitration awards is not to review the merits of the arbitrator's decision, explained Mr. Justice Douglas's opinion. Rather, it is to assure that the arbitrator has been faithful to his duty to draw the essence of the award from the collective bargaining agreement. "A mere ambiguity in the opinion accompanying an award, which permits the inference that the arbitrator may have exceeded his authority, is not a reason for refusing to enforce the award."[14] The parties, Douglas reminds us, have bargained for the arbiter's interpretation of the agreement, not the court's.

Again, Mr. Justice Whittaker, alone, dissented from the Court's decision. His complaint was not with the entire arbitration award but only with that part that provided a remedy for the period of time after the termination of the collective bargaining agreement. According to Mr. Justice Whittaker's analysis, no benefits could have accrued to the employees under the collective bargaining agreement after that agreement had expired. Hence, he argued, beyond the termination date of the collective agreement from which the arbitrator's own power is derived, there is no basis for finding that the arbitrator has power to order the employer to either reinstate the workers nor the pay them back wages for a period subsequent to that termination date.

In *John Wiley & Sons, Inc. v. Livingston*, 376 U.S. 543 (1964), the Supreme Court again examined the extent to which courts must enforce agreements to arbitrate without themselves examining the merits of the matter being submitted to arbitration. *Wiley* involved the claim of a union that employees covered by a collective bargaining agreement containing an arbitration clause were entitled to certain rights against a new employer. Wiley had acquired the first employer's business. The union asserted its claim against Wiley even though the new employer did not have a collective agreement with the union and even though the collective agreement with the first employer expired a few days after filing the suit seeking enforcement of the arbitration agreement.

The Court, in an opinion by Mr. Justice Harlan, accepted as correct the position taken by both sides to the effect that it is for the courts to decide whether there exists an enforceable agreement to arbitrate. "The duty to arbitrate being of contractual origin, a compulsory submission to arbitration cannot precede judicial determination that the collective bargaining agreement does in fact create such a duty."[15] The Court concluded that in light of the statutory policy favoring labor arbitration, the arbitration agreement between the union and Wiley's predecessor was an adequate basis on which to impose upon Wiley the contractual duty to arbitrate with the union respecting what rights, if any, survived the change of ownership and expiration of that collective bargaining agreement.

Further, the Court rejected Wiley's argument that the particular grievances asserted by the union went beyond the duty to arbitrate as established in the arbitration clause of the collective agreement. "Whether or not the Union's demands have merit will be determined by the arbitrator in light of the fully developed facts. It is sufficient for present purposes that the demands are not so plainly unreasonable that the subject matter of the dispute must be regarded as nonarbitrable because it can be seen in advance that no award to the union could receive judicial sanction."[16]

Finally, Wiley had argued that it did not have to arbitrate because the union had failed to satisfy certain procedural conditions to the arbitration duty as established under the collective agreement. Here, too, the Court said that the objection being raised was a matter properly for the arbitrator, not for the courts. The Court's reasoning emphasized the danger of trying to decide procedural questions divorced from the context of the merits of the dispute. Since it is improper for the courts to get involved in weighing the merits of disputes that the parties by agreement assented to submit to arbitration, so, too, it is unwise, stated Mr. Justice Harlan's opinion, for the judiciary to undertake resolution of procedural issues that may be intertwined with the substantive merits. Moreover, Harlan's opinion makes it clear that, in deciding this case, the Court was guided by a desire to adopt a rule that would encourage the speedy resolution of labor disputes by arbitration and that does not create opportunities for delay of the process while "procedural" differences make their slow progress through the judicial mechanism.

Wiley represented a unanimous decision by the Court. But this had not been the situation respecting an arbitration issue decided by the Court less than three months earlier. That case was *Carey v. Westinghouse Electric Corp.*, 375 U.S. 261 (1964), which drew the dissenting votes of Justices Black and Clark and a brief note by Mr. Justice Harlan to the effect that the question was close but that "at this early stage of experience in this area" he thought the majority had made the better choice.

The International Union of Electrical Workers (I.U.E.), of which Carey was president, had a collective bargaining agreement with Westinghouse under which I.U.E. was recognized as the collective bargaining representative of all production and maintenance employees at various locations. At one of these locations, another union was the certified bargaining representative of all salaried technical employees. A dispute arose as to whether certain employees in the engineering laboratory at this location came under the jurisdiction of the I.U.E. or its competitor. Westinghouse dealt with the other union respecting these employees and I.U.E. grieved by complaining that this was in breach of the collective bargaining agreement. When the employer rejected the grievance, I.U.E. demanded that the question be submitted to arbitration pursuant to the broad arbitration clause of its collective agreement with the company. Westinghouse refused to arbitrate this question and argued that only the NLRB could properly resolve such an issue.

In labor parlance, the dispute at Westinghouse involved a "jurisdictional" issue. Machinery, or at least partial machinery, is provided under the National Labor Relations Act for dealing with "juridictional" disputes. But the existence of such machinery does not readily clarify the obligation of the respective parties. First it must be determined which type of "jurisdictional" dispute is involved. Next to the extent that the particular statutory machinery for that type of dispute provides a remedy, the question remains as to whether that statutory remedy is the only available avenue for relief.

In *Carey*, Mr. Justice Douglas, in his majority opinion, first noted that there are two categories of jurisdictional disputes. One is where a union claims that certain work should be performed by the employees covered by its collective bargaining agreement and not by other workers – That is, the dispute concerns the question of whether the work belongs to those who are under the jurisdiction of the particular collective bargaining agreement. The other category of jurisdictional dispute involves the question of whether employees doing certain work are subject to the exclusive bargaining representation of a particular union. These questions can arise when the choice is between union and nonunion work or where more than one union is vying for the work or workers.

As discussed in greater detail in chapter 7, the National Labor Relations Act makes it an unfair labor practice for a union to use strike pressure to get an employer to assign work to employees except where the employer is violating an NLRB certification by making the particular work assignment. When such a strike occurs, the Act gives the NLRB authority to determine which employees should be doing the work. However, the Act encourages the parties to voluntarily use some settlement process other than the Board's decision-making authority. The NLRB has held, and the Supreme Court has elsewhere supported its position, that for such voluntary adjustment machinery to be controlling, all parties to the dispute must bind themselves to submit the dispute through that settlement process. Thus, in the instant case, a decision by an arbitrator in a proceeding under the I.U.E.-Westinghouse contract would not be binding on the other union; therefore, it would not preclude the NLRB from reaching a contrary result. But this possibility was not enough to deter the majority of the Court from giving I.U.E. its crack at an arbitrator. "[T]he arbitration may as a practical matter end the controversy or put into movement forces that will resolve it."[17] Further, Mr. Justice Douglas observed, the policy of the Act concerning work assignment disputes is to more than tolerate arbitration, it is to encourage it.

The National Labor Relations Act also provides machinery for the resolution of those jurisdictional disputes that revolve around the question of which union should be representing the employees who are performing particular work. This can be done either by the complaining union filing a charge asserting that the employer is improperly failing to recognize it as the bargaining representative of these workers, or by the union petitioning the NLRB for an order clarifying the scope of coverage of the board's certificate of representation—should such a certificate have already been issued. But such alternative machinery for resolving the dispute, held the Court, does not bar a suit for enforcement of the collective bargaining agreement. And, Douglas suggested, the intervening award of an arbitrator under the collective agreement might be accepted by the parties, thereby removing the need for an NLRB remedy. In any event, Justice Douglas said, the arbiter's award will have persuasive, though not binding, impact upon the board if the NLRB is later required to rule on the issue.

The majority opinion concluded by observing that although arbitration of the instant dispute might not provide a dispositive result, it might help to resolve the issue and such help is to be encouraged. Even if the superior authority of the NLRB must ultimately be invoked, the "therapy of arbitration" will have been given its opportunity to work a cure. Thus, the majority ruled that I.U.E. was entitled to have this jurisdictional dispute submitted to arbitration.

The dissent by Mr. Justice Black, joined by Justice Clark, complained that the Court had gone too far in its preference for labor arbitration. Subjecting the employer to a procedure that will not have a final and binding result is, he stated, a deprivation of Westinghouse's right to due process of law.

This dissenting position received the support of a number of commentators who expressed the opinion that subjecting the employer to arbitration that can later be reviewed by the NLRB constitutes unnecessary harrassment of the employer and is contrary to the notion that arbitration is a process for the speedy, *final* resolution of differences. These critics were able to find support, too, in the subsequent history of the I.U.E.-Westinghouse dispute. The arbitrator's award split the disputed work between the two bargaining units at Westinghouse and was later rejected by the NLRB on the grounds that it did not clearly reflect the board's standards for resolving jurisdictional questions.[18]

If the arbitration clause is given by management in exchange for the no-strike clause, as the majority of the Supreme Court has asserted in several of the previously discussed decisions, then to what extent can and will the arbitrator and courts use their power to assure obedience to the no-strike obligation? This question has been before the Supreme Court on several occasions with the rule established on the first such occasion being later reversed.

The first of these cases was *Sinclair Refining Co. v. Atkinson*, 380 U.S. 195 (1962), a 5 to 3 decision with Mr. Justice Frankfurter not participating. The Court, in an opinion by Mr. Justice Black, held that the Norris-La Guardia Act's restraints on the power of federal courts to issue injunctions in labor disputes bars a federal court injunction of a union from striking in breach of the no-strike clause even where the union has agreed through its collective bargaining agreement that all disputes shall be resolved by binding arbitration. The key argument put forth in favor of injunctions in such situations was that the term "labor disputes," used in the Norris-La Guardia Act, should not be construed to include situations in which an injunction would promote the process of collective bargaining rather than inhibit it. The greater the benefits of having arbitration substitute for strikes, it was argued, the more attractive is the collective bargaining process. This leads to the conclusion that the Norris-La Guardia restrictions upon labor injunctions should not apply where a federal court's order merely forces the union and its members to abide by their no-strike promises made in the collective agreement. To this argument Justice Black replied that the considerations presented were directed at what might be a more desirable labor policy under the circumstances of current labor-management behavior. But the argument was not, he said, based on an accurate analysis of congressional intent when Norris-La Guardia was adopted.

Further, the majority refused to find that the Norris-La Guardia restraints upon labor injunctions were partially repealed, by implication, when section 301 of the Labor-Management Relations Act was adopted in 1947. In the 1947 statute, Congress had expressly given to the federal courts injunctive power over certain types of labor disputes where such relief is requested by the NLRB. "If Congress had intended that §301 suits should also not be subject to the anti-injunction provisions of the Norris-La Guardia Act, it certainly seems likely that it would have made its intent known in this same express manner."[19] Moreover, Black noted, when the 1947 legislation was being considered, proposals had been put forward and were weighed by Congress that would have repealed Norris-La Guardia to the extent of suits based on breach of collective bargaining agreements. But these proposals were eventually deleted from the statute, reassuring the majority of the Court in *Sinclair* that its interpretation of congressional intent was sound.

It will be recalled that in *Lincoln Mills* Mr. Justice Frankfurter had similarly argued, in dissent, that in adopting section 301 of the Labor-Management Relations Act, Congress had no intention of repealing the Norris-LaGuardia Act's restraints on federal labor injunctions and that, accordingly, a federal court could not order a party to submit to arbitration. Argueably, therefore, the majority in *Sinclair Refining* was adopting the theory of the dissent in *Lincoln Mills*. To avoid any such implication, Mr. Justice Black stated that there was no inconsistency

in the Court's decision in the two cases because *Lincoln Mills* was distinguishable from *Sinclair Refining.* The order to arbitrate issued in *Lincoln Mills* did
not, he pointed out, interfere with the sort of activities protected from federal
court injunctions under the Norris-LaGuardia Act—work stoppages, picketing
and encouragement of those activities. Such activities were, however, involved
in the *Sinclair* case.

Black acknowledged that there might be merit in the view that injunctive
relief should be available to end strikes in breach of no-strike agreements, particularly where the parties have previously agreed upon arbitration machinery
for settling the underlying dispute. However, he rejected the notion that it was
for the Court to mold any such change.

This last assertion to the effect that policy changes are for the Congress, not
for the Bench, is often made by the Court. As explained by Mr. Justice Black,
himself a former United States Senator: "The question of what change, if any,
should be made in the existing law is one of legislative policy properly within
the exclusive domain of Congress—it is a question for lawmakers, not law inter-
preters. Our task is the more limited one of interpreting the law as it now stands.
In dealing with problems of interpretation and application of federal statutes, we
have no power to change deliberate choices of legislative policy that Congress
has made within its constitutional powers. Where congressional intent is discern-
ible—and, here it seems crystal clear—we must give effect to that intent."[20]

But that congressional intent, which was "crystal clear" to a majority of
the Court, led Justices Brennan, Douglas, and Harlan to an opposite conclusion.
For these dissenting members of the Court, the decision did not end with the
conclusion that Congress had not intended to "repeal" part of Norris-LaGuardia
when it adopted the 1947 legislation. Although Congress did not intend to repeal the anti-injunction provisions, explained Mr. Justice Brennan, when it
adopted the Labor-Management Relations Act, Congress did create a conflict
in the statutory law governing labor relations in cases such as the instant one.
Accordingly, he asserted, the proper role for the Court is to seek an accommodation between the two enactments. Because the availability of the injunctive
remedy is far more important to accomplishing the section 301 purpose of
enforcing collective agreements than is its presence a detriment to the goals of
Norris-LaGuardia, Brennan urged, the proper accommodation of the two statutes
is to allow the injunction in enforcement of a no-strike clause where the parties
have themselves provided a method for resolving the underlying labor dispute.

As for the force of the legislative history, Mr. Justice Brennan declared that
it favored his view. The mere fact that Congress declined to repeal part of Norris-
LaGuardia, he stated, is no reason to assume that Congress intended that the
power of the federal courts to enforce collective agreements under section 301 of
the Labor-Management Relations Act would involve anything less than the regular arsenal of remedies. "That would mean, of course, that injunctive relief could
be afforded when damages would not be an adequate remedy."[21] Rather than

engage in a blanket repeal of Norris-LaGuardia, according to Justice Brennan, Congress preferred to have the courts make such necessary accommodations between the policies of the two acts in light of the particular labor relations setting of each case.

The *Sinclair Refining* decision did not, of course, leave employers totally helpless in face of strikes in breach of no-strike clauses. The employer could still sue the union for money damages, or bring a claim before an arbitrator seeking damages, based on the breach of the no-strike clause. In *Drake Bakeries v. Local 50, American Bakery Workers,* 370 U.S. 254 (1962), the Court held that an arbitrator, not a court, should assess such damages where both sides have agreed to take all disputes under the collective bargaining agreement to arbitration.

In addition, as noted in an earlier chapter, the employer could also discharge the strikers for having broken the no-strike condition of employment, which condition was established by the collective agreement.[22]

Further, it was suggested that if the collective agreement made provision for an extra-speedy arbitration procedure by giving an arbiter the power to issue interim orders staying any strike activity during the life of the no-strike clause, then a federal court would be able to issue an order requiring the employees and union to adhere to the arbitrator's order. Such a court order would in effect constitute an injunction of the strike pending the completion of arbitration (and thereby evade the *Sinclair* rule). Nevertheless, it could be rationalized as being outside of the restraints of Norris-LaGuardia on the grounds that the court would not be resolving a labor dispute; rather, it would simply be enforcing an arbitrator's resolution of a contractual dispute arising under the collective agreement. This rationalization for permitting such strike injunctions when in support of an arbitrator's award was given approval by the U.S. Court of Appeals for the 5th Circuit.[23]

Still another suggestion made for maintaining the viability of no-strike clauses was for the employer to secure injunctive enforcement, pending arbitration, in the state courts. The Norris-LaGuardia Act would appear to be inapplicable to such injunctions, since its restraints are directed at federal court jurisdiction only.

The Supreme Court held that the existence of federal jurisdiction to enforce labor arbitration clauses in collective agreements does not preclude the state courts from enforcing them so long as the state courts apply rules of law consistent with federal labor policy. [E.g., *Local 174, Teamsters Union* v. *Lucas Flour Company,* 369 U.S. 95 (1962).] Although a number of states have their own so-called little Norris-LaGuardia statutes barring the courts from issuing injunctions in labor disputes except under very narrowly confined circumstances, this form of state court remedy from breaches of no-strike clauses was often successfully pursued after the decision in *Sinclair Refining.* And, one scholar has estimated that in all but about fourteen states, an injunction can properly be issued against a strike that breaches a no-strike clause.[24] However, to the chagrin of employers, astute union lawyers were often able to evade state injunctive enforcement of no-strike clauses by using the device of "removing" the case to federal court.

When an action is brought in state court but could have been brought in federal court, the defendant is entitled to make a motion in federal court asking that the case be "removed" to the latter court's jurisdiction. As a result, subsequent to *Sinclair Refining* if an employer secured a state court injunction of the strike pending arbitration, because the employees were striking in alleged breach of contractual no-strike and arbitration clauses, the well-informed union attorney would respond by filing a motion in federal court to have the action removed to the federal tribunal. Generally, when this happened, the state court would either itself dissolve its injunction of the strike, on the grounds that it no longer had jurisdiction over the case, or the federal district court, in protection of its own jurisdiction over the removed case, would order that the state injunction be dissolved. And, of course, pursuant to the *Sinclair Refining* decision, the federal court was not able to substitute its own injunction against the strike. Thus, removal provided a means of evading state court injunctions.

The legality of the removal maneuver was raised before the Supreme Court of the United States in *Avco Corporation* v. *Aero Lodge No. 735, I.A.M., 390 U.S. 557 (1968)*. The Court unanimously upheld the validity of the removal tactic but avoided reaching two related questions raised in the litigation. The opinion of the federal Court of Appeals for the Sixth Circuit, which had decided the *Avco* case below, contained a suggestion that because federal labor policy must be respected by the state courts in the enforcement of arbitration agreements, the Norris-LaGuardia restraints upon injunctive remedies applies to the state courts in such cases. The Supreme Court expressly declined to comment on this part of the lower court's opinion. Since the union had in fact elected to remove the case to federal court, the contention concerning the applicability of the Norris Act to state courts was not properly before the Supreme Court.

The question had also been raised in the *Avco* litigation as to whether it had been necessary for the federal district court to dissolve the state injunction or whether that court could have left the state injunction stand despite the removal of the action to federal court. The Supreme Court ruled that at the very least the district court had the power to dissolve the state injunction as a matter of discretion and that because the court had in fact dissolved the state court order, it was not necessary for the High Court to consider whether the district court was required to do so as a matter of law.

But perhaps the most significant aspect of *Avco* was the concurring opinion by Mr. Justice Stewart. He observed that the Supreme Court would no doubt have a future opportunity to reconsider the continuing validity of the *Sinclair Refining* decision. He was joined in this observation by Justices Harlan and Brennan, who had dissented in *Sinclair*. But it was especially interesting that the suggestion came from the pen of Mr. Justice Stewart, inasmuch as he was a member of the slender majority that had decided *Sinclair.*

That opportunity for reconsideration of *Sinclair Refining* came in *Boys Markets, Inc.* v. *Retail Clerks Union,* 398 U.S. 235 (1970), where the Court decided to overrule its earlier position. In *Boys Markets,* Mr. Justice Brennan, the author of the *Sinclair Refining* dissent, was permitted to fully savor his triumph, the task of preparing the Opinion of the Court having been assigned to him.

With true judicial grace, without gloating over his victory Mr. Justice Brennan examined the basic considerations put forth by the majority in *Sinclair* and by the dissent in *Boys Markets.* He attributed the change in the Court's position not to the overwhelming persuasiveness of his earlier dissent, but rather to the asserted insight gained from the intervening experience under the *Sinclair* rule. This experience had, Brennan explained, instructed the Court regarding the shortcomings involved in the policy of the *Sinclair Refining* decision.

Perhaps the single largest hurdle for the majority in *Boys Markets* was posed not by the doctrinal or historic considerations set out in the Court's *Sinclair Refining* opinion, but rather by the fact that the principle of *stare decisis* arguably prevented the Court from overruling its earlier decision, particularly in light of the fact that Congress had allowed that decision to stand even though it had been urged to adopt legislation specifically giving the courts power to enjoin strikes in such situations.

Quoting from an earlier decision, Mr. Justice Brennan responded by cautioning that it is too speculative to attempt to discern Congressional intent from the mere failure of Congress to act on a particular proposal. Rather, he asserted, it had become more and more clear that the *Sinclair* decision was itself a departure from the otherwise consistent interpretation of Congressional policy and it was this discovery that compelled the Court to reconsider its resolution of the *Sinclair* case. Further, he said, the union practice under the combined decisions of *Sinclair* and *Avco,* of immediately removing to federal court any injunctive actions brought in state court to enforce no-strike arbitration clauses, was undermining Congress's desire to permit the enforcement of collective bargaining agreements in the state as well as the federal courts.

Mr. Justice Brennan recognized that one route for removing the dilemma posed to continued state court participation in these cases was to decide that the *Sinclair Refining* decision applied to state actions as well as to federal court proceedings—that is, that the Norris-LaGuardia Act's restraints on injunctive remedies for labor disputes could not be undermined by the state courts. This solution was rejected, however, on the grounds that Congress had no intention of imposing such restraints upon the state courts either when it adopted Norris-LaGuardia nor when it enacted section 301 of the Labor-Management Relations Act.

One might suspect that the change of the Court's position between *Sinclair* and *Avco-Boys Markets* was motivated not so much by a reevaluation of

congressional purpose nor by concern over the preservation of state court jurisdiction, but rather by a reappraisal of the wisdom of withholding the injunctive
remedy in such situations. The Court's opinion in *Boys Markets* openly admits
to such judicial concern over the impact of its prior decision. The damages
remedy for breaches of the no-strike clause, which continued to be available
under *Sinclair,* had not proved adequate observed the Court. Citing to reports
of bar committees and the observations of scholarly commentators, Justice
Brennan noted that: "[A]n action for damages prosecuted during or after a
labor dispute would only tend to aggravate industrial strife and delay an early
resolution of the difficulties between employer and union."[25] Thus, the
Court concluded "that *Sinclair* does not make a viable contribution to federal
labor policy." [26] Finally, not to totally neglect the foresight of his dissent in
Sinclair, Brennan reiterated the doctrinal and interpretive points made there in
support of the position that Norris-LaGuardia does not bar federal injunctions
of strikes which breach no-strike clauses.

So as not to unduly encroach upon the Congressional policies of Norris-
LaGuardia, the *Boys Markets* decision stressed that the availability of an injunction in support of a no-strike agreement is conditioned upon the presence of
several factors such as the availability of settlement through arbitration and
the employer's willingness to arbitrate the underlying dispute. Nor even then
will the injunction be available as a matter of course. The judge must in each
case weigh all of the equities bearing on the situation such as the relative burden
upon the parties of granting or withholding the injunctive relief.

Neither the post-*Sinclair* experience nor the majority's narrowly drawn
exception to the Norris-LaGuardia Act persuaded Mr. Justice Black, the author
of the majority opinion in *Sinclair Refining,* of the error at that decision. In a
strongly worded dissent, Justice Black asserted that since the time of the decision in *Sinclair* the only thing of significance to change had been the membership of the Court and the position of one justice (Stewart). He stated that even
if *Sinclair* had been wrongly decided, the

"... subsequent 'reinterpretation' of the statute is gratuitous and
neither more nor less than an amendment: it is no different in effect
from a judicial alteration of language that Congress itself placed in
the statute. ... It is the Congress, not this Court, that responds to the
pressures of political groups, pressures entirely proper in a free society.
It is Congress, not this Court, that has the capacity to investigate the
divergent considerations involved in the management of a complex
national labor policy. And it is Congress, not this Court, that is elected
by the people. This Court should, therefore, interject itself as little as
possible into the law-making and law-changing process. Having given
our view on the meaning of a statute, our task is concluded, absent
extraordinary circumstances. When the Court changes its mind years

later, simply because the judges have changed, in my judgment, it takes upon itself the function of the legislature."[27]

Mr. Justice Black similarly asserted that the constitutional doctrine of separation of powers among the three branches of government presents a more important policy to be upheld than does any adverse consequences resulting from an erroneous interpretation of labor legislation.

Finally, Black argued that the consequences of *Sinclair* and *Avco* were not as severe as the majority portrayed. The no-strike clause could still be enforced by a damages remedy, the union could be ordered to arbitrate and the employer could resort to his own self-help measures by discharging the strikers. However, Mr. Justice Black provided no hints in his dissent as to whether, in the face of the Norris-LaGuardia Act, he would have permitted a court to issue an injunction in support of an arbitrator's back-to-work order.

Mr. Justice White, the only other dissenting member of the Court, did not join in the strong language of the Black dissent. Rather, he simply noted that he relied on the reasons set forth in Mr. Justice Black's opinion for the majority in *Sinclair Refining*.

Because Mr. Justice Marshall did not participate in the *Boys Markets* decision, had Chief Justice Burger and Mr. Justice Blackmun, both of whom were appointed to the Supreme Court subsequent to the *Sinclair Refining* case, felt bound by the doctrine of *stare decisis* to adhere to the Court's prior decision, then the result in *Boys Markets* would have been a 4 to 4 split. In such situations, the decision of the lower court prevails. In this case, that decision, in accord with the *Sinclair* doctrine, was to deny the injunctive remedy. Thus, the departure from the established precedent on this issue resulted in principal part from the votes of Burger and Blackmun, two Nixon appointees. There was some irony in this inasmuch as in making his nominations to the Supreme Court, President Nixon had emphasized that in searching for persons to nominate to this high office he sought, among other things, men who believe strongly in the concepts of strict interpretation of the law and judicial restraint. Whatever one might think of the merits of overruling the *Sinclair Refining* decision, it is difficult to characterize *Boys Markets* as the product of either the philosophy of strict judicial interpretation or of judicial restraint.

The Court has unquestionably played an activist role in the development of the law of labor arbitration. And amongst those "activists" have numbered such jurists of conservative reputation as Clark, Harlan, Burger and Blackmun. To date, Congress has not rebuffed the Court's creative explorations in this area, thus, indicating that Congress has either concurred in the Bench's interpretation of congressional purpose, or that it has tacitly accepted the wisdom of the Court's policy formulations, or that it has not found sufficient motivation to overturn the Court's action through new legislation.

It is probably fair to assume that in enacting the governing legislation respecting judicial enforcement of labor arbitration clauses, Congress did not foresee the precise issues which the Court has had to resolve. Accepting this assumption, is it wrong for the Court to engage in some legislative type activity so long as it seeks to shape policy in the manner in which it anticipates that Congress would have decided had the specific question been raised when the legislation was being considered? Mr. Justice Black's answer in *Boys Markets* is a resounding: "Yes, it is wrong!" It is interesting to observe that the answer of the majority of justices who decided *Boys Markets* would probably be in accord with Justice Black if the question was put as stated above. It should be noted, for example, that Justice Brennan's opinion is developed not in terms of justifying the result because it reflects a meritorious policy concerning questions which were overlooked by Congress; rather, Brennan's opinion analyzes the issue in terms of discovering the true intent of Congress in the course of accommodating two somewhat conflicting expressions of that intent.

One might argue that the position taken by the majority in *Boys Markets* is disingenuous and, as Black suggests, a threat to democratic institutions. The Congress of the United States has a vast responsibility and is a very complex institution. To secure a change in legislation is normally an undertaking that requires a very considerable commitment of time, energy and finances, and even then is unlikely to succeed—despite the fact that the legislative goal is meritorious. Thus, the policy adopted through judicial activism is likely to prevail due to the burdens of overcoming legislative inertia. This holds true, moreover, irrespective of how far removed the Court's policy making is from legislative purpose.

On the other hand, because of the very cumbersomeness of the legislative process, because of the very burdens that make it so difficult to successfully usher any legislative proposal through Congress, it may well be that judicial activism of the sort displayed in *Boys Markets* is an absolutely essential ingredient in the survival of the American governmental system. If the Court, based upon a judicial philosophy of adhering to the letter of legislation until clarified by Congressional amendment, were to impose solutions that it deems unsatisfactory and it doubts would receive approval were the precise issue placed before Congress, then the end results could be disastrous not only for the parties regulated in the particular situations but for the entire system of government. In such circumstances, we would be doomed by the inefficiencies of the legislative process to live under undesirable rules, not because such rules accord with the intent of the elected lawmakers, but because they accord with the clear meaning of laws written and adopted to govern other situations but which are, nevertheless, on their face applicable to the matters brought before the courts.

The problem of governing the United States is too vast to be handled by a single legislative branch of government if the system permits only that branch the authority and responsibility of governing wisely. Though literal adherence to the doctrines of judicial restraint might bring dire results upon the lives of the governed and eventually upon the entire system of governance, nevertheless one cannot deny that there are real dangers of autocracy in judicial activism and that Mr. Justice Black's warnings in the *Boys Markets* dissent deserve careful consideration.

There is no way of determining with accuracy the impact of the Supreme Court's decisions upon the extent to which labor arbitration is utilized in the United States. It was widely used for resolving disputes prior to the Court's entry into the field. Its use has increased since the *Lincoln Mills* decision, so that today it is exceptional for a collective bargaining agreement not to provide for the arbitration of at least some types of differences arising under the contract. Though the impact of the Court's decisions in this area cannot be measured, it is reasonable to assume that it has, at least to some extent, contributed to the growth of labor arbitration.

Although estimates vary, each year American labor arbitrators probably issue between 15,000 and 20,000 awards. Normally the parties accede to the obligation to submit to arbitration and abide by the award. Therefore, litigation concerning labor arbitration continues to be relatively infrequent. Rather, the focus of attention has shifted to the extent to which administrative agencies and courts should stay their hand in favor of the arbitral process even in those situations in which these other tribunals are not legally required to give deference to the arbitrators. In such situations, arbitration has received a mixed response.[28]

The National Labor Relations Board, however, has become progressively more receptive to arbitration in recent years. It has moved from a position of deferring to arbitration only in those situations in which an award consistent with the Board's own policies had already been issued prior to the issuance of an unfair labor practice decision, to a policy of now staying its own proceedings in many categories of cases if the matter is being pressed to binding arbitration.[29]

To the extent that judicial and administrative tribunals continue to expand the role of labor arbitration, clearly much of that trend can be attributed to the stature to which arbitration was raised by the Supreme Court's opinion in *Lincoln Mills,* the *Steelworkers Trilogy, Carey,* and *Wiley.*

6 Change of Ownership and Other Business Alterations

"Employee turnover" is a term commonly used to denote the occurrence of a worker leaving his present job for a new one, for retirement, for unemployment, or to denote the event of the employee's death. Its counterpart term, "employer turnover," while less commonly used, also describes a normal occurrence in business affairs. Employer turnover can take a variety of forms. In the first six months of 1975, for example, some 5,500 business failures were recorded in the United States.[1]

Employer turnover, of course, is not without its impact on the workers. For example, when a business fails, the employees of that business must find new jobs and, hence, there is resulting "employee turnover" as well.

The merger of different business entities into a new single enterprise constitutes another form of employer turnover. Though merger will often have but slight consequences for the employees, at least in the short run, occasionally such changes can have very considerable impact upon employee welfare. Because of a merger, for example, changes might be made in the manner in which work is performed or the way in which supervisory decisions are made. Such changes can in turn, result in loss of jobs, alteration of assigned work tasks, and modification of the terms and conditions of work.

Sale of a business's operating property to a new owner constitutes another form of employer turnover. For example, this can take the form of the sale of part of the plant equipment or of an operating unit such as a plant or store. It can also involve the sale of all of the employer's plant and equipment. As with a merger, the sale of business assets may be accompanied by serious alterations of the terms and conditions under which people are employed. To illustrate, the new owner may not want to continue to employ those who formerly operated that plant and equipment, or the new owner might have radically different ideas from the previous owner concerning personnel policies or the manner in which work is to be performed. Indeed, the new owner may use the plant and equipment to perform different operations from those previously conducted at the plant.

Still another form of employer turnover occurs when an employer moves the business to a new location. Such moves can be motivated by any one or a combination of considerations such as the need for new plant or equipment, or for access to different or better sources of supply or more favorable markets. Changes in such costs of doing business at the old locale, such as tax rates, utility rates, and prevailing wage rates, too, might motivate a move. Obviously,

127

therefore, employer turnover is a significant event in labor-management relations, often involving a complicated setting in which the grounds for decision may be hard to unravel and the impact upon employees even harder to predict.

Runaway Shops

As can be seen from the above, one possible motive leading to employer turnover is the desire to escape the consequences of unfavorable employment conditions. The theme that one cannot run from his problems is a subject for Biblical text as well as moral tracts and psychological treatices. The response of fleeing from a problem may reveal an underlying physiological reflex and undoubtedly is a common response to situations involving stress, but in any event, employer flight has been an ever present facet of labor relations in the United States.

For example, in the first year of the National Labor Relations Act, S & K Kneepants Co., Inc. was accused by the Amalgamated Clothing Workers of America of moving its plant from Lynchburg to Culpepper, Virginia so as to avoid bargaining with the union. The union represented about 85 percent of the company's workers. In labor parlence, the union was accusing S & K of being a "runaway shop."

After holding a hearing, the NLRB determined that S & K Kneepants Co. was indeed guilty of running from the union's successful organization of the employees.[2] Moreover, the Board found that this was not the first time that S & K had moved in an attempt to rid itself of the obligation of dealing with a union. In 1930 S & K had been operating in New York City where its employees were union represented. In December of that year, the company moved to Lynchburg, Virginia "in search of unorganized and cheaper labor." After the National Industrial Recovery Act had been declared unconstitutional in 1935, S & K increased its work hours from thirty-six to forty-five per week and cut its employees' wages in many instances from $12 a week to as low as $5 a week. Sometime thereafter its workers began joining the Amalgamated Clothing Workers Union, which eventually sought to bargain with the company and claimed that it represented a majority of the workers. The company's refusal to bargain was met by a strike. The employer continued in its refusal to recognize the union or to sign any agreement, eventually modifying its position to insistence that the union leave the scene. After the union faded into the background, the company signed an agreement with a committee of its employees, giving an assurance that no worker would be discharged for having taken part in the union activities and granting some improvements in the terms of employment. Shortly after signing this agreement, the company began making arrangements to close the plant and move the operation to a new factory in Culpepper, Virginia.

As a result of the above described sequence of events, the NLRB concluded that the company's purpose in closing its Lynchburg plant was to avoid bargaining with the union representing the majority of its workers and that, therefore, the company was in violation of the National Labor Relations Act. To remedy this violation, the NLRB ordered that upon the reopening of the Lynchburg plant, the employer would have to reinstate the employees who had previously worked there. In the alternative, the Board ruled, if the company resumed its operations at another location, the Lynchburg employees would have to be offered jobs at the new location and the employer would have to pay the reasonable transportation expenses for moving the employees and their families to the new location.

The *S & K Kneepants* case set the pattern for future NLRB decisions dealing with runaway shops. One variation in the remedy, later devised by the board, has been to require the employer who moves to a new location within reasonable commuting distance from the original site, to reimburse the employees for increased traveling expenses in going to and from the new plant location.

The problem of dealing with the runaway shop becomes more difficult to resolve when the employer's anti-union motivation is combined with economically sound reasons for moving the business. The guideline adopted by the NLRB and the Courts of Appeals has been that the employer is free to move if economic necessity is the predominant motive. [E.g., *Local 57 I.L.G.W.U.* v. *National Labor Relations Board*, 374 F.2d 295 (D. C. Cir. 1967)].

The Supreme Court has never found it necessary to deal directly with the runaway shop issue. However, in the course of deciding cases involving related problems, the Court has indicated that it approves the approach taken by the NLRB and the U.S. Courts of Appeals in resolving this question.[3]

Contracting Out

A less drastic step than the runaway shop, but a closely related measure, is for the employer to contract out to a nonunion company, or to an employer who has a less onerous collective bargaining agreement, some or all of the work otherwise performed by his own employees. It was this sort of decision which precipitated the leading case of *Fibreboard Paper Products Corp.* v. *National Labor Relations Board*, 379 U.S. 203 (1964).

The Fibreboard company had a plant in Emeryville, California, in which the maintenance employees had been represented since 1937 by a United Steelworkers of America local union. The latest collective bargaining agreement covering these maintenance employees was scheduled to expire on July 31, 1959, and negotiations for a new contract were begun in early June. The union's list of proposed modifications of the collective agreement was sent on June 15th, but until July 27th the union was unsuccessful in its efforts to arrange a bargaining meeting with the employer. When the parties did meet on the 27th, the company notified the union that effective August 1st the company would no longer perform its own maintenance work but would arrange to have that work performed by an outside contractor. The union protested that the company could not lawfully do this and the union and company representatives agreed to meet again on July 30th for further discussion.

By July 30th, Fibreboard had entered into an agreement with Fluor Maintenance, Inc., for the latter company to perform the maintenance work at Fibreboard's plant, Fluor to be paid on a costs plus fixed fee basis. At the July 30th meeting, the company explained that because it would no longer be employing the maintenance employees represented by the union, it would be pointless to discuss a new collective bargaining agreement.

Fibreboard obviously felt justified in its action. For some time, the company had been calling upon the union to help improve the efficiency of the plant maintenance work. Fluor, the new maintenance contractor, had assured Fibreboard that Fluor would successfully reduce maintenance costs by reducing the size of the maintenance staff, decreasing overtime work, getting the work done for less in fringe benefits payments, and by more efficiently preplanning and scheduling the work to be performed. Fibreboard estimated that it was saving about $225,000 annually by transferring this work to the Fluor company.

Charges were filed by the union with the NLRB, and the General Counsel issued a complaint against Fibreboard that asserted that the company's action interfered with the employees' right of self-organization, discriminated against the employees' union activities, and breached the company's statutory duty to bargain in good faith with the union.

The Board ruled against the union, relying on prior decisions respecting the employer's right to unilaterally determine to subcontract work so long as that determination was not designed simply to avoid dealing with unionized employees. Shortly after deciding the *Fibreboard* case, however, the NLRB reconsidered its position on this question and reversed itself in *Town & Country Mfg. Co.,* 136 NLRB 1022, 1027 (1962), stating: "[T]he elimination of unit jobs, albeit for economic reasons, is a matter within the statutory phrase 'other terms and conditions of employment' and is a mandatory subject of collective bargaining within the meaning of Section 8(a) (5) of the Act."[a] In the meantime, the union's lawyers had petitioned the NLRB for reconsideration of the *Fibreboard* decision and, proving that persistency is an important trait in a lawyer, the NLRB agreed to reconsider the case. Upon that reconsideration, the Board reversed its previous ruling.

This second *Fibreboard* decision was appealed and reached the Supreme

---

[a]Section 8(a) (5) makes it an unfair labor practice for an employer to refuse to bargain in good faith with the duly designated collective bargaining representative concerning wages, hours, and other terms and conditions of employment.

Court, which unanimously affirmed the result in the board's second ruling and upheld the NLRB remedy requiring Fibreboard to resume its maintenance operation, reinstate the maintenance workers with back pay, and bargain with the union.

Chief Justice Earl Warren delivered the majority opinion for the Court and a concurring opinion was offered by Mr. Justice Stewart, joined by Douglas and Harlan. Mr. Justice Goldberg, who had been counsel for the union at the time the case arose, did not participate in the decision.

Warren's opinion reasoned that the contracting out in this situation inevitably meant the termination of these employees' jobs and that job termination has traditionally been treated as a subject requiring collective negotiation. "To hold, as the Board has done, that contracting out is a mandatory subject of collective bargaining would promote the fundamental purpose of the Act by bringing a problem of vital concern to labor and management within the framework established by Congress as most conducive to industrial peace."[4] Further, Warren noted that provisions dealing with the contracting out of work could be found in numerous collective bargaining agreements thereby demonstrating, he said, that the subject is amenable to the collective bargaining process. The Chief Justice cautioned that the Court was not suggesting that the employer would have to reach agreement on this issue. Its only obligation under the Act is to bargain in good faith. "[A]lthough it is not possible to say whether a satisfactory solution could be reached, national labor policy is founded upon the congressional determination that the chances are good enough to warrant subjecting such issues to the process of collective negotiation."[5]

Obviously conscious of the complexity of the related issues and the potential scope of what was being decided, Warren stressed that the Court's decision went only to the question of whether an employer must bargain prior to replacing the employees in an existing bargaining unit with those of an independent contractor to do the same work under similar working conditions. "Our decision need not and does not encompass other forms of 'contracting out' or 'subcontracting' which arise daily in our complex economy."[6]

It was this potential breadth of the precedent established by *Fibreboard* that caused three members of the Court to join in a separate concurrence. In that concurring opinion, Justice Stewart stated that it was worthy of note that the statutory language respecting the duty to bargain is shaped in words of limitation—that is, the Act sets forth specific (though vaguely defined) subject categories concerning which the parties are obliged to negotiate, with the implication being that the duty is confined to those categories only. This implication, he explained, is supported by the history of the statute as it was discussed and modified in the process of being adopted by Congress. The vague language of the Act is susceptible to very expansive interpretation, Stewart observed, but, "Only a narrower concept of 'conditions of employment' will serve the statutory purpose of delineating a limited category of issues which are subject to the duty to bargain collectively."[7] The fact that a managerial decision affects job security is not, of itself, reason to make that decision a subject for compulsory collective negotiation. "Decisions concerning the volume and kind of advertising expenditures, product design, the manner of financing, and sales, all may bear upon the security of the workers' jobs."[8] Some decisions, Stewart added, will even more directly affect job security. Such decisions could include the decision to invest in labor-saving machinery or to liquidate assets. Nevertheless, Mr. Justice Stewart argued: "Nothing the Court holds today should be understood as imposing a duty to bargain collectively regarding such managerial decisions, which lie at the core of entrepreneurial control. . . . If . . . the purpose of § 8(d) [the provision defining the duty to bargain in good faith] is to describe a limited area subject to the duty of collective bargaining, those management decisions which are fundamental to the basic direction of a corporate enterprise or which impinge only indirectly upon employment security should be excluded from that area."[9] Because the instant case involved a decision falling short of questions such as what shall be produced or how capital shall be invested, Stewart explained that he was able to concur in the result.

Not to be vulnerable to charges of narrowness of perspective, Mr. Justice Stewart added that he was fully aware of the impact that technological change has upon job security and the resulting concern that organized labor has regarding this problem. "It is possible that in meeting these problems Congress may eventually decide to give organized labor or government a far heavier hand in controlling what until now have been considered the prerogatives of private business management. That path would mark a sharp departure from the traditional principles of a free enterprise economy."[10]

In other Western nations this sort of governmental and union intervention into job security issues is an accepted part of the employment structure. In the Netherlands, for example, the employer cannot discharge a worker without government approval and, similarly, the worker cannot quit without such approval. Other European countries statutorily impose minimum periods of discharge notice that must be given prior to releasing an employee, and these notice periods can often be quite lengthy. But the type of procedure Justice Stewart proclaimed to be too removed from American traditions to be read into the Act, absent clear legislative intent, most resembles the codetermination approach and Works Council systems that have been developed in several Western European nations. Variously, these approaches either require union participation in all managerial decisions affecting a substantial number of employees, or condition discharge on either prior consultation with or prior approval of an employee selected committee.

Surely Mr. Justice Stewart is correct in declaring that such methods of operation are alien to our American free enterprise tradition; but if those traditions are to be dated from the time of the promulgation of the Wagner Act, or even the Taft-Hartley Act, then it also can be argued that the notion that an employer must bargain with a union representative rather than directly with his own workers, too, is a sharp departure from our traditional ideas concerning the prerogatives of business ownership. Thus, the very adoption of the National Labor Relations Act was itself a break with those traditions. It is apparent, therefore, that to the extent that "traditional principles of a free enterprise economy" guide the justices in cases such as *Fibreboard,* the Court is not dealing with self-evident or unambiguous points of reference. Rather, such "traditional principles," selected by the Court in determining what it will permit by statutory implication and what will be allowed only if statutorily specified, are themselves reflections of the judges' own experiences and value systems.

While examining *Fibreboard,* it is also worth noting, for those who are too ready to pin ideological labels on members of the Court, that Stewart and Harlan, both popularly denominated as conservatives, were joined by Justice Douglas in this separate concurring opinion. Even though Justice Douglas was popularly labeled as a liberal—and by some as a radical—he joined forces with the more conservative Stewart and Harlan in calling for a limited construction of the Court's decision so as to avoid an excessive encroachment upon management's right to control capital investment and direct the enterprise. Nor was Justice Douglas' position in *Fibreboard* an aberration. Frequently, in labor relations cases, Douglas would find it necessary to remind the Court and the country that Congress has traditionally accepted management's role as designed to determine where, when and how to invest capital, and labor's role as designed to maintain pressure on management to share its income.

Plant Closings

As previously observed, escape is a normal response to stress, though sometimes it takes an abnormal form. Suicide is the most extreme type of escape; psychopathic withdrawal is another variation. To avoid combat, soldiers have been known to maim themselves; to escape capture, animals have been known to chew off their limbs. It is for the reader to decide whether any of these extreme forms of escape conduct bear analogy to the actions of Darlington Manufacturing Company when on September 6, 1956, the Textile Workers Union narrowly won an NLRB election entitling it to be recognized as the exclusive bargaining representative of the employees working in the Darlington textile mill.

The Darlington company was part of a corporate complex controlled by Deering Milliken & Co., which was, in turn, controlled by the Milliken family. Through various corporate entities, Deering Milliken operated 27 textile mills and marketed the cloth produced by them. When the results of the NLRB election were announced, a meeting was called of the Darlington board of directors at which it was proposed that the mill be closed and the business liquidated. The corporate directors voted to close the mill, and this decision was approved by the stockholders about a month later. From the time of the directors' decision to close the plant, no new orders were taken and the employees were gradually discharged as outstanding orders were fulfilled. By November, operations had ceased and the following month the plant equipment and machinery were sold at auction.

The NLRB found that prior to the election the company had threatened to close the mill if the union won. It found, also, that after the directors voted to close, the employees were told that that decision had resulted from the employees' vote to be union represented. The company refused to bargain with the union on the grounds that there was nothing to bargain about. The union filed charges with the NLRB asserting that the employer's conduct constituted unlawful discrimination against protected union activity including an unlawful refusal to bargain with the duly certified bargaining representative.

The NLRB held against the company but was reversed by a divided vote in the Court of Appeals for the Fourth Circuit. Actually, that court initially had upheld the board 2 to 1, but it was decided that the case merited *en banc* consideration—that is, consideration by all five members of that court. The additional two members of the court joined the original dissenter so as to change the result. This particular *en banc* reconsideration became a matter of considerable political debate several years later when Judge Hainsworth of the Fourth Circuit was nominated to the Supreme Court by President Nixon.

Judge Hainsworth was not on the panel that originally heard the Darlington case. When it was reargued *en banc* he voted contrary to the original panel, and in favor of the company. When he was being considered for the Supreme Court, a few years later, it was revealed that Judge Hainsworth owned a considerable amount of stock in, and was on the board of directors of, a company that did a sizable amount of its business with the Deering Milliken corporate group. Union leaders and civil rights leaders who opposed Hainsworth's appointment to the Court cited his participation in the *Darlington* case and argued that ethical standards dictated against his participation. This charge likely played an important role in the Senate's rejection of the Hainsworth nomination. In many ways the episode was reminiscent of the events, discussed in chapter 1, which kept Judge John Parker off the Supreme Court in 1930.

About eight years after the NLRB election at the Darlington mill, the case was argued before the Supreme Court. There was a time when members of the United States Senate with some frequency appeared as advocates before the Supreme Court of the United States. But that practice had fallen into dissuse by the mid-twentieth century. Nevertheless, it was revived by Senator Sam Ervin, Jr., of North Carolina (the site of the Darlington mill) who argued the cause on behalf of the company. Senator Ervin's high repute as a former jurist not withstanding, the Supreme Court of the United States issued a decision unanimously supporting the union's challenge to the Darlington closing.[11] This decision was not a total victory for the union, however, and did not bring the case to its final conclusion.

A central concern of the Supreme Court in its decision was the extent to which an employer is free to terminate its business. The Court's first premise, which it announced with almost no discussion, was that "an employer has the right to terminate his business, whatever the impact of such action on concerted activities, if the decision to close is motivated by other than discriminatory reasons."[12] The discrimination referred to is, of course, anti-union discrimination. Based on this proposition, the Court then moved to weigh the question of whether an employer can go completely out of business if the employer's motive is to avoid unionization. The NLRB had found that such had been the motive of Darlington as evidenced by the statements made to employees. Thus, if an anti-union motive is an unlawful basis for going out of business, then the union would have proved its case.

But the Supreme Court was not prepared to give the union such an easy victory. In its opinion, by Mr. Justice Harlan, the Court labeled this claimed blanket restraint upon an employer's decision to terminate business as "a startling innovation." So startling, the Court insisted, that it could be maintained only if clearly supported by evidence concerning Congress's intent in adopting the National Labor Relations Act, or at least, unequivocal prior judicial interpretation of the statute. The Court stated that it could find neither form of support for this contention of the union. And in reviewing the case precedent asserted by the union as being in support of its position, Mr. Justice Harlan rejected, as inapplicable, the NLRB and lower court decisions respecting a runaway shop.

Nevertheless, the Court was clear that although the Act does not interfere with an employer's determination to go out of business, even for anti-union purposes, this prerogative is available to the employer *only if* it involves a *total* termination of business. In explanation of this distinction the Court stated: "[T]he force of such a closing is entirely spent as to that business when termination of the enterprise takes place. On the other hand, a discriminatory partial closing may have repercussions on what remains of the business, affording employer leverage for discouraging the free exercise of § 7 rights among remaining employees of much the same kind as that found to exist in the 'runaway shop' and 'temporary closing' cases."[13]

Accordingly, the Court ruled that a partial closing of a business is a violation of the section 8(a) (3) prohibition against employer discrimination for union activity if that partial closing is motivated by a purpose to chill unionism in any remaining part of the employer's enterprise *and if* the employer can reasonably foresee the closing as having such an effect. Further, the Court held, this restraint on closing part of a business applies even though the closed operation is legally a separate corporate entity and even where the closed operation is not affiliated with or engaged in the same commercial line as the rest of the enterprise. Rather, the critical factors are that those who close the operation have enough interest in other businesses so that they can expect to benefit from the discouragement of unionization caused by the closing, and close the entity for the purpose of producing such discouragement. Finally, for the employer to be guilty, it must be realistic to expect the employees of the remaining operations to be put in fear of similar retribution should they engage in union activities.

Because the standards set down in the *Darlington* decision were not established at the time the facts were weighed by board, the Supreme Court sent the case back to the NLRB for further findings and disposition in light of the Supreme Court's clarification of the law governing the issue. On remand, the NLRB found Darlington guilty on the grounds that the closing was cited by affiliated Deering Milliken companies to their employees as an example of what happens when a union comes into a mill. The company again appealed to the federal courts but the NLRB decision was upheld, the final disposition of the case coming in 1968. Thus, some 12 years after the union won the election at Darlington, the NLRB's order was enforced. That order provided the remedy of back pay to the discharged employees until they found substantially equivalent work or were placed on preferential hiring lists at other Deering Milliken plants. It also required Deering Milliken to bargain with the union concerning the details of compliance with that remedy.

If the Darlington closing succeeded in discouraging unionization at other Deering Milliken operations, it clearly had ample time to work its benefits for the enterprise. The remedy, even assuming its effectiveness at countering the discouragement of union activity, was deferred for a dozen years. If the ultimate resolution of the dispute between the company and the union achieved any form of justice, surely it was justice delayed. And if the adage about "justice delayed is justice denied" has any validity, it is clear that the significance of the *Darlington* decision must be found in some direction other than its impact upon the former employees of the Darlington mill or upon the union. That significance is, of course, to be found in the Court's policy pronouncements, in the case, regarding the extent to which the statutory protections granted to workers and unions to organize for collective labor activity has imposed restraints on the traditional right of the owner of property to control its disposition. The Court's resolution left the owners of employment capital neither with their full prerogative to withdraw from an enterprise wholly intact nor wholly destroyed. The Court's resolution in effect tells the owners of employment capital that they can do as they like with their property so long as in acting from anti-union motive, they do not exploit the power of withdrawal so as to personally benefit from the anti-union impact.

If the congressional purpose in adopting the national labor laws was to protect employee freedom of choice respecting collectivization of the economic power of labor, then is that goal not defeated whenever employer conduct has an impact of discouraging union activity, irrespective of whether the perpetrator of that discouragement benefits from his misdeed? When one enters the market place and commits wealth to commercial activity, a wide variety of restraints are by law imposed upon the owner's control of that wealth. Thus, the owner must accurately advertise the nature of his commercial activity; the owner must avoid creating danger to health or safety resulting from his activity; the owner must maintain various sorts of records of his activities; the owner must refrain from selecting employees on the basis of race, sex, religion, youth, or union activity; the owner must permit his property to be inspected in various ways, and the like. Is it any more of a restraint upon the prerogatives of ownership, therefore, to say that just as your employment of your property is regulated, so too is your withdrawal of it from the market place subject to restrictions justified by the interest of public well-being? The Court's assertion in *Darlington* that it is a startling innovation to assert that an employer cannot abandon business activity if the motive is anti-union, therefore, is supported more by emotional response than by a neutral evaluation of the scope of property rights afforded in the modern corporate state and managed economic system.

On the other hand, if faced with the same choice respecting the owner's option of totally withdrawing from the marketplace irrespective of the motive, is it likely that Congress would have chosen any differently from the unanimous Court in *Darlington*? Or, to put it another way, to the extent that the lines drawn in *Darlington* regarding the right of property holders to use their power vindictively against pro-union workers are lines drawn on the basis of emotional response to personal value systems, it is probable that the value base from which the Court operated in issuing its decision is parallel to the values guiding congressional action. Thus, while one can point to the logical structure of the National Labor Relations Act, in light of its stated purposes, as a basis for refuting aspects of the Court's decision, that language and the art of logic, if the sole framework for decision making, would achieve a less accurate result in truly reflecting the legislative intent than has the Supreme Court's decision in *Darlington*.

Business Transfers and Bargaining Status

When employer turnover leaves the workers with a changed employer, rather than wholly abandoned, a different set of questions arise. And the issues become somewhat complicated to the extent that the new employer has an existing collective bargaining relationship or to the extent that at the time of the change there are unresolved disputes concerning the status of union activity at the employment establishment.

It is a long established policy of the NLRB that where the change of ownership does not alter the business operations or employment characteristics in any material way, then the new owner is in the same shoes as its predecessor.[14] Thus, the board will amend a certification of a union's representative status, in such cases, to show the name of the new owner or entity.[15] Similarly, the NLRB has held that in such cases the successor employer must remedy any unfair labor practices committed by the previous owner or entity if the successor either knew about the improper employer conduct at the time of change or if charges were filed against the predecessor at the time of the change. This is referred to by labor lawyers as the *Perma Vinyl* doctrine.[16] Though the federal appellate courts have disagreed with the board's application of this policy to the facts in particular cases, the courts have accepted the underlying principle that where there is not significant change in the structure and conduct of the employing operation, then the rights and responsibilities of the workers, the union, and the employer under the National Labor Relations Act should remain unchanged.[17]

In *Regal Knitwear Co. v. National Labor Relations Board*, 324 U.S. 9 (1945), the Supreme Court held that a cease and desist order issued by the board against an employer and its "successors and assigns," can in fact be enforced, at least in some circumstances, against a business that purchases the company that had committed the unfair labor practices. *Regal Knitwear*, however, raised the successor issue as an abstract question, and it was not until late 1973 that this principle was reviewed by the Supreme Court upon a record presenting a concrete factual setting.

The case before the Court, *Golden State Bottling Co., Inc. v. National Labor Relations Board*, 414 U.S. 168 (1973), on the other hand, did not place the full scope of the *Perma Vinyl* doctrine under the High Court's scrutiny inasmuch as the evidence showed that the principal officer of the successor employer had actual knowledge of the pending NLRA charge when it purchased the employing enterprise. Yet the broad language of the Court's unanimous decision supporting the *Perma Vinyl* doctrine as applied to the facts in *Golden State*, indicate that the Court is prepared to approve its application as well in situations in which the successor does not have actual knowledge of the charged misconduct so long as the unfair labor practice charges were filed prior to the transfer of ownership.

In explaining its position, the Court emphasized that the goal of the Act is to protect employees in their exercise of the statutory right to engage in concerted activity and that the intimidation of the employees is not necessarily lessened by the mere sale of the business by those who owned it when the misconduct took place. "[T]he employees may well perceive the successor's failure to remedy the predecessor employer's unfair labor practices . . . as a continuation of the predecessor's labor policies."[18] Moreover, the Court observed that because the board's doctrine assures that the successor will be in a position to at least learn about this potential liability prior to buying the business, the successor can protect itself by reflecting that potential liability in the price it pays for the business or by including in the sales contract a provision requiring the predecessor to indemnify the successor for any liability that might arise due to the former's unfair labor practices.

But not all protections of employee benefits are derived from the labor statutes. Many of the most important aspects of the collective bargaining relationship are established not by the National Labor Relations Act, but rather by the collective bargaining agreement negotiated between the union and employer. To what extent, then, does a change in business ownership alter any of these contractual rights?

John Wiley & Sons, Inc. v. Livingston, 376 U.S. 543 (1964), placed before the Court an employer turnover situation with an amply complicated factual setting. From these well knotted threads, the Court began to weave the doctrine to govern the impact that employer turnover has upon the employer-union-employee contractual relationship.

John Wiley & Sons is a large publisher of technical books. For what were admitted by all concerned to be valid business reasons, it acquired, through corporate merger, the business previously operated by Interscience, Inc., a smaller publisher of technical books. At the time of merger, Interscience had about eighty employees, half of whom were represented by District 65, Retail, Wholesale and Department Store Union, AFL-CIO. District 65 had a collective bargaining agreement with Interscience covering these employees. The agreement was silent as to its affect in the event of a sale or other change in the business ownership. None of the Wiley employees were union represented.

Several months before the expiration of the current collective bargaining agreement, Wiley and Interscience commenced merger discussions. The union negotiated with Interscience concerning the impact of the merger upon the union represented workers but no agreement was reached. The union sought to continue its representation of these employees after the merger, which took place almost four months before the expiration of the collective bargaining agreement, and asserted that that agreement continued in full force and affect as against Wiley. Wiley, on the other hand, rejected the union's claim to representational status after the merger and insisted that the employees' collective bargaining benefits ceased with the termination of Interscience as a business entity.

After the merger, Wiley retained most of the Interscience employees, though eleven accepted severance pay in an amount in excess of that required by the District 65 - Interscience collective bargaining agreement. As to the remaining employees previously under that agreement, District 65 asserted that they were entitled to their former seniority rights even though now employed by Wiley, and that the same was true with respect to accrued vacation rights based on the collective bargaining agreement. The union also demanded that Wiley continue in the future to pay these workers on the basis of the pay schedule established with Interscience, continue to make contributions into the pension and welfare plans as before, continue to grant severance benefits as in the Interscience collective agreement, and continue the job security and grievance procedures under the old contract in so far as the former Interscience employees were concerned. Wiley rejected the union's claims, whereupon the union sought to process them as grievances under its collective bargaining agreement with Interscience. Finally, when the new employer thwarted this approach, the union filed a suit in federal court seeking to compel Wiley to arbitrate these grievances pursuant to the arbitration clause of the collective agreement with Interscience. The suit was filed one week before that collective bargaining agreement was due to expire.

The theory of the union's suit was that Wiley, as Interscience's successor, was responsible for performing the terms of the collective bargaining agreement, including that part of the agreement under which the parties had committed themselves to place before an arbitrator, for final and binding decision, "any differences, grievance or dispute between the Employer and the Union arising out of or relating to" the collective agreement or its application or interpretation. As discussed in a previous chapter, it had been settled under prior case decisions that the federal courts have the power to enforce such provisions by ordering the recalcitrant party to submit to arbitration. Wiley resisted the suit on the grounds that the union claims were directed at a contract with Interscience, not Wiley. The case was resolved favorably to the union, without dissent.

Leaving aside the Court's discussion of the respective roles between the judiciary and arbitrators, the crux of its holding in *Wiley* regarding a successor employer's responsibilities is that "the disappearance by merger of a corporate employer which has entered into a collective bargaining agreement with a union does not automatically terminate all rights of the employees covered by the agreement . . . ."[19] The duty to arbitrate, explained the Court, can only result from a contractual undertaking.

Here there was a contract with the predecessor employer, Interscience, and therefore the crucial question was whether that contract could operate against Wiley. The fact that Wiley had not signed that collective bargaining agreement was not a sufficient defense against the duty to arbitrate, held the Court, because collective bargaining agreements are not ordinary contracts. Thus, it would be for an arbitrator to decide whether any of the unions claims concerning seniority rights, severance pay and other benefits for the former Interscience employees survived the change of ownership due to rights bestowed in the agreement between Interscience and District 65.

The Court's opinion does not provide any clear, concrete criteria for determining when a successor will be bound by the previous employer's agreement nor whether the successor's responsibility can run beyond the agreement's provisions respecting the submission of outstanding disputes to arbitration. Rather, the Court's opinion is filled with words of mystique concerning the nature of collective agreements and with hints as to possible distinctions between the facts in *Wiley* and other types of situations. Nevertheless, it is clear in the Court's discussion that the duty to arbitrate, if not other parts of the collective bargaining agreement, survives the change of business so long as there is "substantial continuity of identity in the business enterprise before and after" the change in ownership.

When the Court, through its decision in *Wiley*, gave the contractual obligation to arbitrate disputes arising under the collective bargaining agreement a status independent of the parties signatory to the contract, its choice, though contrary to commercial notions of contractual relations, was not alien to traditional concepts of the law of property. A lease of realty is a contract that under the law of property creates rights and obligations that run with the land irrespective of who owns the land—that is, though the signatories to the actual leasing contract no longer hold the ownership rights to the land (or the lease), the leasehold obligations and rights are enjoyed by the present parties occupying those positions.

It is arguable that the purposes of the NLRA are best served by such a rule that draws on this analogy to the law of property. The rights and obligations created by the collective bargaining agreement run with the employment establishment irrespective of union identity or business ownership, just as rights and obligations of a lease run with the land irrespective of who holds the lease or owns the land. And by this line of reasoning, the entire collective agreement would bind all successors. Such a rule has the virtue of stabilizing the collective bargaining relationship by assuring that the terms and conditions of employment fixed by the collective agreement will be invulnerable to any alteration due to changes in the collective representative or business ownership. On the other hand, at least part of the balanced formula so proposed is negated by section 8(d) of the National Labor Relations Act where, in the course of establishing that the duty to bargain collectively includes the duty to refrain from making unilateral changes in existing collective agreements, the statute expressly excepts those situations in which a union has been superseded as the collective bargaining representative of the employees. Thus, total adoption of this analogy to the law of leaseholds does not seem to be possible in light of the specific language of the Act.

The concept that the collective agreement follows the employing unit, rather than being limited just to the parties signatory to the contract, is one that has been adopted for the regulation of labor relations in other countries. To illustrate, in Belgium the labor relations code specifically states: "In case of the total or partial transfer of an undertaking, the new employer shall be bound to observe the terms of the agreement which bound the former employer, until the agreement is no longer in force."[20] Moreover, it is common under the laws of other industrial nations for the collectively negotiated terms of employment to be made applicable, either by judicial decrees or by ministry directive, to all employees in an industry irrespective of whether their particular enterprise participated in the union-management bargaining.

The above discussed potential expansion of the *Wiley* decision was pursued by the NLRB several years later when it ruled in the *Burns* case that successor employers and the incumbent union are bound by the existing collective bargaining agreement where a change in business ownership has not substantially altered the nature of the employing enterprise.[21] According to the board's analysis in *Burns,* the collective bargaining agreement regulates the terms and conditions of employment for the "employing industry" and is part of what the successor takes over in the course of taking over the employing industry.

In justification of its position, the board explained that the successor stands in the shoes of the prior owner and "can make whatever adjustments the acceptance of such obligation may dictate in his negotiations concerning the takeover of the business. Normally, employees cannot make a comparable adjustment. Their basic security is the collective-bargaining agreement negotiated on their behalf."[22] This argument was not sufficiently persuasive, however, to win the support of the Supreme Court of the United States.

Before discussing the Supreme Court's rejection of the board's decision in *Burns*, it is important to understand the very special factual situation involved in that case. Burns did not buy either the property or corporate shares of its predecessor, nor did it merge with its predecessor. Thus, *Burns* is not a typical successorship situation. Rather, what happened in *Burns* was that it replaced its predecessor as the company responsible for performing plant security services at a Lockheed Aircraft facility at the Ontario International Airport in California. More precisely, the security services for Lockheed at this facility had for some time been performed under contract by the Wackenhut Corporation. Four months after the United Plant Guard Workers of America had been certified by the NLRB as the exclusive bargaining representative of the forty or so security guards employed by Wackenhut at this facility, the Wackenhut contract to supply these services terminated. Wackenhut and Burns International Security Services, Inc., both submitted bids for a new contract to provide security services at the Lockheed facility and Burns was the successful bidder.

Upon taking over the security services for Lockheed, Burns hired twenty-seven former Wackenhut guards who had been working at this facility. However, the remaining fifteen guards employed by Burns for the Lockheed contract were not former Wackenhut employees. At other operations Burns had collective bargaining agreements with the American Federation of Guards. Upon hiring the former Wackenhut employees, Burns informed them that it could not live with the agreement between Wackenhut and the United Plant of Guards if they wanted to work for Burns. Burns thereafter recognized the American Federation of Guards as the collective bargaining agent of its employees at this Lockheed facility and rejected the demands of the United Plant Guards that Burns recognize that union pursuant to the NLRB certification. Burns also rejected the union's demand that Burns honor the collective bargaining agreement which the union had negotiated with Wackenhut.

The NLRB had found that Burns was guilty of an unfair labor practice in having assisted the American Federation of Guards and having recognized that union after such assistance. This finding was upheld by the appellate court and was not appealed to the Supreme Court.

The Board had also held that Burns committed an unfair labor practice in refusing to recognize the United Plant Guards as the collective bargaining agent of its workers at the Lockheed facility. This holding, too, was accepted by the Court of Appeals. An appeal was taken to the Supreme Court on this issue and a majority of the Court agreed that under the circumstances "it was not unreasonable for the Board to conclude that the union certified to represent all employees in the unit still represented a majority"[23] of them. Its discussion of this issue noted that there was no finding of any significant change in the operational structure for providing the security services and that a majority of the Burns employees were former members of the Wackenhut bargaining unit. The Court also pointed out that had Burns refused to hire anyone because they were members of the United Plant Guards, then this would have constituted an unfair labor practice.

Four members of the Supreme Court, the Chief Justice and Justices Brennan, Powell, and Rehnquist, would have disposed of the *Burns* case by finding that the successorship doctrine was inapplicable and that there was insufficient continuity in the employing entity or the employee unit in this situation to warrant holding that Burns had a duty to continue to recognize the United Plant Guards, let alone a duty to honor the existing collective bargaining agreement.

The majority, however, having found that the United Plant Guards continued to be entitled to recognition as the collective bargaining agent of the employees who performed the security services at this Lockheed facility, had to reach the question of whether the union was also entitled to enforce against Burns the collective agreement that it had negotiated with Wackenhut. On this point, the Supreme Court found itself in disagreement with the decision of the National Labor Relations Board.

Rejecting the NLRB's assertion that *Wiley* supported the result of binding Burns to the Wackenhut collective agreement, the Supreme Court distinguished the *Wiley* holding on the grounds that there the Court was accommodating the employer's freedom to contract with the "judicial preference for peaceful arbitral settlement of labor disputes."[24] That accommodation was accomplished in *Wiley* not by holding the successor bound by the predecessor's collective bargaining agreement but rather by holding that it was for an arbitrator to determine the extent, if any, to which the provisions of that prior collective agreement survived the merger and were applicable to the successor. Moreover, the Court emphasized in its *Burns* decision, *Wiley* was decided under a situation in which the merger had taken place under a state law that generally imposes the predecessor's contractual obligations upon the surviving corporation. "Here there was no merger or sale of assets, and there were no dealings whatsoever between Wackenhut and Burns. . . . Burns purchased nothing from Wackenhut and became liable for none of its financial obligations."[25]

Whereas the Court had found the guiding policy in *Wiley* to be the preference for settling labor relations disputes by arbitration, a policy which it had previously found sanctioned by the Labor Management Relations Act (but which in *Burns* it referred to as a "judicial preference"), in *Burns* it found the guiding policy to be contained in the section 8(d) definition of the phrase "to bargain collectively." In that definition, Congress expressly rejected the notion that either party to collective bargaining has a statutory obligation to agree to any proposal or make any concessions. That policy of protecting the parties from official compulsion respecting any particular concessions would be violated, reasoned the Court, if Burns were to be held bound by the provisions of the Wackenhut agreement. The purpose underlying this policy, explained the Court, is to minimize labor strife by allowing the agreement to reflect the economic power realities of those governed by the collective bargaining agreement. The Court noted, accordingly, that an existing collective agreement might well reflect concessions by a union which it would not have made had it faced a financially healthier employer. Or, the terms may reflect the concessions of an economically weak predecessor that would dissuade a new employer from replacing it if it had to operate under such employment terms and conditions. "Strife is bound to occur if the concessions which must be honored do not correspond to the relative economic strength of the parties."[26]

But having based its holding on the rather broad policy implications just enumerated, the Supreme Court then proceeded, in the *Burns* case, to narrow the scope of its holding. If the policy of the Act is to bind the parties to agreements only where they reflect the economic power realities of labor and capitol, logically that policy should be equally applicable to all forms of successorship. The economic realities of the respective bargaining power of the United Plant Guards and Burns would have changed from the balance of power between the United Plant Guards and Wackenhut had Burns come to control the employment at the Lockheed facility by absorbing the corporate stock of Wackenhut or by purchasing its assets, just as it changed due to the transfer of ownership in the form of succession which in fact had occurred in the case.

Of course, the nature and degree of alteration in the balance of bargaining power might vary depending on the form of takeover. Thus, had Burns acquired the contract by absorbing the Wackenhut company into the Burns corporate structure, Burns would clearly have gained a considerable increase in bargaining power because of the concomitant increase in its size and dominance of the security industry. On the other hand, it would have been possible in the circumstances presented in the case as it came to the Court, for Burns to have been in a weaker bargaining position than that of Wackenhut. Accordingly, the same considerations that caused the Court to decide against imposing the Wackenhut collective agreement on Burns should cause the Court to refuse to impose a predecessor's collective agreement upon the parties in any sort of successorship situation. Yet the Court refrained from allowing the language of its decision to carry the full scope of these implications. Said the Court: "[I]n a variety of circumstances involving a merger, stock acquisition, reorganization, or assets purchase, the Board might properly find as a matter of fact that the successor had assumed the obligations under the old contract."[27]

Of course, just because the Court narrowed its decision in *Burns*, so as to avoid enunciating a rule that is to control other types of successorship situations, does not mean that when such cases finally do come before the Court it will respond any differently from the way in which it decided the *Burns* case. Rather, the Court was simply assuring future flexibility for dealing with such cases. In this way the Court protected itself from being concerned in such future decisions with discovering and explicating the sort of distinction which it found necessary to spell out in *Burns* in order to show why the Burns situation was not controlled by *Wiley*.

The Court must constantly make this sort of choice as to whether to narrow a decision so as to avoid commiting judicial policy along the lines of apparent implications flowing from the present determination. Arguing for the technique of avoiding the possibility that its decision will be given a broad interpretation is the sort of experience reflected in the sequence of questions from *Wiley* to *Burns*. Without a concrete set of facts before it, the Court cannot fully appreciate the impact of its decision upon alternative situations. In the mean time, though, the broad language of prior decisions may give false guidance to lower courts, to administrative agencies such as the NLRB, and to lawyers advising their clients. Then, when finally faced with the concrete facts of a new case, the Court may discover considerations which it failed to weigh when it dealt with the earlier factual setting, and those considerations will give the Court new insight into the impact of alternative policy choices. Thus, though *Fibreboard*, *Wiley* and *Burns* in a broad sense all dealt with the impact of employer turnover upon collective bargaining agreement commitments, the thrust of the Court's primary concerns expressed in *Wiley* and *Fibreboard* — protecting contractually established employee rights from changes due to conditions over which employees have little or no control — were very different from those expressed in *Burns*. The primary concerns of the Court expressed in *Wiley*, if broadly construed and applied, could have led to a result in *Burns* which was unacceptable to the Court. Therefore, in *Burns* it became necessary for the Court to reshape the doctrinal considerations previously announced so as to accommodate the desired results in both situations.

In contrast to the danger of misleading the courts, agencies, and regulated parties, which is the risk of broadly stated Supreme Court opinions, is the burden of opinions such as *Burns* that expressly restrict the doctrine being applied to the precise type of facts involved in the matter before the Court. Decisions such as *Burns* leave the lower courts, the administrative agencies and the regulated parties with a void respecting the rules by which they are to be governed. It is certainly debatable whether such calculated uncertainty is any less disruptive than providing guidance through a doctrine that eventually is declared to be misleading.

Respecting the uncertainty created by the *Burns* decision, the burden is not as severe as one might at first glance suppose. Because the Court's orientation has been one of applying traditional notions of contractual obligations, or more accurately, the limits thereof, it is safe to assume that where the parties to a collective bargaining agreement expressly make provision in their agreement for the event of succession, the Court will allow the parties' contractual resolution to control. Thus, a union that wants to assure its members of the benefits of the bargain for the full period of the agreement might attempt to provide protection by insisting that the collective agreement state that it is binding on the successors of the employer as well as upon the actual party signing the document.

Of course, even such a successorship clause probably would not have saved the Wackenhut agreement for the United Plant Guards inasmuch as the Court would likely reject the notion that Wackenhut had the power to tie the hands of its competitor, absent some direct transfer of corporate stock or property between them. That exception aside, though, by writing a successorship clause into the collective agreement, a union would have cause to expect that it could save itself from any uncertainty created by the Court's opinion in *Burns*. Even if the courts were to decide not to enforce the clause by making the collective agreement enforceable against the successor, such a clause should, at the very least, provide the union with a basis for suing the predecessor for any damages suffered as a result of the successor's failure to honor the collective agreement.

By the same device of a specific clause in the collective bargaining agreement covering succession, the current employer can assure that the agreement will be binding on the union in relation to any successor of the employer, thereby enabling the current employer to negotiate with a potential successor using as a selling point any beneficial aspects of the collective agreement (that is, beneficial from the employer's viewpoint).

And, of course, should the Supreme Court ultimately decide that *Burns* is the exceptional situation, that in the more common forms of employer turnover the successor will be bound by the collective agreement entered into by the prior owner, then, too, it can be anticipated that the parties will nevertheless still have the power to avoid the impact of the Court's rule by contractually providing for the agreement to terminate and cease to be binding upon the change of the employer's identity. Accordingly, the choices to be made by the Supreme Court in refining the rules announced in *Burns* will likely govern only those situations in which there are no provisions in the collective agreement regarding the issue of whether the contractual rights and obligations of that agreement are to continue in effect in the event of employer turnover.

Inasmuch as the Supreme Court's rule concerning successorship will govern the parties' rights and obligations absent a special contractual provision, that determination will at the very least affect the parties' bargaining position concerning this issue. For example, should *Burns* prove to be the exception, then an employer who wishes to contractually avoid this result will have to offer the union something in return. Alternatively, if the Court decides that the *Burns* result is equally applicable to other forms of employer turnover, then a union that wants to be assured of the continued viability of the collective agreement, irrespective of employer turnover, will have to offer the current employer something in exchange for that sort of contractual variation from the norm established by the Court's ruling. Thus, whichever way the Supreme Court eventually resolves the questions left open by the *Burns* case, its decision will have a direct impact on the respective bargaining power and burdens of parties negotiating collective agreements.

In addition to the questions left unresolved by *Burns* is the question of the extent to which the *Burns* decision may have reopened the issue previously decided in *Wiley*. After the *Burns* case was decided, some observers suggested that despite the Court's express effort to distinguish the *Wiley* decision, there was too much inconsistency between the principles underlying the two opinions to support *Wiley's* continued viability. A test of this contention came before the Court in *Howard Johnson Company, Inc.* v. *Detroit Local Joint Executive Board,* 417 U.S. 249 (1974).

Prior to June 1972, the Grissom family employed 53 persons in connection with a motel and restaurant that it operated pursuant to a franchise agreement with the Howard Johnson Company. On June 16, 1972, the Grissoms entered into an agreement to sell to Howard Johnson Co., Inc., all of the personal property used in connection with operating the motel and restaurant and to lease the underlying land to Howard Johnson. The latter expressly disclaimed all obligations respecting any labor agreements between the Grissoms and any labor organization. Howard Johnson Co., Inc., then proceeded to hire and train its own work force. It hired forty-five employees, only nine of whom had worked for the Grissoms.

The union thereafter brought a suit to require Howard Johnson to arbitrate with it under the labor agreement with the Grissoms the union arguing that Howard Johnson's failure to hire all of the former workers constituted a lockout in violation of that collective agreement. The suit was brought against both the Grissoms and Howard Johnson. With respect to the obligation of the latter, the union relied in part on the fact that the collective agreement explicitly provided that successors of the Grissoms would be bound. The lower federal courts, relying on *Wiley*, held that *Howard Johnson* was required to arbitrate. The Supreme Court reversed with Mr. Justice Marshall presenting the Opinon of the Court.

Neither *Burns* nor *Wiley* supported the result below, stated Justice Marshall. Whereas *Wiley* involved a merger, with the resulting disappearance of the predecessor employer, Marshall explained, the present case involved "only a sale of some assets" with the prior employer remaining in existence enriched by the income from the sale and lease to Howard Johnson. Moreover, Marshall observed, unlike *Wiley*, Howard Johnson had hired few of the seller's employees. Accordingly it could not be said that there was a substantial continuity of identity in the business of Howard Johnson with that of the Grissoms. In this regard the Court noted that it would be an unfair labor practice for Howard

Johnson to refuse to hire the former Grissom employees in order to avoid recognizing the union or in order to avoid having workers who are union members. But the Court stated that there was "no suggestion in this case that Howard Johnson in any way discriminated in its hiring against the former Grissom employees because of their union membership, activity, or representation."[28] Because of this lack of continuity of identity, the obligation to arbitrate found in *Wiley* was not applicable in this case.

Mr. Justice Marshall's opinion did not discuss the impact of the successor clause in the collective agreement. However, he pointed out that the Grissoms had conceded that they were compelled to arbitrate any union grievances arising out of the transfer of ownership, thereby implying that the union might be entitled to a remedy against the Grissoms due to their sale of the business to a party who disclaimed the labor agreement.

Justice Douglas filed a vigorous dissent. Under his analysis of the facts there was "a substantial continuity — indeed identity — of the business operation under Howard Johnson. . . ."[29] Mr. Justice Douglas found it most significant that the Grissoms had been a franchisee of Howard Johnson. He noted that that franchise agreement had provided Howard Johnson with authority to determine and approve standards of operation and service, and that Howard Johnson had a right of first refusal in the event of a sale of the business and was required to approve any successor. When it took over its franchisee's business, he concluded, Howard Johnson also took over the duty to arbitrate. "Any other result makes nonsense of the principles laid down in *Wiley*."[30] The majority's position, he asserted, gives the successor the ability to avoid all obligations under the collective agreement "by the simple expedient of arranging for the termination of all of the prior employer's personnel."[31]

There have been several successorship situations in which the NLRB has held the new employer guilty of unfair labor practices in systematically avoiding the seller's employees when hiring a work force. The remedy has included the obligation of hiring the predecessor's employees. Thus, it may not be quite as easy as Justice Douglas indicated for a successor to avoid the obligations of its predecessor's collective agreement. On the other hand, how come Howard Johnson did not hire a more substantial number of the experienced Grissom employees? The majority's opinion stated that there was "no suggestion" of discrimination against the Grissom employees because of the union activity. But did not the very pattern of Howard Johnson's conduct in explicitly disclaiming any obligations under the labor agreement and hiring so very few of the Grissom employees suggest a discriminatory purpose?

There are other possible explanations for a successor's failure to hire many of the predecessor's workers. For example, the successor might think that those employees are inept or dishonest. Obviously more than a pattern of conduct suggesting a design to avoid the obligations of a collective agreement is needed to persuade the Court that the successor must at least justify its failure to hire a substantial number of the experienced employees who worked for the seller.

Mr. Justice Marshall's opinion spoke, at one point, of the successor's "right to operate the enterprise with his own independent labor force."[32] Perhaps, when all is said and done it will be this last statement that will emerge as the key to the Court's judgment in *Howard Johnson*. And, perhaps, more and more, successor employers will avail themselves of that "right" so as to avoid the duty of bargaining with the union representing the predecessor's employees as well as avoid the collective agreement between the union and the precessor. Should this be the impact of the Court's opinions in *Burns* and *Howard Johnson*, then clearly the concern for preserving the ready transferability of capital will have prevailed over the concern for employment stability. The economic repercussions of such a policy choice likely will eventually be felt in the political arena. Ultimately, therefore, Congress may be asked to judge whether it wishes to reverse the Court's judgment on this issue.

7

The NLRB as Overseer of Personnel Arrangements

A principle often cited as permeating labor-management relations in the United States is self-determination. It is the operative guideline both with respect to the decision as to whether worker interests will be collectively represented and with respect to the resolution of terms and conditions of employment when the parties engage in collective bargaining. Accordingly, although the legislation in this area establishes procedural boundary lines for the negotiating process and for waging economic warfare, generally the National Labor Relations Act does not attempt to fix, or permit government interference with, the setting of the actual terms and conditions of work. But the Taft-Hartley amendments to the National Labor Relations Act did include some inroads upon the concept of self-determination with the result that the self-determination principle does not operate as an absolute rule.

Antifeatherbedding Provision

With respect to a number of areas, the statute does limit the terms and conditions of employment to which the parties can agree or assigns to the agency responsibility for occasionally resolving such matters. For example, Congress has made it an unfair labor practice to pressure an employer to pay for services that are not performed. This provision was designed to eliminate, at least in part, the so-called practice of "featherbedding" — that is, requiring an employer to pay wages for work which is not performed.[a]

The practice of featherbedding falls into several categories. At one extreme is the corruptly motivated collusion between management and union officials to place on the payroll persons designated by the union who perform no work. This sort of arrangement is a means of paying the union officials for illegal or improper services such as agreeing to a collective contract which accomplishes less for the employees than could have been obtained through rigorous negotiations. The nonworking "employees" might be close friends or relatives of the union officials or simply subordinates who "kick-back" all or most of these wages to the officials themselves. Similarly, the featherbedder can be a wholly fictitious person whose paycheck is given to and cashed by the union officer.

At the other extreme is the employee who performs work that his fellow

---

[a]Instead of working, the employees are able to stretch out on a feather bed.

employees think is important but the employer claims has no functional value to
the enterprise. The elevator operator assigned to a newly automated machine
but whose personality is enjoyed by those confined to the moving cubicle
several times a day might be an example of such a "feather bedding" situation.
The truck driver's helper whose main responsibility is to keep the driver awake
on long hauls is another example. Somewhere in between these extremes is the
job that produces no profit for the employer but that the union seeks to preserve in order to save a member from the unemployment rolls (or to keep a member on the dues-paying roll).

In 1946 Congress passed a very particularized antifeatherbedding statute,
the Lea Act, which made it a crime to coerce a broadcasting station to employ
persons whose services are no longer needed by the station. The statute was
clearly designed to combat efforts by the musicians' union to preserve broadcasting studio musicians' jobs whose positions were being displaced by improved
technology for sound recording and replay.

James C. Petrillo, President of the American Federation of Musicians, reportedly set out to test the new law's constitutionality by demanding that as a
condition of reaching agreement on a new collective agreement, a particular radio
station hire three new musicians. Petrillo was charged with criminal violations
under the Lea Act, and he defended himself by arguing that the prosecution had
to be dismissed because the statute was unconstitutional. Mr. Justice Black
wrote the opinion for a five judge majority which rejected Petrillo's challenge.[1]
Douglas did not participate in the decision and Reed wrote a dissent in which he
was joined by Justices Rutledge and Murphy.

The dissent is of particular interest here because it explored the difficulties
in ascertaining when a job preservation demand can truely be classified as
"featherbedding." Reed's opinion charged that the statute was unconstitutionally vague. How, he asked, is the jury to determine when the union's demands
are justified by the fact that a smaller number of employees are not capable of
performing a given task? If a union demands shorter hours, and thereby more
workers, can the jury find that such a demand against a broadcaster is unlawful?
In determining whether the union is demanding jobs for persons with no service
to perform, Mr. Justice Reed continued, is the demand to be weighed on the
basis of management skill or employee performance? In other words, what is
the legal effect upon the union demand where the employee's lack of value is
due to managerial ineptitude rather than due to an inherent lack of value in
having the additional worker. Some managers no doubt are more skilled than
others in organizing employees to be productive. Skilled management of such
variables as the division of labor, job training, job direction, production mix,
and production goals might turn unproductive workers into productive ones.
Accordingly, Reed concluded, the Lea Act is without standards having the constitutionally required degree of precision.

This challenge, posed by Reed's dissenting opinion, was avoided rather than answered by the majority in *Petrillo*. Mr. Justice Black explained that at the procedural stage of the constitutional challenge that was before the Court, the specifications of the charges could still be amended and the pleadings and proof could later narrow the issue with sufficient precision so as to avoid the constitutional issue of vagueness. Accordingly, Black concluded that the statute was not overly vague on its face and the case was returned to the lower court for further proceedings. (It is interesting to note that in later years, when confronted with a statute challenged as deterring the exercise of civil liberties because of lack of precision in defining the prohibited conduct, Mr. Justice Black could normally be counted on to cast his vote with those who would strike down the law for excessive vagueness.) Petrillo was subsequently tried and acquitted on the grounds that there was no proof that he knew that the radio station in question had no need for three additional musicians.

Not long after the adoption of the Lea Act, Congress passed the Taft-Hartley Act amendments to the National Labor Relations Act. The amendments added a provision making it an unfair labor practice to require an employer to pay for services which are not performed. Within a few years the Court had to resolve the question of whether this prohibition reached all featherbedding activities or just some. It dealt with this issue through two cases. In both cases, the NLRB had concluded that the union demands in question were not unfair labor practices and in both cases the board's decision was upheld by a divided Supreme Court.

One of these cases, *American Newspaper Publishers* v. *National Labor Relations Board*, 345 U.S. 100 (1953), involved a challenge, under the NLRA's anti-featherbedding provision, to the legality of the newspaper typographical workers' insistence on the "right" to set so-called bogus type. This practice stemmed from the union's efforts to preserve job oppotunities for typesetters and compositors against the tide of technological change that for over half a century had been threatening to displace many of their job skills with increasingly more efficient equipment. One concession won by the union was the right of compositors to set type for local advertising mats even though the mats used for printing the newspaper had been previously set by a more efficient duplicating technique.

The court's opinion noted that the cost of this bogus work for the Chicago Herald-American was about $50,000 a year and for the New York Times about $150,000 per year. The majority of the Supreme Court held, however, that the union's insistence on continuing the practice of setting bogus type for local advertising did not conflict with the antifeatherbedding provision of the National Labor Relations Act. The Court's conclusion was based in part on the history of the legislation in relation to the *Petrillo* case.

One of the arguments raised concerning the Lea Act, as we have seen, was that it created excessive discretion on the part of the prosecutor and jury with respect to how many employees is too much and as to what number is reasonable for performing a particular task. In examining the typographical case, the Court explained that when Congress wrote the Taft-Hartley antifeatherbedding pro-vision, the bill's sponsors intended to avoid the prospect of a *Petrillo* type challenge being made to the effect that their proposal gave too much discretion to the NLRB with regard to when the work force size has gone beyond what is permissible. Accordingly, the Court explained, Congress intended to confine the antifeatherbedding provision of the National Labor Relations Act to those situations in which payment is demanded though no service at all has been or will be rendered. For this reason, held the Court, the conduct of the type-setters and compositors' union did not violate the Act inasmuch as they intended to perform the work of setting the bogus type in exchange for the compensation sought.

In the companion case, *National Labor Relations Board* v. *Gamble Enter-prises, Inc.*, 345 U.S. 117 (1953), the Court ruled that it was not a violation of the antifeatherbedding provision of the NLRA for the musicians' union to insist that theatres using live musical performances employ a minimum number of musicians. The Court explained that the musicians' union, according to the NLRB's findings of fact, had proposed a variety of ways in which those musicians, whom the employers claimed were in excess of the show's needs, could be usefully utilized. Accordingly, the Court held, the musicians were demanding paid work, not pay for no work, and therefore their demands were not an unfair labor practice under the National Labor Relations Act.

Mr. Justice Douglas concurred with the Court's result respecting the musi-cians but not with regard to the typesetters and compositors. The distinction, as he saw it, was that the musicians' work has some potential utility, though per-haps not enough to always make their employment profitable to the employer. In contrast, he argued, the setting of bogus type has no usefulness whatsoever. Congress, he asserted, intended to prohibit the demand for compensation without giving a service in return. When the work performed has no utility, then it is not a service performed for the employer under the meaning of the statute.

Mr. Justice Jackson's analysis led him to the opposite result from Mr. Justice Douglas. Jackson accepted the lawfullness of the demand for bogus type setting work and explained his conclusion on the basis that this was an ancient practice that had become part of the industry's operations. The musicians' demand, however, was a new device for securing compensation to do unwanted work and therefore, Jackson asserted, it violated the intent of the antifeatherbedding clause.

Chief Justice Vinson and Mr. Justice Clark rejected the majority position with respect to both the typesetters and the musicians, accusing the Court of twisting "the law by the tail." For them the test of featherbedding under the Act is whether the employer wants or needs the employees. While recognizing that their interpretation would place a very difficult judgment upon the NLRB in particular cases, they could find no such difficulty involved in the situations at issue.

After the above two decisions, the antifeatherbedding provision of the NLRB seemed headed for the scrap heap. It was another twenty years before such charges were to advance far enough to even require an NLRB decision.[b] Although it is possible that this signifies that the Act has effectively deterred unions from pressing featherbedding demands, it is equally possible to conclude that this signifies that the Court's ruling in *Gamble* and *American Newspaper Publishers* stripped any meaningful dimension from the provision's protective effect. In this connection, some consideration should be given to the fact that within a decade after these two decisions, theatre entertainment involving live musical groups declined almost to the point of novelty and there was a most substantial withering of the newspaper industry both in terms of numbers of papers and the financial stability of the survivors. In each instance, much of the cause has been attributed by management to the uneconomical work rules imposed by union demands. There is considerable credibility to this assertion that the unions eventually deprived their members of jobs by insisting on the perpetuation and even extention of featherbedding practices. On the other hand, in both situations the competitive impact of the growth of the television industry undoubtably also did considerable damage.

Machinery for Resolving Jurisdictional Disputes

In a prior discussion, we have characterized American labor relations law as a Code of Conduct intended to reduce the casualty count in labor-management conflicts while, at the same time, permitting the parties to flex and use economic muscle in seeking mutually acceptable accords. To carry the rules of combat analogy just a bit further, this Code of Conduct recognizes the presence of neutrals and offers them some special protection from lethal fallouts. But the analogy to the battlefield ends here because in labor warfare a party who is a combatant with regard to one aspect of interaction may be a neutral with respect to other dimensions. Thus, an enterprise will sometimes find itself unwillingly caught in the midst of an open conflict amongst competing unions or clashing groups of employees. Sections 8(b)(4)(D) and 10(k) of the National Labor Relations Act, which were added by the Taft-Hartley amendments to the Act, are designed to provide a rescue mission for employers caught in the middle of that form of interunion or interemployee struggle known as "jurisdictional

---

[b]See the Developing Labor Law at 692 (C. Morris ed. 1971). In 1973, in two cases, the NLRB adopted Administrative Law Judges' findings of featherbedding violations. The union did not seek the board's review in one case (*International Longshoremen's and Warehousemen's Union, Local 91*), and the Board affirmed in the other [*Metallic Lathers Union of New York and Vicinity*, 207 NLRB 631 (1973)].

disputes."[c] These provisions are also designed to help the disputing parties disengage from this form of internecine combat.

As described in an earlier chapter, "jurisdictional disputes" can involve two types of questions: (1) which union is entitled to represent workers doing particular work, and (2) which workers are entitled to do particular work. To illustrate, suppose that an enterprise manufactures sliding doors and that its employees are represented by two different unions; one union is the spokesman of the production workers while the other bargains on behalf of the machinists – a group of skilled, specially trained employees responsible for repairing, maintaining, and resetting and recalibrating the production equipment. Let us further assume that the employer buys a new, highly automated piece of production equipment that recalibrates and resets itself upon the press of a button. Finally, let us assume that this machine requires a single operator whereas the equipment it replaced was operated by four persons. Accordingly, this new machine is displacing some of the work previously performed by machinists and other work previously performed by production personnel. Who should operate the new machine, a former production worker or a machinist? Moreover, which union should represent the person awarded the job of operating this new machine, the production workers' union or the machinists' union? If the unions cannot agree respecting the first of these questions, they have a jurisdictional dispute over a work assignment; if they cannot agree respecting the second question, they have a jurisdictional dispute over representation. It takes little imagination to anticipate that the unions might not be able to agree on the answer to either of these questions and thus will have a jurisdictional dispute of a dual nature. Such jurisdictional disputes often are highly charged matters. They reflect a tendancy of American workers to feel and assert a proprietary interest in their job responsibilities.

For years the labor federations struggled rather unsuccessfully with the problem created by jurisdictional disputes. Efforts by these federations of unions to bring peace in such situations met with some success but were too often frustrated by power politics set in motion by the competing vested interests of the component unions constituting the federations. Moreover, there were two major contending labor union federations during much of the period preceding the Taft-Hartley amendments to the National Labor Relations Act, and considerable jurisdictional rivalry existed between the two federations. Thus, in one highly publicized conflict, carpenters and teamsters belonging to the American Federation of Labor refused to handle the products of seven large sawmills in Oregon whose workers were represented by a union belonging

---

[c]Some types of jurisdictional disputes can be resolved by the NLRB through the unit clarification procedure. The board's power as to such matters arises under section 9 of the Act, not under the provisions cited in the preceding text.

to the Congress of Industrial Organizations. In retaliation, the CIO-affiliated longshoremen refused to handle the products of those mills that were organized by AFL affiliates. This stand-off lasted for three months and caused considerable economic dislocation in Oregon, a state in which the lumber industry has a significant financial impact.

Prior to Taft-Hartley, the National Labor Relations Board kept out of such disputes on the grounds that jurisdictional differences are best solved by the parties themselves. Thus, in *Axton-Fisher Tobacco Company*, a case found in the first volume of the Labor Board's reports, the agency refused to determine whether those who repaired machines on the production lines, as contrasted with those who repaired them in the machine shop, were properly encompassed by the union certified to represent the machinists or by the union certified as the representative of production workers. In an early comment on the board's attitude in this area, Louis Jaffe noted: "It is basic to our liberalistic philosophy that it is worth paying high to allow a maximum of self-government."[2] Nevertheless, he went on to observe that the history of such jurisdictional conflicts indicated that too often the self-governing machinery was incapable of functioning with regard to these issues.

Accordingly, although jurisdictional disputes accounted for but a small portion of lost work days, those intent on imposing legal constraints upon all facets of labor union activity found in such conflicts a convenient focus of attack in the lobbying efforts leading up to the Taft-Hartley amendments. Even President Truman, who opposed much of the Taft-Hartley changes, supported the idea of imposing a final resolution of jurisdictional disputes upon those who failed to reach a voluntary settlement.

As previously stated, Congress adopted two provisions in 1947 designed to deal with jurisdictional disputes. Section 8(b)(4)(D) copes with the problem by making it an unfair labor practice for a union to coerce an employer into assigning particular work to a particular group of employees or to the members of a particular bargaining unit. And section 10(k) establishes a special procedure giving the Board power to determine which group of employees or which bargaining unit in question is entitled to the disputed work. Under this provision, the parties can avoid the board's authority over such questions by themselves agreeing upon a binding method for adjusting their jurisdictional conflict.

The scheme of dismissing disputes if the parties agree upon a means of voluntary settlement is a unique feature in the Labor Act. It is true, of course, that unfair labor practice proceedings are frequently dismissed because of a private adjustment of the dispute. In such situations, however, the dismissal is discretionary with the Regional Director of the NLRB who must decide whether dismissal serves the public interest. Section 10(k), on the other hand, makes dismissal of the unfair labor practice mandatory if, within ten days after the charge has been filed, the conflict is settled by, or scheduled to be settled by, some form of binding adjustment. In effect, then, Congress has deemed it to always be in the public interest for such matters to be resolved by private machinery if that is possible.

Another aspect of this procedural requirement is to place all of the regulatory emphasis upon preventing *future* strife due to differences over union and work jurisdiction. The focus is upon the parties finding a means of adjusting their dispute or being faced with a resolution imposed by the NLRB. Curing of damage caused by past misconduct involving such conflicts is removed from the board's remedial consideration in such cases. That is not to say that Congress has not provided a remedy for such past damage. It is possible to secure a remedy for the damage caused by such past misconduct by bringing an independent private suit under a wholly separate provision of the Taft-Hartley Act, section 303. And it was with respect to the interaction of section 303 with the NLRB's responsibilities under the Act that the first case involving a jurisdictional dispute found its way to the Supreme Court.

The case referred to, *International Longshoremen's & Warehousemen's Union* v. *Juneau Spruce Corp.*, 342 U.S. 237 (1952), involved a suit by a lumber milling company against a union whose members refused to unload the company's barges because the company used nonunion personnel to load the barges at its mill. This suit was brought under section 303 of the Labor-Management Relations Act on the basis that the union's refusal to work the barges constituted an unlawful attempt to force the company to assign the loading work to a group having no enforceable claim to that work. In addition to bringing this suit, the company filed charges with the National Labor Relations Board and asserted that the union was engaging in unlawful coercion in connection with a jurisdictional dispute.

The NLRB determined that the union was not entitled to the disputed work. Thereafter the section 303 suit went to trial. At that trial, the union contended that damages could be assessed only with respect to its activities subsequent to the NLRB's resolution of the dispute in the 10(k) proceeding. The trial court, however, allowed the jury to assess damages from the onset of the union's jurisdictional pressure tactics and the jury returned a verdict for the company in the amount of $750,000 plus costs. That judgment was upheld by both the U.S. Court of Appeals and by the Supreme Court.

Two independent forms of remedy are provided in jurisdictional disputes, explained the Court. An administrative remedy is provided through the NLRB's 10 (k) and unfair labor practice proceedings in the form of a cease and desist order, whereas a judicial remedy in the form of monetary damages is provided through a section 303 suit in federal district court. "The fact that the two sections have an identity of language and yet specify two different remedies is strong confirmation of our conclusion that the remedies provided were to be independent of each other."[3] Quoting from Senator Taft, the Court further pointed out that although the administrative remedy was added to the law by the Taft-Hartley Act, the section 303 damages provision was a retention of an existing common-law right of employers to sue unions for injury caused by a jurisdictional strike. Thus, the Court's decision left an employer with two means of combatting union coercion in jurisdictional controversies: a threat to sue for damages, plus an administrative resolution of rights together with a cease and desist order against coercive conduct on the part of a union having no lawful claim to the disputed work.

Although the Labor-Management Relations Act created a new role for the NLRB in combatting jurisdictional disputes, the agency proved to be a reluctant recipient of the section 10(k) peace-making authority over these matters. It construed its responsibility as being limited to determining whether the juris-dictional demands being charged as unfair conduct were in fact unsupported by either a prior NLRB unit certification (issued in conjunction with a union election victory) or a collective bargaining agreement provision describing the recognized unit as being represented by the union being charged. If the board decided that the certification or the collective agreement supported the accused union's jurisdictional claim, then it dismissed the charge; if it found no such support for the jurisdictional claim, then it issued a determination that the accused union was not entitled to the work. But the latter determination did not necessarily mean that the competing union assigned the work by the em-ployer was entitled to it. This issue was left in the air by the board, which declined to make an affirmative award of the disputed work to one of the com-peting unions.

The board's post-Taft-Hartley policy respecting jurisdictional proceedings was well illustrated in *National Labor Relations Board* v. *Radio and Television Broadcast Engineers Union*, 364 U.S. 573 (1961), (generally known as the *CBS* case). There, charges were filed by Columbia Broadcasting System, the employ-ing television network, against a technicians' union whose members refused to operate TV cameras. This refusal was in protest against the network's assign-ment of certain lighting work to stagehands rather than to technicians. These two groups—the technicians and the stagehands—had for several years been waging running warfare over the right to operate the electric lighting equipment for various forms of broadcasts. CBS was unsuccessful in its effort to keep both sides happy by dividing the work between them.

When the NLRB made its determination respecting the technicians' right to the disputed work, it focused its attention solely on the scope of the union's certification as a bargaining agent and the scope of the employer's recognition of the union as contained in the collective agreement. The board refused to consider any facts reflecting upon the respective merits of the technicians' verses the stagehands' claim to the work and refused to issue an award of the lighting work to any particular group of employees. Finding no support for the technicians' claim in either the collective agreement or the technicians' unit certification, the board determined that the technicians' union was not entitled to the lighting work.

The effect of the board's approach, as described above, was to make the employer's work assignment decisive—that is, unless the union charged with unfair conduct in support of its work assignment claim could find support in either the board's certification of its authority as bargaining agent or in the employer's expressed recognition of the union as bargaining agent, a cease and desist order would be issued against the union. Thus, absent such clear administrative or contractual basis for a particular union's claim, the employer's work assignment would govern situations involving ambiguous union jurisdiction. It is understandable that unions would be less than satisfied with this state of affiars.

Employers, too, had cause for dissatisfaction with the board's approach inasmuch as it left open the question of the ultimate merits of a group's claim to particular work. As a result, the employer could anticipate, and CBS experienced, a continuing series of outbreaks of self-help efforts by the rival labor groups, with each determined to vindicate its "rightful" claim to the work.

The technicians' union refused to obey the board's order in the *CBS* case by arguing that the order was defective because the union was not given a chance to establish that it had the more meritorious claim to the work and because the board failed to issue a determinitive award of the disputed work. The NLRB petitioned the United States Court of Appeals for the Second Circuit in seeking a court order enforcing its decision. The Second Circuit, however, agreed with the union's contentions and therefore refused to grant the requested order. Two other Circuits had previously reached the same conclusion but still another Court of Appeals, subsequent to the Second Circuit's decision, resolved the question in favor of the board. Accordingly, the agency's decision predictably would or would not receive judicial support, depending upon which federal appellate court received jurisdiction to review the board's determination in such a proceeding. With the issue in this posture there was clear need for a definitive resolution of the question by the Supreme Court. Absent the high court's decision, what was intended to be a single national law regulating labor-management relations was functionally two different laws fragmented along the regional boundaries demarking the various federal apellate circuits.

A unanimous Supreme Court ruled in favor of requiring the NLRB to go beyond its practice of issuing limited determinations in jurisdictional disputes. The statutory requirement that the Board "hear and determine the dispute," held the Court, conveys "not only the idea of hearing but also the idea of deciding a controversy."[4] The Court explained that this meant that in order to quiet the underlying quarrel between the conflicting labor groups, Congress expected the board to end the uncertainty by deciding which group is entitled to the work.

It is often asserted that governmental bodies tend to expand their jurisdiction whenever possible. If this is so, why was it necessary to the Supreme Court to, in effect, order the NLRB to play a more expansive role in an area over which it had been given apparent statutory authority? The answer might be found in the fact that the jurisdictional dispute procedure places the board in a very different sort of decision-making role than it usually exercises under the Act.

In deciding bargaining unit and unfair labor practice questions, the NLRB normally shapes the labor-management relationship with regard to collective activities. However, when it decides the merits of a jurisdictional controversy, as in *CBS*, the Board is faced with making a personnel determination on behalf of the parties. In arguing its position before the Supreme Court, the NLRB suggested that out labor relations laws were drafted with a presumption that certain managerial decisions belong solely to management and that consistent with that presumption it is the employer, not the board, who has the ultimate say as to whom to hire and what work the employees should perform. The board's lawyers, arguing before the Court, noted, too, that Congress gave no standards in the Act to guide the agency in making a substitution of its judgment for the employer's regarding work assignments.

Responding to this line of argument, the Court reassured the board of its competence to handle such matters by stating: "[A] dministrative agencies are frequently given rather loosely defined powers to cope with problems as difficult as those posed by jurisdictional disputes and strikes."[5] Beyond its own experience, suggested the Court, the NLRB can find the necessary guidance in the standards used by labor arbitrators, unions, and employers in settling such conflicts when such matters are adjusted by private machinery. Moreover, the Court dismissed the board's solicitude for management's prerogative to regulate its work force by noting that most of these cases reach the agency for the very reason that without government intervention the employer will likely not be able to exercise the very choice with which the board does not want to interfere.

Still another contention of the NLRB for resisting the demand that it affirmatively award the disputed work was that its policy had promoted private settlement of jurisdictional disputes and that such private adjustment of differences was to be preferred over governmentally imposed solutions. In support of this argument, the board cited to the fact that of the over 1,100 jurisdictional dispute cases initiated between 1947 and 1959, only 95 required board action in a 10(k) determination. In the rest, either the charges were withdrawn or the parties agreed on a private means of adjustment which thereby resulted in dismissal of the charge. If the board began issuing affirmative awards of disputed work, insisted its lawyers, many more parties would select NLRB resolution rather than find a private means for adjustment.

The Court's answer was to the effect that Congress had already weighed that possibility and had resolved it by imposing this additional function on the board. It is interesting to note that the board's prediction of less frequent resort to private adjustment machinery in jurisdictional disputes has proved accurate, although that increase has not been especially dramatic and has not overwhelmed the agency. Whereas the portion of such disputes actually going to the board for determination in the 1947-59 period was about 9 percent, the portion for the three year period of 1968-70 had increased to about 15 percent.

Critics of the Labor Board have asserted that in carrying out the responsibility for adjusting disputed work assignments, the board has followed a practice of giving almost total deference to the employer's preference—that is, they claim that the agency continues to be governed by its stated assumption in the *CBS* case that work assignments are properly a prerogative of management. The board has denied that it gives undue weight to the employer's preference in work assignment determinations. However, surveys of its decisions in this area show that in a very substantial majority of situations, the board's analysis of the merits has supported the employer's assignment of the disputed work.

As previously explained, a jurisdictional dispute brought under section 10(k) of the Act must be dismissed if within ten days the parties have agreed to resolve the conflict by means of their own adjustment machinery. The statute, however, does not spell out who are the "parties" to the dispute. Arguably the "parties" are the competing labor groups. Alternatively, the parties are those labor groups plus any employer or employers caught in the midst of the jurisdictional battle. This question was not authoritatively resolved by the United States Supreme Court until 1971 when a unanimous Court decided *National Labor Relations Board* v. *Plasterers' Local Union No. 79*, 404 U.S. 116 (1971), in favor of the second definition.

In the previously mentioned case, two employers in the business of laying title and terrazzo were picketed by a plasterers' union because the tile companies employed members of a tile setters' union to apply mortar and plaster bases on which the tile was laid. This work, claimed the plasterers, properly belonged to their trade. They had previously brought their claim to the National Joint Board for the Settlement of Jurisdictional Disputes and had prevailed except to the extent that the Joint Board awarded to the tile setters that laying of material which was to take place on the same day as the setting of the tile.

This Joint Board had been established in 1948 under an agreement between the American Federation of Labor and several national associations representing employers in the building and construction industry. Pursuant to the AFL-CIO constitution, the two unions were bound by the Joint Board's determination. Under the Joint Board arrangement, the employers could have participated in the dispute resolution procedure. However, in these particular cases, the employers had not bound themselves to taking such matters before the Joint Board and, in fact, did not participate in the Joint Board's process.

When the tile setters did the disputed work in violation of the Joint Board's award (though, in conformance with their collective agreements with these employers) and the plasterers picketed the job sites in protest of this violation, the employers filed charges against the plasterers thus initiating a 10(k) proceeding.

The plasterers contended that the NLRB was compelled to dismiss the unfair labor practice charges filed by the employers and dismiss the 10(k) proceeding. The plasterers' union argued that the Joint Board's determination of the dispute was a private adjustment by the parties and that since its action was consistent with that adjustment, its picketing activity was not an unfair labor practice. In effect, it argued that the work belonged to it under the Joint Board award and that it was, therefore, lawfully free to use picketing, boycotts, strikes, and the like, to force the employer and the tile setters' union to abide by that award. This position was rejected by the NLRB on the grounds that although employers are permitted to be parties to Joint Board determinations, in these cases the employers had not agreed to abide by such adjustment machinery and, therefore, the Joint Board's decision did not constitute a bar to the 10(k) determination. In other words, the private adjustment machinery did not include all of the "parties" and, hence, did not constitute an award that could be recognized under 10(k).

Accordingly, the NLRB proceeded to examine the jurisdictional controversy. To the plasterers' chagrin, after citing to such factors as the collective agreement between the employers and the tile setters, the ability of the tile setters to handle this work skillfully and efficiently, and to past practices of these employers and of the industry, the Board declined to follow the decision of the National Joint Board for the Settlement of Jurisdictional Disputes. Instead, it awarded all of the disputed work to the tile setters.

The plasterers' union refused to abide by the NLRB's decision. It appealed to the appellate court and the agency cross-petitioned, thereby requesting an order enforcing the Board's determination of the dispute. The plasterers triumphed in the U.S. Court of Appeals only to have their victory reversed by the Supreme Court of the United States.

A key argument supporting the plasterers' position was that in the *CBS* case the Court had emphasized the neutrality of employers in jurisdictional disputes. If the employer is neutral, argued the plasterers, then the employer is not a necessary party to the dispute resolution machinery. Presenting the Opinion of the Court, Mr. Justice White noted that although employers who are caught in the midst of a jurisdictional dispute often have no interest in the outcome other than that it be promptly made, at other times the outcome carries considerable economic consequences for the employer. In the instant situation, he stated, the record established that a victory for the plasterers meant both a substantial increase in costs to the tile and terrazzo companies, as well as potential loss of business to plastering contractors. The Court asserted that the ordinary meaning of the term "the parties to the dispute," as used in section 10(k), includes the employer inasmuch as management has material interests at stake. "It would . . . be myopic," stated Justice White, "to transform a procedure that was meant to protect employer interests into a device that could injure them."[6] And, White added, the *CBS* decision was not inconsistent with this conclusion. *CBS*, he pointed out, was a case in which the employer had no quarrel with either possible award since it had contracts with both unions and both groups of workers could do the disputed work with equal skill and efficiency. Hence, in that case the Court was not concerned with the instant issue regarding the affect of a private resolution in which the employer had not participated.

Among the other arguments posed by the plasterers was the assertion that by requiring the NLRB to recognize the Joint Board's resolution, even absent the employer's participation in that private adjustment proceeding, employers would feel a greater sense of compulsion to participate in such proceedings. This, in turn, would further the Congressional policy of promoting private resolution of such disputes by the parties themselves. A number of commentators had expressed support for this position. Rejecting this argument, Mr. Justice White stated that although the Court recognizes a policy of promoting private settlement of labor disputes, voluntariness is a central characteristic of such favored private dispute settlement mechanisms. "[W]e decline," he said, "to narrow the Board's powers under § 10(k) so that employers are coerced to accept compulsory private arbitration when Congress has declined to adopt such a policy."[7] The latter reference was to a proposal strenuously supported by Senator Wayne Morse during the consideration of the Taft-Hartley legislation dealing with jurisdictional disputes, a proposal which eventually was rejected by Congress.

Contractual Arrangements to Promote Union Membership

As described earlier, when the 1947 Labor-Management Relations Act version of the National Labor Relations Act was adopted, it was widely hailed by conservatives and employers as a reasonable and long overdue adjustment that brought a measure of balance and equity to the nation's labor laws. Liberals and unions were equally emphatic in their condemnation of the new law as a tool designed to repress and destroy the American Labor movement.

A characteristic feature of Taft-Hartley, cited by unions as proof of their contention, was the outlawing of the closed shop. A closed shop is an arrangement between a union and an employer under which the employer agrees to hire union members only (often with the added stipulation that management will confine its hiring to those union members referred to it by the union). This latter feature is called a union hiring hall. Under this arrangement, the union provides a job referral service—the hiring hall—for its members, and the employer agrees to do its recruiting exclusively from the union referrals.

Sections 8(a)(3) and 8(b)(2) of the NLRA, as revised by Taft-Hartley, prohibit an employer from refusing to hire because the applicant either is or is not a union member. It does, however, permit the union and employer to enter into an arrangement requiring the worker to become a union member after thirty days of employment.[d] This provision clearly outlaws the closed shop and the use of those hiring halls that are available to union members only. This change in the law was justified by Taft-Hartley supporters as an appropriate protection (and, if anything, an insufficiently rigorous protection) of the worker's freedom of association. It was further justified as a necessary check upon overbearing union conduct and dangerous growth of monopolistic union control over the work force. Unions, on the other hand, insisted that elimination of the closed shop was nothing less than a strategy to destroy union activity in a variety of industries in which that form of union security was a structural necessity for union survival.

The union's case in support of the closed shop rested largely on two sorts of situations. One situation involves industries with rapid job turnover due to brief job duration. An example is found in the building construction industry where tradesmen such as electricians and plumbers often are needed on a project for no more than a few days or a few weeks. Similarly, the longshoring industry in the United States traditionally has hired its work gangs on a daily basis with the number hired depending on the cargo, number, and size of the ships in port on that day. Ships' crews are hired for longer durations but normally such hire is based on the length of the voyage. With modern technology, that period is frequently less than the thirty days established under the Taft-Hartley Act as the minimum time before an employee can be required to obtain membership. Under circumstances such as those just described, unions fear that many workers will try to avoid their collective responsibilities and that employers can easily take advantage of the situation to discourage and dissipate union support. For related reasons, unions assert that the closed shop is also necessary to provide a reasonable degree of job security and union security in those situations in which craftsmen are faced with rapid technological obsolescence. The printing industry provides a good example of this type of situation cited by unions as justifying the closed shop.

In the industries previously mentioned, as well as others, unions at various times have resorted to a variety of techniques to evade the restraints that Taft-Hartley placed upon the closed shop. One approach was to secure agreements from employers giving hiring preference to workers previously employed in the industry and to give that preference on a seniority basis. Where the industry had previously been thoroughly unionized, this had the effect of a "union members only" provision. Similarly, a maritime union obtained an agreement from the Pacific Shipowners' Association to give hiring preference to sailors with prior experience on their own vessels or with ships owned by other members of the association. Still another device, one used widely by the building and

---

[d]Pursuant to section 14(b) of the statute, such arrangements can be outlawed by state law.

construction unions, was to get the employers to limit hiring to certified crafts-men and apprentices having training in trade schools operated jointly by the employers and the unions. Finally, unions continued to enter into exclusive hiring hall agreements with employers and would give preferential treatment to their members in providing job referrals from the hiring hall.

Eventually, the building and construction unions were able to lobby some relief for themselves by securing a concession in the 1959 Landrum-Griffin amendments to the Labor Act that permits unions to enter into collective agree-ments covering such workers even though the union does not represent a majority of the employees when the agreement is executed. This modification further permits such agreements to require that building and construction workers become union members after seven days as contrasted with thirty days in all other industries.

With the rhetoric concerning closed shop and hiring hall arrangements that surrounded the debate over Taft-Hartley, it was not surprising that of the three cases involving charges against unions decided by the NLRB within the first year of the Act's passage, one case, *National Maritime Union*, 78 NLRB 971 (1948), resulted in an unfair labor practice finding based on the union's insistence upon retaining a hiring hall arrangement that gave favored treatment to union members.

The United States Supreme Court, on the other hand, did not review this aspect of the Taft-Hartley Act amendments until over a decade later. The even-tual vehicles for Supreme Court review were *Local 60, Carpenters* v. *National Labor Relations Board*, 365 U.S. 651 and *Local 371, IBT* v. *National Labor Relations Board*, 365 U.S. 667 (1961). Both cases involved union challenges to the NLRB's regulation of those hiring hall activities that the agency regarded as an evasion of the closed shop prohibition.

The first case, *Local 60*, did not challenge the board's finding of an unlaw-ful closed shop arrangement. That arrangement consisted of requiring the employer to hire exclusively from union referrals where in fact the union gave preference to its own local members in making such referrals. In issue, instead, was the agency's remedy requiring the union to reimburse the union dues paid by members starting six months prior to the filing of the unfair labor practice charge that led to the board's dissolution of this unlawful preferential hiring system. This remedy was rejected by a divided Supreme Court on the grounds that it was punitive, not remedial, and that the agency is empowered to remedy the victims of unlawful union conduct but not to punish the wrongdoers.

The Court's conclusion that the board's dues reimbursement order was punitive, was based upon the agency's failure to find that anyone had joined the union in order to get employment under the unlawful preferential hiring arrangement. So far as the record stood, there was no evidence to show that any union members first started paying dues within the period set by the board for reimbursement. Moreover, the Court emphasized that during all of this time for which the board sought dues reimbursement, the members were receiving services and other benefits from the union as a result of their dues payments.

The board lost the second case as well. In that situation a Teamsters local union had hiring hall arrangements that recognized seniority on an industrywide basis in giving hiring preference. The hiring hall provision, however, was expressly applicable irrespective of whether the job applicant was a union member. This arrangement was ruled unlawful by the NLRB even though the agency failed to find that the union discriminated against nonmembers in operating its hiring halls. Rather, the board applied a previously announced doctrine that it would treat hiring hall agreements as *per se* illegal unless certain precautions were taken to reduce the prospects for abuse. In addition to requiring that the arrangement expressly assures nondisciminatory referrals, the board required that the employer expressly retain the right to reject any person referred and that notices be posted informing job applicants of the hiring hall arrangements and of the safeguards against preferential treatment for union members. These precautionary steps had not been followed by the Teamsters local and a majority of the Supreme Court held that such precautionary steps could not be imposed by the NLRB.

In rejecting the board's view, the Supreme Court, in an opinion by Mr. Justice Douglas, noted that Senator Taft had been amongst those who, during the debates over the Taft-Hartley amendments, acknowledged that not all hiring hall practices were bad and that the hiring hall system did have a legitimate and valuable purpose in aiding job placement and promoting employment security. In light of such recognition of the legitimate role of hiring halls, the maority of the Court refused to allow inferences of improper conduct to be applied by the NLRB, especially in the presence of express guarantees in the hiring hall agreement against discrimination due to lack of union membership.

The Court majority did admit that the very existence of a hiring hall does encourage union membership. Nevertheless, Douglas explained, this alone is not enough to warrant the board's exercise of pervasive regulation of such institutions inasmuch as many other aspects of union-management relations equally encourage union membership. Thus, the very fact that a union has been recognized by an employer or that a union has obtained bargained benefits from the employer encourages employees to join the union. Yet, such common forms of employer "aid" to the union's status have not traditionally given rise to presumptions of unlawful conduct by the union or employer in participating in such processes.

Justices Harlen and Stewart, though joining the majority, issued a concurring opinion in which they emphasized the fact that the board had not presented evidence showing that the parties had entered into the hiring hall agreement because of a motivation of encouraging union membership. Because the hiring hall arrangement can readily be justified by substantial and legitimate employer and union considerations, they explained, it should be necessary for the agency to prove improper motive if the board is to be allowed to label the arrangement as an unfair labor practice.

Two members of the Court, however, saw considerable merit in the NLRB position. Justices Clark and Whittaker insisted that agency expertise, practical experience and common sense, supported the inferences drawn by the board with regard to the probable impact that the very existence of a hiring hall arrangement has upon substantially encouraging job applicants to join the union. Accordingly, they agreed with the board's insistence that unions and employers adopt the prescribed safeguards against the coercive implications inherent in such arrangements.

Divided Loyalties of Employees

Unlike some other nations' labor relations systems, American labor law generally draws a sharp line separating the statutory status of supervisory personnel from that of the so-called rank and file workers. The protections of the National Labor Relations Act do not extend to supervisory personnel. Nevertheless, section 14(a) of the Act explicitly permits supervisors to be union members. This does not mean that the employer must accede to the supervisor being a union member. The employer can discriminate against union members with respect to supervisory personnel because they are not "employees" as defined by the NLRA. Therefore, such discrimination is not an unfair labor practice. Similarly, there is nothing in the statutes requiring a union to accept supervisors as members. Thus, section 14(a) simply allows a supervisor to be a union member if the union accepts such members and if the supervisor's employer does not object. This is not to say that the section is without significance. Absent the express permission contained in section 14(a), it could be argued that union membership for managerial personnel constitutes unlawful assistance to a labor organization.

Supervisory personnel promoted from the ranks may have a variety of reasons for retaining their union membership. Occasionally it may be ideological. In other situations that membership may be the best means for obtaining particular financial benefits attached to union membership such as participation in a union sponsored low premium group life insurance or medical insurance program. Or union membership may provide access to certain discount retailing operations or consumer cooperatives. Some unions in large urban areas operate excellent moderate rent housing facilities. Some have attractive recreational facilities for members. In a few industries the principal private pension program available to workers is the program sponsored by the union for union members.

A key reason for the last situation is that in some industries employees are constantly changing their employer. In such situations pension and health insurance programs based upon employer contributions are very difficult to administer. Instead, the union operates the group benefit program. In such situations it is also common for the same person to work as a supervisor for one employer and in a nonsupervisory capacity for a different employer. Thus, the musician who books a band date will normally function as band leader for that job but will be just another hired musician the next night if the job has been booked by someone else. Similarly, in the building construction trades, a journeyman may work for one employer for a week or two as foreman and have a nonforeman's position with a different employer during the next few weeks. Indeed, it is not uncommon for such tradesmen to function as sub-contractors employing their fellow tradesmen for brief periods, while alternative-ly working in an employee capacity for other subcontractors when they do not have subcontracts of their own. Because the workers are frequently moving in and out of the supervisory, or even employer, positions, it is impractical to con-stantly resign and then renew union membership. Hence, such workers will for this reason, too, want to avail themselves of the permission granted by section 14(a) to retain their union membership irrespective of their current employ-ment status.

The supervisor-union member has potentially conflicting loyalties. The union insists that as a union member he has a responsibility to act in concert with his fellow members whereas the employer may insist that as a supervisor he has a responsibility to resist such concerted action. Likely because of that very conflict of interests, unions on occasion have attempted to compel employ-ers to select their supervisors solely from amongst union members and to require that foremen be union members.

The NLRB has treated efforts involving restrictions upon the group from which supervisors can be recruited as a violation of section 8(b)(1)(B) of the Act. That section makes it an unfair labor practice for a labor organization to restrain or coerce an employer "in the selection of his representatives for the purposes of collective bargaining or the adjustment of grievances."

In dealing with another situation, the NLRB ruled that section 8(b)(1)(B) prohibits a union from imposing fines or suspending or expelling supervisor-union members as a disciplinary sanction for assigning work in a manner that the union deemed to be contrary to the collective agreement. This board decision came to be known as the *Oakland Mailers* doctrine. The board also applied the *Oakland Mailers* doctrine to situations in which supervisor-union members were disciplined by the union for working during a strike.

The Supreme Court of the United States, however, dividing 5 to 4, rejected the Labor Board's extension of the *Oakland Mailers* doctrine in the last situation. Two cases served as the Supreme Court's vehicle for considering this issue which was decided under the heading *Florida Power & Light Co.* v. *International Brotherhood of Electrical Workers,* 417 U.S. 790 (1974).

A novel aspect of the first case involved in the *Florida Power & Light* decision was the fact that the employer, Illinois Bell Telephone Company, not only permitted all of its supervisors to be union members, it actually required union membership of its lower ranking supervisory personnel. The union's constitution provided for disciplinary action, including fines, to be imposed upon members committing any of twenty-three enumerated offenses. Working for an employer whom the union had "declared in difficulty" with the union was one such offense.

In 1968, in the course of negotiating a new collective agreement, the union engaged in a four-and-a-half-month strike against Illinois Bell Telephone. The employer informed its supervisors that it wanted them to come to work during the strike but that the choice was their's and that they would not be penalized for not working. The union, on the other hand, warned supervisor-members that they would be disciplined by the union if they worked during the strike. Some supervisor-members crossed union picket lines and were fined $500 each by the union for doing so. The majority of the NLRB held this to be a union unfair labor practice under section 8(b)(1)(B).

In the case involving Florida Power & Light Company the employer did not require any supervisors to be union members, but it did permit such membership. Moreover, it had a collective agreement with the union covering aspects of the terms and conditions for the employment of its lower level supervisors. On the other hand, the collective agreement expressly provided that supervisors were not to be "disciplined through union machinery for the acts they may have performed as supervisors acting in the Company's interests." Nevertheless, when supervisors crossed union picket lines during a strike, the union brought charges under its disciplinary procedure with the result that it expelled and imposed fines in amounts ranging from $100 to $6,000 on those supervisors who, in crossing the picket lines, engaged in nonsupervisory bargaining unit work. Charges were then filed with the NLRB, which held that the union's conduct violated section 8(b)(1)(B) of the National Labor Relations Act.

The majority of the Supreme Court, in explaining its rejection of the Labor Board's position, stated that Congress's concern in protecting employers from union interference with supervisory personnel had focused on two specific activities — collective bargaining and grievance adjustment. The Court concluded from this that "a union's discipline of one of its members who is a supervisory employee can constitute a violation of § 8(b)(1)(B) only when that discipline may adversely affect the supervisor's conduct in performing the duties of, and acting in his capacity as, grievance adjuster or collective bargainer . . . ."[8] Because the supervisors in question were not disciplined for activity related to either of these functions, the Court concluded that the disciplinary action was not in violation of the Labor Act.

The error of this conclusion, argued the dissent, is that the economic pressure created by supervisors performing bargaining unit work is part and parcel of the collective bargaining process. Thus, they explained, performing such work is a facet of representing the employer's collective bargaining interests. At the very least, argued Mr. Justice White's dissenting opinion, the Board's interpretation of the Labor Act was a reasonable reading of the statute and, therefore, it was inappropriate for the Court to act as a super-board by substituting one reasonable construction for another.

Florida Power & Light did not leave employers with a strict either-or choice of either allowing supervisors to be union members and suffer the loss of their "loyalty" during strikes, or prohibiting such membership and thereby penalize supervisors by depriving them of the various potential benefits of union membership. The alternative, noted the majority opinion, is to negotiate with the union for a provision exempting supervisor members from being disciplined for carrying out supervisory duties. This, indeed, is what Illinois Bell had done. But whether that exemption permitted its supervisors to engage in bargaining unit work during a strike was a matter of construing the collective agreement. Resolution of that issue of contractual interpretation, suggested the Court by way of a footnote, was a matter to be taken up through the grievance-arbitration machinery of the contract between the union and the employer, not by means of the unfair labor practice proceeding based on section 8(b)(1)(B).

Reviewing the four areas covered by the discussion in this chapter, we find a singular lack of pattern to either the Court's or the NLRB's policy choices. In all four situations, the Act arguably requires that the agency intervene in matters that affect working arrangements but also could be worked out by the parties at the bargaining table. At what might be called one extreme, the featherbedding situation, both the agency and the Court have given the statute a narrow reading, thereby returning the particular type of dispute back into the parties' hands. In the other three situations, jurisdictional disputes, hiring hall agreements and union disciplining of supervisor-members, the NLRB and the Supreme Court selected opposite policy alternatives. On the issue of jurisdictional disputes, the agency sought the narrower view of leaving the parties to suffer with or to work out arrangements themselves. The Court, however, insisted that the law required the NLRB to regulate such conflicts by itself adjusting the underlying controversy whenever the parties fail to rapidly agree upon their own adjustment machinery. On the hiring hall question, it was the Court that took the narrower, nonintervention (or, at least, reduced intervention) approach as contrasted with the NLRB's attempt to actively regulate this form of union-management arrangement for personnel recruitment. And in the situation involving union discipline of supervisor-members, the Court rejected the agency's effort to insulate the question from the bargaining process but instead, once again, left the issue to the parties' own processes for adjustment.

Clearly, the respective positions of the Court and the board on these questions suggests lack of merit to accusations that either of these decision making bodies is mastered by a pro-union or anti-union predilection nor is there evidence from the Court's track record that it has a pro-NLRB bias. Moreover, both the Court and the Board have at times taken a cautious view and at other times a generous view of the NLRB's capacity to serve as an active regulatory body in governing these aspects of the terms or conditions of employment. In light of the fact that the NLRB is selected and structured essentially to carry on the rule of an adjudicative body, as contrasted with a regulatory role, it is a bit surprising that the Court ever shapes decisions with a view toward the board being required to serve the regulatory type of function of overseeing the personnel arrangements contractually reached by the parties. Congress, however, has not yet balked at such interpretations of the NLRB's scope of responsibility and the Court's action may be reflecting a conviction, shared by some commentators in the labor relations field, that a more active regulatory sort of NLRB enforcement of national policy would have a beneficial impact upon labor-management relations.

8 Conclusion

When compared with the labor-management relations systems of other industrial nations, ours is characterized, amongst other ways, by the frequency and extent to which policy choices have been made and shaped by the judiciary. A similar observation can be made when comparing the field of labor-management relations with other areas of American law in which the public interest has been entrusted to administrative representation and in which enforcement takes place in the first instance at the level of an administrative tribunal.

Although the impact of the National Labor Relations Board's authority reaches a very considerable portion of the nation's business enterprises, the impact of other agencies such as the Federal Trade Commission, the Social Security Administration and the Internal Revenue Service is considerably more extensive. In like respect, the economic influence of policy choices made by agencies such as the Securities and Exchange Commission, the Internal Revenue Service, and the Federal Communications Commission is undoubtedly even more significant than is the impact of such choices made by the NLRB. And, although the number of cases annually handled by the NLRB is substantial, its docket is not as large as that administered by agencies such as the Social Security Administration and the Internal Revenue Service. Yet, judicial review of the NLRB's policy choices, and its application of settled rules of law, plays a far more significant role in the dockets of the federal courts than does review of the comparable actions of other federal agencies. Thus, in recent years, almost half of all cases heard by the U.S. Courts of Appeals involving review of federal agency decisions were cases that originated in the National Labor Relations Board. Similarly, typical of the relative role of NLRB cases in the Supreme Court's docket, in recent years, was the docket of the 1973-74 Term of Court when only tax cases as a category equalled the number of NLRB cases reviewed by the Court on the merits.

This pattern is not easily explained. Certainly, the high frequency of judicial review of NLRB decisions cannot be attributed to a deficiency in the quality of the agency's work relative to that of other federal agencies. Unlike most other federal agencies, the board has never been the subject of scandal involving a breach of duty, conflict of interest, or other indication of corruption. Although management representatives are frequently heard accusing the board of a pro-union bias and the opposite charges are often leveled by union representatives, detached observers have rarely accused the NLRB of being a captive of the parties it is intended to regulate—a charge often made by such observers respecting most other government agencies. And, the competence of the NLRB at both the staff and member levels can fairly be evaluated as being at least as good as that of the other federal agencies. Finally, the NLRB wins a very substantial majority of those of its cases that are reviewed by the federal courts. Accordingly, the frequency of judicial review of NLRB decisions cannot be explained by the quality of the board's work product.

As already observed, neither can the explanation for the special judicial attention bestowed upon the NLRB's activities be explained by the importance of its activities or the burden of its case docket. Less judicial scrutiny is bestowed upon the activities of agencies having an even more important impact upon our lives and having even larger case dockets.

Nor is an explanation to be found in either the complexity or vagueness of the statutory enactment administered by the agency. The texts of a number of other laws administered by government agencies involve both greater complexity and less precise statement of policies or standards.

The answer, therefore, does not lie not in the structure of our labor law or in the system for its administration. Rather, the answer would appear to lie in the attitude of the parties and in the attitude of the judiciary itself. The policy choices in the labor relations field involve factors with respect to which the moving parties have an especially deep personal commitment. Losses are not easily accepted. The fight is continually renewed. Moreover, these policy choices involve factors that frequently are closer to the personal experiences of the judiciary than are those involved in other areas of administrative law, thereby permitting the justices to feel a greater sense of expertise and confidence in their decisions in this area. The frequent division of the different U.S. Courts of Appeals respecting the "right" choice amongst alternative interpretations of the National Labor Relations Act no doubt has encouraged the parties to pursue labor cases to the court of last resort, and that same division has necessitated at least some of the Supreme Court's activism in the labor field.

Perhaps, too, the justices have been encouraged to continue to be activists in this area inasmuch as in recent decades judicial management in the labor relations field has produced a number of successful innovations that have received the acquiescence of the legislature and the acclaim of scholars.

Whatever the reason, though, there can be little question but that the Supreme Court will continue for some time to shape our economic, social, and political policies in the course of serving as a court of last resort in labor-management relations cases. And equally certain is that the personal experiences, philosophies, and predilections of the Supreme Court justices will continue to be reflected in the decisions with which they review the administrative and judicial refinement of the broad and vaguely defined statutory policies adopted by Congress for the regulation of this field.

Notes

Notes

Chapter 1
Historic Perspective

1. E.g., *Worley* v. *State,* 11 Humph. 172 (Tenn. 1850), II H. Catterall, *Judicial Cases Concerning American Slavery and the Negro* 545 (1929) (owner guilty of mayhem for castrating an "unmanageable" slave); *State* v. *Will,* 1 Dev. & Bat. 121 (N.C. 1834), H. Catterall, id. at 2-3, 70 (attempt to take slave's life is attempted murder); *State* v. *Hoover,* 4 Dev. & Bat. 365 (N.C. 1839), H. Catterall, id. at 85-86 (death of slave due to vicious punishment constitutes murder); *accord, State* v. *Bradley,* 9 Rich. 168 (S.C. 1855), H. Catterall, id. at 446.

2. 2 Blackstone, *Commentaries* 428 (Tucker ed. 1803).

3. F.T. Carlton, *The History and Problems of Organized Labor* 14 (1911); M. Farrand, *The Laws and Liberties of Massachusetts—Masters, Servants, Labourers (1630)* § 5 at p. 38 (1929).

4. J. Grossman, *Wage and Price Controls During the American Revolution,* Monthly Lab. Rev. 3-7 (Sep. 1973).

5. 2 Blackstone, *Commentaries* 428-29, n. 10-13 (Tucker ed. 1803).

6. Kan. Acts of 1859 ch XIII §§ 8, 12.

7. Ill. Rev. Stat. of 1845 § 11.

8. Kan. Acts of 1859, id. n. 6; Ill. Rev. Stat. of 1845 § 15. See generally, Bureau of Labor Statistics, *History of Wages in the United States* 34-36 (1934) (republished by Gale Research Co. 1966).

9. 2 Blackstone, n. 5 supra.

10. W. Bailey, *Master's Liability for Injuries to Servant* 2-3 (1894); C. Labatt, I *Master and Servant* 18 (1904); *Wright* v. *N.Y. Cent. R.R.,* 25 N.Y. 562, 565-66 (1862).

11. H. Carman & H. Syrett, II *A History of the American People* 4-8 (1953); J.W. Hurst, *Law and the Conditions of Freedom in the 19th Century United States* 15-16 (1956); id., *The Growth of American Law* 63 (1950); C.P. Magrath, *Yazoo* (1966) (passim).

12. F.T. Carlton, supra n. 3 at 157.

13. Id. at 16-17.

14. C. Dankert, *An Introduction to Labor* 122-124 (1954).

15. Generally known as the *Philadelphia Cordwainers* case, this 1806 decision

is reported in 3 J. Commons & E. Gilmore, *A Documentary History of American Industrial Society* 68 (1910).

16. *The Labor Injunction* (1930).
17. Id. at 2.
18. Id. at 3; E. Witte, *Early American Labor Cases,* 35 Yale L.J. 825, 826-27 (1926).
19. Frankfurter & Greene, supra n. 16 at 3 n. 10.
20. E. Witte, supra n. 18 at 828.
21. 4 Metc. 111 (Mass. 1842).
22. See, e.g., L. Reynolds, *Labor Economics and Labor Relations* 277-78 (2d ed. 1954) and C. Gregory & H. Katz, *Labor Law: Cases, Materials and Comments* 30-31 (1948).
23. E. Witte, *Early American Labor Cases,* 35 Yale L.J. 825, 828-32 (1926); F. Frankfurter & N. Greene, *The Labor Injunction* 137 (1930); J. Landis *Cases on Labor Law* 34-35 (1934).
24. *Walker* v. *Cronin,* 107 Mass. 555 (1871).
25. J. Landis, *Cases on Labor Law* 36 (1934). F. Carlton, supra n. 3 at 158.
26. J. Landis, id. at 832.
27. Id. at 833.
28. *Barr* v. *Essex Trades Council,* 30 Atl. 881 (N.J. Ch. 1894).
29. *Vegelahn* v. *Guntner,* 44 N.E. 1077, 1081 (Mass. 1896) (dissent).
30. Ibid.
31. Id at 1082.
32. Frankfurter & Greene, supra n. 23 at 18-19; J. Landis, supra n. 25 at 510 n. 5; *In re Debs,* 158 U.S. 564, 597-98 (1895).
33. *In re Debs,* 158 U.S. 564, 586-87 (1895).
34. Quoted in Frankfurter & Greene, supra n. 23 at 19-20 n. 79.
35. C. Gregory, *Labor and the Law* 102-03 (rev. ed. 1949).
36. 208 U.S. at 175.
37. Id. at 178.
38. Id. at 189.
39. Id. at 190.
40. 235 U.S. 522 (1915).
41. 208 U.S. at 301.
42. W. Merritt, *Destination Unknown* 24 (1951).
43. H. Shulman, *Labor and the Antitrust Laws,* 34 Ill. L. Rev. 769, 771 (1940).
44. F. Frankfurter & N. Greene, *The Labor Injunction* 141 (1930).
45. Id. at 143, 143 n. 36.
46. Id. at 145.
47. 254 U.S. at 483.
48. Id. at 480-81.
49. *American Steel Foundaries* v.*Tri-City Central Trades Council,* 257 U.S. 184

(1921); *Bedford Cut Stone Co.* v. *Journeymen Stone Cutters Ass'n.* 274 U.S. 37 (1927).

50. Frankfurter & Greene, supra note 44 at 173-74 n. 159.
51. Id. at 9 n. 48.
52. Id. at 176.
53. J. Landis, *Cases on Labor Law* 182 (1934).
54. 236 U.S. at 20.
55. Id. at 28.
56. 245 U.S. at 250-51.
57. Id. at 254.
58. Id. at 271.
59. 247 U.S. 184 (1921). It is noteworthy that Chief Justice Taft's opinion acknowledged the necessity of unions to aid workers in combatting the power of capital and unfair and arbitrary employer treatment.
60. C. Summers & H. Wellington, *Labor Law* 394 (1968); H. Millis & E. Brown, *From the Wagner Act to Taft-Hartley* 18 (1950).
61. 281 U.S. at 570.
62. H. Millis and E. Brown, *From the Wagner Act to Taft-Hartley* 19-20 (1950).
63. F. Frankfurter & N. Greene, *The Labor Injunction* (1930); E. Witte, *The Government in Labor Disputes* (1932).
64. A. Schlesinger, Jr., *The Coming of the New Deal* 138-139 (1958).
65. Id. at 101.
66. Id. at 145.
67. H. Millis & E. Brown, *From the Wagner Act to Taft-Hartley* 24 (1950).
68. Schlesinger, supra n. 64 at 398-400.
69. Id. at 404-05.
70. 79 Cong. Rec. 7565, 7567, May 15, 1935.
71. Gregory, supra n. 35 at 324.
72. 295 U.S. at 546.
73. Id. at 548-50.
74. 301 U.S. at 31.
75. *Washington Coach Co.* v. *NLRB,* 301 U.S. 142 (1937).
76. *Associated Press* v. *NLRB,* 301 U.S. 103 (1937).
77. 301 U.S. at 78.
78. C. Gregory & H. Katz, *Labor Law* 848 (1948).
79. 301 U.S. at 94.
80. Id. at 96-97.
81. Id. at 99.
82. Gregory, supra n. 77.
83. 301 U.S. at 41.
84. Ibid.
85. Ibid.

86. Id. at 43.
87. Id. at 132.
88. See generally H. Millis & E. Brown, *From the Wagner Act to Taft-Hartley* 271-81 (1950); R.A. Lee, *Truman and Taft-Hartley* 11-19 (1966).
89. Lee, id at 61-63.
90. Id. at 88-96.
91. D. Bok & J. Dunlop, *Labor and the American Community* 57 (1970).
92. Id. at 12.

Chapter 2
Regulation of Picketing and Other Union
Organizing Activities

1.   *Schneider* v. *Irvington,* 308 U.S. 157, 163 (1939).
2.   *Cafeteria Union* v. *Angelos,* 320 U.S. 293, 295 (1943).
3.   *Bakery Drivers Local* v. *Wohl,* 315 U.S. 769, 772 (1942).
4.   Id. at 775.
5.   *Giboney* v. *Empire Storage and Ice Company,* 336 U.S. 490, 502-03 (1949).
6.   *United Association of Journeymen Plumbers* v. *Graham,* 345 U.S. 192, 200 (1953).
7.   Id. at 202.
8.   Id. at 202-03.
9.   *International Brotherhood of Teamsters* v. *Vogt,* 354 U.S. 284 (1957).
10. *Logan Valley Plaza, Inc.* v. *Amalgamated Food Employees Union,* 227 A.2d 874, 876 n. 3 (Pa. 1967).
11. *Amalgamated Food Employees Union Local 590* v. *Logan Valley Plaza, Inc.,* 391 U.S. 308, 319 (1968).
12. Id. at 319-20.
13. *Republic Aviation Corp.* v. *NLRB,* 324 U.S. 793, 802 n. 8 (1945).
14. *NLRB* v. *Stowe Spinning Co.,* 336 U.S. 226, 229 (1949).
15. *NLRB* v. *Babcock & Wilcox Co.,* 351 U.S. 105, 113 (1956).
16. *Central Hardware Co.* v. *NLRB,* 407 U.S. 539, 548 (1972).
17. *Lloyd Corp., Ltd.* v. *Tanner,* 407 U.S. 551, 564-65 (1972).
18. Id. at 580.
19. Ibid.
20. Id. at 586.
21. Id. at 584.

Chapter 3
Supremacy of Federal Power

1.   *Hill* v. *Florida,* 325 U.S. 538 (1945).

2.   *Garner* v. *Teamsters, Chauffeurs & Helpers Local Union No. 776 (AFL)*, 346 U.S. 485, 487 (1953).
3.   Id. at 499.
4.   *Weber* v. *Anheuser-Busch, Inc.*, 348 U.S. 468, 481 (1955).
5.   Id. at 481.
6.   E.g., *Linn* v. *United Plant Guard Workers*, 383 U.S. 53 (1966); *Vaca* v. *Sipes*, 386 U.S. 171 (1967).
7.   *San Diego Building Trades Council* v. *Garmon*, 359 U.S. 236, 243-44 (1959).
8.   See *Wisconsin Employment Relations Board* v. *Automobile Workers*, 336 U.S. 245 (1949).
9.   359 U.S. at 244-45.
10.   Id. at 245.
11.   Id. at 245–46.
12.   Id. at 250.
13.   *Motor Coach Employees* v. *Lockridge*, 403 U.S. 274, 277 (1971).
14.   Id. at 287.
15.   Id. at 289.
16.   Id. at 297-98.
17.   Id. at 303.
18.   Id. at 304.
19.   Id. at 318.
20.   Id. at 322.
21.   Id. at 326.
22.   Id. at 328.

Chapter 4
Regulating Economic Warfare

1.   *NLRB* v. *Insurance Agents' International Union*, 361 U.S. 477, 488-89 (1960).
2.   *Consolidated Edison Co.* v. *NLRB*, 305 U.S. 197, 236 (1938).
3.   *NLRB* v. *MacKay Radio & Telegraph Co.*, 304 U.S. 333, 347 (1938).
4.   *NLRB* v. *Fansteel Metallurgical Corp.*, 306 U.S. 240, 253 (1939).
5.   Id. at 263.
6.   Id. at 266-67.
7.   Ibid.
8.   Russell Baker, *Observer*, Int'l Herald Tribune, Apr. 30, 1973.
9.   *Southern Steamship Co.* v. *NLRB*, 316 U.S. 31, 51 (1942).
10.   *NLRB* v. *International Brotherhood of Electrical Workers*, 346 U.S. 464, 475 (1953).
11.   Id. at 479-80.
12.   *NLRB* v. *Insurance Agents' International Union*, 361 U.S. 477, 482 (1960).

13. Id. at 488.
14. *International Union, U.A.W.* v. *Wisconsin Employment Relations Board,* 336 U.S. 245 (1949).
15. 361 U.S. at 504.
16. *NLRB* v. *Sands Manufacturing Co.,* 306 U.S. 332, 344 (1939).
17. *NLRB* v. *Rockaway News Supply Co.,* 345 U.S. 71, 80 (1953).
18. E.g., *NLRB* v. *The Magnavox Co.,* 415 U.S. 322 (1974).
19. See e.g. *Darling & Co.,* 171 NLRB 801 (1968), enforced *sub nom. Lane* v. *NLRB,* 418 F.2d 1208 (D.C. Cir. 1969); *Inland Trucking Co.,* 179 NLRB 350 (1969), enforced 440 F.2d 562 (7th Cir. 1971).
20. *Ottawa Silica,* 197 NLRB 449, enforced 482 F.2d 945 (6th Cir. 1973) and *Intercollegiate Press,* 199 NLRB 177, affirmed 486 F.2d 837 (8th Cir. 1973).
21. *NLRB* v. *Great Dane Trailers, Inc.,* 388 U.S. 26, 31 (1967).
22. Id. at 33.
23. *NLRB* v. *Fleetwood Trailer Co.,* 389 U.S. 375, 381 (1967).
24. *NLRB* v. *Servette, Inc.,* 377 U.S. 46, 50 (1964).
25. *NLRB* v. *Fruit & Vegetable Packers & Warehousemen, Local 760,* 377 U.S. 58, 62 (1964).
26. Id. at 63.
27. Id. at 64.
28. Id. at 78-79.
29. Id. at 80.
30. *American Bread Co.,* 170 NLRB 91, enforced 411 F.2d 147 (6th Cir. 1969); *Dow Chem. Co.,* 211 NLRB no. 59 (1974). One might question whether, in such cases, the "secondary" employer's business is not so entwined with that of the struck employer so as to constitute such picketing as "primary" and, therefore, not subject to the restraints of § 8(b) (4). *Dow* has been reversed on the broader principle that peaceful picketing directed only at the struck product is always protected. 524 F.2d 853 (D.C. Cir. 1975).

Chapter 5
Creating a Law of Labor Arbitration

1. *International Ass'n of Machinists* v. *General Electric Co.,* 406 F.2d 1046, 1049 (2d Cir. 1969).
2. *Textile Workers Union of America* v. *Lincoln Mills of Alabama,* 353 U.S. 448, 451 (1957).
3. Id. at 452.
4. Id. at 453.
5. Id. at 455.
6. Id. at 458.
7. Id. at 463-64.

8. Id. at 469.

9. *United Steelworkers of America* v. *American Manufacturing Co.,* 363 U.S. 564, 568 (1960).

10. Id. at 573.

11. *United Steelworkers of America* v. *Warrior & Gulf Navigation Co.,* 363 U.S. 574, 576 (1960).

12. Id. at 584-85.

13. Id. at 580.

14. *United Steelworkers of America* v. *Enterprise Wheel & Car Corp.,* 363 U.S. 593, 598 (1960).

15. *John Wiley & Sons, Inc.* v. *Livingston,* 376 U.S. 543, 547 (1964).

16. Id. at 555.

17. *Carey* v. *Westinghouse Electric Corp.,* 375 U.S. 261, 265 (1964).

18. *Westinghouse Electric Corporation,* 162 NLRB 768 (1967).

19. *Sinclair Refining Co.* v. *Atkinson,* 370 U.S. 195, 204 (1962).

20. Id. at 214-15.

21. Id. at 220.

22. *NLRB* v. *Rockaway News Supply Co.,* 345 U.S. 71 (1953).

23. *New Orleans Steamship Ass'n* v. *General Longshore Workers,* 389 F.2d 369, cert. denied, 393 U.S. 828 (1968).

24. Bartosic, *Injunctions and Section 301,* 69 Colum. L. Rev. 980, 1001-06 (1969).

25. *Boys Markets, Inc.* v. *Retail Clerks Union,* 398 U.S. 235, 248 (1970).

26. Id. at 249.

27. Id. at 257-58.

28. Compare, *Gateway Coal Co.* v. *United Mine Workers,* 414 U.S. 368 (1974), (resolution of safety issue is a matter for arbitration and not a matter exclusively controlled by the Occupational Safety and Health Act); *Alexander* v. *Gardner-Denver Co.,* 415 U.S. 36 (1974), (arbitration award in favor of employer does not bar an action or bind the court in a later suit by an employee alleging violation of the Equal Employment Opportunity Act).

29. *Jos. Schlitz Brewing Co.,* 175 NLRB 141 (1968); *Collyer Insulated Wire,* 192 NLRB 837 (1971). This shift in NLRB policy toward greater deference to arbitration has stimulated a large body of commentary, some of which is supportive and some of which is antagonistic to the board's new position.

Chapter 6
Change of Ownership and Other Business Alterations

1. Wall Street Journal Index, 1975.

2.   *S & K Kneepants*, 2 NLRB 940 (1936).
3.   *Textile Workers* v. *Darlington Mfg. Co.*, 380 U.S. 263, 271-72 (1965).
4.   *Fibreboard Paper Products Corp.* v. *NLRB*, 379 U.S. 203, 211 (1964).
5.   Id. at 214.
6.   Id. at 215.
7.   Id. at 221.
8.   Id. at 223.
9.   Ibid.
10. Id. at 225-26.
11. *Textile Workers* v. *Darlington Manufacturing Co.*, 380 U.S. 263 (1965).
12. Id. at 269.
13. Id. at 274-75.
14. *Chas. Cushman Co.*, 15 NLRB 90 (1939).
15. *Johnson Ready Mix*, 142 NLRB 437 (1963).
16. *Perma Vinyl Corp.*, 164 NLRB 968 (1967).
17. E.g., *NLRB* v. *Alamo-White Truck Service*, 273 F.2d 238 (5th Cir. 1959);
     NLRB v. *Zayre Corp.* 424 F.2d 1159 (5th Cir. 1970).
18. *Golden State Bottling Co., Inc.* v. *NLRB*, 414 U.S. 168, 184 (1973).
19. *John Wiley & Sons, Inc.* v. *Livingston*, 376 U.S. 543, 548 (1964).
20. Belgium, Act Respecting Collective Industrial Agreements and Joint
     Committees at Art. 20.
21. *William J. Burns International Detective Agency, Inc.*, 182 NLRB 348
     (1970).
22. Id. at 350.
23. *NLRB* v. *Burns International Security Services, Inc.*, 406 U.S. 272, 278
     (1972).
24. Id. at 286.
25. Ibid.
26. Id. at 288.
27. Id. at 291.
28. *Howard Johnson Company, Inc.* v. *Detroit Local Joint Executive Board*,
     417 U.S. 249, 262 n. 8 (1974).
29. Id. at 267.
30. Id. at 268.
31. Id. at 269.
32. Id. at 264.

Chapter 7
The NLRB as Overseer of Personnel Arrangements

1.   *United States* v. *Petrillo*, 332 U.S. 1 (1947).
2.   Jaffe, *Inter-Union Disputes in Search of a Forum*, 49 Yale L.J. 424, 431
     (1940).

3. *International Longshoremen's & Warehousemen's Union* v. *Juneau Spruce Corp.*, 342 U.S. 237, 244 (1952).
4. *NLRB* v. *Radio and Television Broadcast Engineers Union*, 364 U.S. 573, 579 (1961).
5. Id. at 583.
6. *NLRB* v. *Plasterers' Local Union No. 79*, 404 U.S. 116, 130 (1971).
7. Id. at 133-34.
8. *Florida Power & Light Co.* v. *International Brotherhood of Electrical Workers*, 417 U.S. 790, 804.

Index

Adair v. *United States,* 13, 17, 23-24, 29
A.F. of L. v. *Swing,* 43, 47, 49
AFL-CIO, 162
Allen-Bradley Local No. 1111 v. *Wisconsin Employment Relations Board,* 59
American Civil Liberties Union, 39
Amalgamated Food Employees Union Local 590 v. *Logan Valley Plaza Inc.,* 47-60, 69
American Federation of Labor, 6, 14, 21, 35, 156-157, 162
American Liberty League, 30
American Newspaper Publishers v. *NLRB,* 153-155
American Plan. *See* yellow-dog contract
American Ship Building Company v. *NLRB,* 91-93, 95
American Steel Foundries v. *Tri-City Central Trades Council,* 20-21, 29
arbitration, 2, 12-13, 22, 27, 36, 38, 67, 87, 105-125, 139-141, 143, 147-148, 161-164, 171
Arbitration Act. *See* United States Arbitration Act
Avco Corporation v. *Aero Lodge No. 735, I.A.M.,* 120-121, 123
Axton-Fisher Tobacco Company, 157

Babcox & Wilcox Co., NLRB v., 53-56
Bakery Drivers Local v. *Wohl,* 44-45
bargaining. *See* collective bargaining
bargaining unit, 29
Belgium, 141
Biddle, F., 28
Black, Mr. Justice, 26, 42-46, 58, 77, 79, 83, 85, 102-103, 110, 114, 116-118, 122-125, 152-153
Blackman, Mr. Justice, 58, 66 123
Blue Eagle campaign, 28
Board of Railroad Wages and Working Conditions, 22
boycotts, 9, 14-16, 34-35, 37, 40, 97-104
Boys Markets, Inc. v. *Retail Clerks Union,* 121-125
Brandeis, Mr. Justice, 15-16, 20-21
Brennan, Mr. Justice, 55, 57, 90, 101, 111-112, 118-122, 124, 143
Britain. *See* England
broad decisions, 145

Brown case, 89-93, 95
Buffalo Linen case. *See NLRB* v. *Truck Drivers Local Union No. 449*
Burger, Chief Justice, 58, 66, 123, 143
Burns case, 141-148, 149
business closing, 135, 137
business turnover. *See* change of ownership
Butler, Mr. Justice, 33, 43

Carey v. *Western Electric Corp.,* 114-116, 125
Carlson v. *California,* 43
Carter v. *Carter Coal Co.,* 31
Case Act, 36
CBS case, 159-164
Central Hardware Co. v. *NLRB,* 54-56
change of ownership, 127-149
civil rights law, 40
Clark, Mr. Justice, 63, 114, 116-118, 123, 154, 168
Clarke, Mr. Justice, 15
Clayton Act, 14-16, 20, 23-24
closed shop, 37, 164-165
collective agreements, 5, 22-23, 38, 72, 82, 106-125, 139-149, 159, 162-168, 170-171
collective bargaining, 5, 22-23, 29, 36-38, 71-105, 110, 117, 122, 130-149, 151, 170-171
Collins, Thomas v., 47
Commonwealth v. *Hunt,* 7
Commonwealth v. *Pullis,* 6
company union, 23, 27
conciliation. *See* mediation
Congress of Industrial Organizations (CIO), 35, 42, 157
Constitution, U.S., Art. I §2, 1; Art. I §9, 1; Art. I §10, 4; 1st Amendment, 31, 34, 51, 58, 101-103; 5th Amendment, 4, 13, 53; 13th Amendment, 3; 14th Amendment, 4, 17, 42-43, 68-69; Supremacy clause, 59-60, 68. *See also* federalism; freedom of expression; preemption; property rights
consumer boycott. *See* boycotts
consumer picketing. *See* picketing, economic; picketing, organizational
contempt of court, 11-12, 26
contracting out work, 129-133

contract, liberty of, 2-4, 17-25
contract of employment. *See* employment
    contract
Coppage v. *Kansas,* 17-18, 23-24, 29
Cordwainers case. *See Commonwealth*
    v. *Pullis*
criminal conspiracy, 6-8

damages remedy, 8-9, 14, 38, 64-65, 67,
    119, 122-123, 146, 158
Danbury Hatters case. *See Loewe* v. *Lawlor*
Darlington case, 133-137
Day, Mr. Justice, 18
Debs, E., 11
Debs, In re, 11, 24
Deering, Duplex Co. v., 15, 20, 24, 29
defamation, 62
Democratic National Platform, 12, 14
disloyalty as cause for discipline, 79-80
Douglas, Mr. Justice, 43-44, 46-47, 55, 57,
    59-60, 66-67, 79, 85, 100, 108-111,
    113, 115-116, 118, 131, 133, 148, 152,
    154, 167
Drake Bakeries v. *Local 50, American
    Bakery Workers,* 119
Duplex Co. v. *Deering,* 15, 20, 24, 29
duty of fair representation, 62, 67
duty to bargain. *See* collective bargaining

employment contract, 2-5, 7, 107
England, 4-5
Erdman Act, 12, 22-24
Erie Resistor Corp., NLRB v., 95
Ervin, S., 39, 134

Fair Labor Standards Act, 40
Fansteel Metallurgical Corp., NLRB v., 75-
    79, 82-83
featherbedding, 151-155, 171
federalism. *See* preemption
Federal Mediation and Conciliation Service,
    38
Fibreboard Paper Products Corp. v. *NLRB,*
    129-133, 145
Fleetwood Trailer Co., NLRB v., 96-97
Florida Power & Light Co. v. *International
    Brotherhood of Electrical Workers,*
    169-171
Fortas, Mr. Justice, 58
Frankfurter, Mr. Justice, 6, 15-16, 20, 25,
    43, 47, 60-64, 79, 81, 109-111, 117
freedom of expression, 31, 34, 42-58, 69,
    101-104
Fruit and Vegetable Packers, NLRB v.,
    99-104

Garmon, San Diego Building Trades Council
    v., 62-68

Garner v. *Teamsters, Chauffeurs & Helpers
    Local Union No. 776 (AFL),* 60-62
Garrison, L., 28
Germany, 5
Giboney v. *Empire Storage and Ice Com-
    pany,* 44-47, 49
Goldberg, Mr. Justice, 90, 92, 107, 131
Golden State Bottling Co. Inc. v. *NLRB,*
    138
Goldwater, B., 39
Gompers, S., 6, 15, 25
good faith bargaining, duty of, 37, 80-82,
    88-90
Great Dane Trailers, Inc., NLRB v., 94
Great Depression, 24-28
Greene, N., 6, 15-16, 20
Gregory, C., 12, 30
Griffin, R., 39

Hague, F., 42
Hague v. *CIO,* 42-43
Harlan (1st Justice Harlan), 13
Harlan (2d Justice Harlan), 58, 63-66, 81,
    95-97, 101-103, 111, 114, 118, 120,
    123, 131, 133, 135, 167
Hartley, F., 36
Haynsworth, C., 134
Hill v. *Florida,* 60-63
hiring hall, 165-168, 171
Hitchman Coal & Coke Co. v. *Mitchell,*
    19-21, 24
Hobbs Act, 36
Holden v. *Hardy,* 4
Holmes, Mr. Justice, 10, 13, 15, 18, 23-24,
    46
Hoover, H., 21, 25
Howard Johnson Company, Inc. v. *Detroit
    Local Joint Executive Board,* 147-149
Hughes, Chief Justice, 18, 23-24, 31-33,
    42, 76
Hughes v. *Superior Court of California,* 45
Hunt, Commonwealth v., 7

indentured service, 1-3
injunctions, 8-12, 14-21, 23-26, 34, 37,
    42-61, 108-109, 113, 117-123
Insurance Agents case, 80-81, 83-84, 92
International Brotherhood of Teamsters
    v. *Vogt,* 46-47, 49, 69
*International Longshoremen's & Ware-
    housemen's Union* v. *Juneau Spruce
    Corp.,* 158-159
interstate commerce, authority to regulate,
    11-14, 23, 29, 31-34
Interstate Commerce Commission, 12
Italy, 5
Ives, I., 39

Jackson, Mr. Justice, 44, 52-53, 61, 154
Jaffe, L., 157
John Wiley & Sons, Inc. v. *Livingston,* 113-114, 125, 139-141, 143, 145, 147-148
Jones & Laughlin Steel Corp., NLRB v., 31-34
Juneau Spruce Corp., International Long-shoremen's & Warehousemen's Union v., 158-159
jurisdictional disputes, 35, 38, 115-116, 155-164, 171

Kennedy, J., 36, 39, 101
Kennedy, R., 39
Keyserling, L., 28

Labor-Management Relations Act, 36-38, 40, 67, 72, 79, 89, 97, 107, 109-112, 117-118, 121, 132, 151, 153-159, 164-167. *See also* National Labor Relations Act
Labor-Management Reporting and Dis-closure Act, 39, 67, 97, 99-104, 166. *See also* Labor-Management Relations Act; National Labor Relations Act
LaFollette, H., 26
LaGuardia, F., 25
laissez-faire, 6, 10, 18, 25
Landrum-Griffin Act. *See* Labor-Manage-ment Reporting and Disclosure Act
Landrum, P., 39
Lea Act, 36, 152-153
legislative control of working conditions, 2-5
Lewis, J., 25-26
Lincoln Mills, Textile Workers v., 107, 109-110, 117-118, 125
Lloyd Corporation, Ltd. v. *Tanner,* 56-58
Local 57 I.L.G.W.U. v. *NLRB,* 129
Local 60, Carpenters v. *NLRB,* 166-168
Local 371, IBT v. *NLRB,* 166-168
lockouts, 87-93, 147
Lockridge, Motor Coach Employees v., 64-68
Loewe v. *Lawlor (Danbury Hatters'* case), 13-14, 24, 29
Logan Valley Plaza case, 47-60, 69
Lucas Flour Co., Teamsters Union v., 109, 119

McClellan, J., 39
MacKay Radio & Telegraph Co., NLRB v., 73-74
McKenna, Mr. Justice, 13
McReynolds, Mr. Justice, 24, 33, 43
Magnavox case, 86
Magruder, C., 28
majority-rule concept, 22, 27-29

managerial decisions, 132
Marshall, Mr. Justice, 51, 55, 57-58, 123, 147-149
Marsh v. *Alabama,* 50-51
Meadowmoor Dairies, Inc., Milk Wagon Drivers Union v., 43, 45, 47
mediation, 12, 22, 27, 36, 38, 105
merger. *See* change of ownership
Milk Wagon Drivers Union v. *Meadowmoor Dairies, Inc.,* 43, 45, 47
Minton, Mr. Justice, 85
Morse, W., 164
Motor Coach Employees v. *Lockridge,* 64-68
Murphy, Mr. Justice, 44, 152

narrow decisions, 145
National Association for the Advancement of Colored People, 21
National Association of Manufacturers, 27
National Catholic Welfare Conference, 37
National Council of Jewish Women, 37
National Industrial Conference Board, 27
National Industrial Recovery Act, 26-30
National Joint Board for the Settlement of Jurisdictional Disputes, 162
National Labor Board, 27-28
National Labor Relations Act, 22, 29-35, 37, 40, 50-56, 59-68, 72-77, 79-101, 108-109, 115-116, 128-138, 141, 143, 151, 153-159, 161-174. *See also* Labor-Management Relations Act
National Labor Relations Board, 27, 29-34, 37-38, 40, 50-56, 61-68, 73-104, 108-109, 115-116, 125, 128-138, 141-145, 148, 154-164, 166-174
National Maritime Union, 166
National Recovery Administration, 26-28
National War Labor Board, 22
negotiation. *See* collective bargaining
Netherlands, 132
New Negro Alliance v. *Sanitary Grocery,* 34
Nixon, R., 36, 123, 134
NLRB v. *Babcock & Wilcox Co.,* 53-56
NLRB v. *Brown,* 89-93, 95
NLRB v. *Erie Resistor Corp.,* 95
NLRB v. *Fansteel Metallurgical Corp.,* 75-79, 82-83
NLRB v. *Fleetwood Trailer Co.,* 96-97
NLRB v. *Fruit and Vegetable Packers,* 99-104
NLRB v. *Gamble Enterprises, Inc.,* 154-155
NLRB v. *Great Dane Trailers, Inc.,* 94
NLRB v. *Jones & Laughlin Steel Corp.,* 31-34
NLRB v. *Local 1229, International Brother-hood of Electrical Workers,* 79-80

NLRB v. *MacKay Radio & Telegraph Co.*, 73-74
NLRB v. *Plasterers' Local Union No. 79*, 162
NLRB v. *Radio and Television Broadcast Engineers Union*, 159-164
NLRB v. *Rockaway News Supply Co.*, 84-87
NLRB v. *Sands Manufacturing Company*, 82-87
NLRB v. *Servette, Inc.*, 98-99
NLRB v. *Stowe Spinning Co.*, 52-54
NLRB v. *Truck Drivers Local Union No. 449*, 87-90
NLRB v. *Washington Aluminum Company*, 83-84
Norris, G., 25-26
Norris-LaGuardia Act, 25-26, 30, 34, 37, 107-109, 117-123
no strike agreement, 109, 111-112, 117-123

Oakland Mailers, 169
Occupational Health and Safety Act, 40
Ordinance of Labourers, 4
organizational activity, 41-58. *See also* picketing, organizational; union, right to join

Parker, J., 21-22, 134
Perma Vinyl doctrine, 138
Petrillo case, 153-154
Petrillo, J., 152-153
Philadelphia Cordwainers case. *See* *Commonwealth* v. *Pullis*
picketing, economic 16, 26, 34, 43-45, 79-80, 84-85, 93, 98-104, 162
picketing, extortionate, 40
picketing, mass, 59
picketing, organizational, 16, 26, 40-41, 43-58, 60-61, 63. *See also* organizational activity
picketing, shopping center, 47-58
plant closing, 133-137
Powell, Mr. Justice, 57-58, 86, 143
preemption, 59-69
property rights, 49-58, 133-137, 141
Pullis, Commonwealth v., 6
Pullman strike, 11-12

racketeering, 38-40
Railway Labor Act, 22-24, 106
Railway Labor Board, 22
Reed, Mr. Justice, 43, 47, 52, 77-79, 83, 152
Regal Knitwear Co. v. *NLRB*, 138
Rehnquist, Mr. Justice, 58, 86, 143
Republic Aviation Corp. v. *NLRB*, 51-52

Richberg, D., 25, 28
Right-to-Work law, 46
Roberts, Mr. Justice, 21-22, 30-31, 42, 47
Rockaway News Supply Co., *NLRB* v., 84-87
Roosevelt, F., 26-29, 77-78
runaway shop, 128-129
Rutledge, Mr. Justice, 152

sale of business. *See* change of ownership
San Diego Building Trades Council v. *Garmon*, 62-68
Sands Manufacturing Company, *NLRB* v. 82-87
Sanford, Mr. Justice, 21
Schechter Poultry Corp. v. *United States*, 28, 31-33
Schneider v. *Irvington*, 43
S & K Kneepants, 129
secondary activity, 35-38, 40-41, 45, 67, 97-104
Senn v. *Tile Layers Protective Union*, 42
Servette, Inc., *NLRB* v., 98-99
Shaw, L., 7
Sherman Act, 14-16
Shipstead, H., 24
Shulman, H., 14, 111
Sinclair Refining Co. v. *Atkinson*, 117-123
sit-down strike, 75-78
slavery, 1-3
social security, 40
Southern Steamship Co. v. *NLRB*, 78-79
Statute of Apprentices, 4
Statute of Labourers, 4
Steelworkers Trilogy. *See United Steel-workers of America* v. *American Manufacturing Co.*; *United Steelworkers of America* v. *Enterprise Wheel and Car Corp.*; *United Steelworkers of America* v. *Warrior & Gulf Navigation Co.*
Stewart, Mr. Justice, 57, 63-64, 66, 86, 95-97, 101-103, 120-122, 131-133, 167
Stone, Chief Justice, 42, 47, 60, 77
Stowe Spinning Co., *NLRB* v., 52-54
strike as mutiny, 78-79
strikers, rights of, 40, 73-87, 93-104, 113, 117-123
strikers, 5, 7, 11-23, 26-27, 35-38, 73-104, 113, 117-123
strikers, hit and run, 81
Sturgis, W., 111
successorship. *See* change of ownership
supervisors, 168-171
Sutherland, Mr. Justice, 33
Swing, A.F. of L. v., 43, 47, 49

Taft, Chief Justice, 22

Taft, R., 36, 158, 167
Taft-Hartley Act. *See* Labor Management Relations Act; National Labor Relations Act
Teamsters Union v. Lucas Flour Co., 109, 119
Teapot Dome, 21
Texas & New Orleans Railroad Co. v. Brotherhood of Railway & Steamship Clerks, 23-24
Textile Workers v. Lincoln Mills, 107, 109-110, 117-118, 125
Thomas v. Collins, 47
Thornhill v. Alabama, 43, 45, 47, 49
Tile Layers Protective Union, Senn v., 42
transferability of capital, 149
Transportation Act, 22
Tree Fruits case. *See NLRB v. Fruit and Vegetable Packers*
Truax v. Corrigan, 42
Truman, H., 36-37, 157

unions, early history, 5-6
union organizing. *See* organizational activity; union, right to join
union, right to join, 7, 13, 17-27, 29-30, 168-172
union, right to not join, 37, 164
union security agreement, 64, 164-168
United Association of Journeymen Plumbers v. Graham, 46, 49
United States Arbitration Act, 106-108, 110
United Steelworkers of America v. American Manufacturing Co., 110-112, 125
United Steelworkers of America v. Enterprise Wheel and Car Corp., 113, 125

United Steelworkers of America v. Warrior & Gulf Navigation Co., 112-113, 125
unprotected concerted activity, 6-11, 14-21, 43, 45, 45-47, 59, 62, 75-87

vagueness, 153
VanDevanter, Mr. Justice, 24, 33
Vinson, Chief Justice, 52, 154
Vogt, International Brotherhood of Teamsters v., 46-47, 49, 69

wage-hour law. *See* Fair Labor Standards Act
Wagner Act. *See* National Labor Relations Act
Wagner, R., 27-29
waiver of protected rights, 84-87, 117-123
War Labor Board, 106
Warren, Chief Justice, 46, 58, 90, 92, 131
Weber v. Anheuser-Busch, 61-62
Welfare and Pensions Disclosure Act, 39
whipsaw strike, 88-91
White, Mr. Justice, 58, 66-68, 90-93, 123, 163-164, 171
Whittaker, Mr. Justice, 63, 81, 112-113, 168
Wiley case. *See John Wiley & Sons, Inc. v. Livingston*
Wilson, W., 15, 22
Witte, E., 25
Wohl, Bakery Drivers Local v., 44-45
work assignment disputes. *See* jurisdictional disputes

yellow-dog contract, 16-22, 24-25, 29

About the Author

Alvin L. Goldman was born, raised and educated in New York City. After three years of law practice there, during which time he began to specialize in the labor relations field, he left to teach law at the University of Kentucky. Although Labor Law has remained Professor Goldman's main teaching, research and writing area, he has also devoted a considerable portion of his professorial efforts to Constitutional Law, the Supreme Court and Administrative Law during the past decade.

Early in his teaching career, the author spent a year as Professor in Residence on the staff of the N.L.R.B. member Sam Zagoria. As a volunteer civil liberties lawyer he has appeared before the Supreme Court, and as an active labor arbitrator he keeps in touch with day-to-day problems of the labor relations field.